Congressional Publications

Congressional Publications
A Research Guide to
Legislation, Budgets, and Treaties

JERROLD ZWIRN

Libraries Unlimited, Inc.
Littleton, Colorado
1983

LIBRARIES UNLIMITED, INC.
P.O. Box 263
Littleton, Colorado 80160

Library of Congress Cataloging in Publication Data

Zwirn, Jerrold.
    Congressional publications.

    Includes bibliographies and index.
    1. United States. Congress--Information services.
2. United States. Congress--Bibliography. I. Title.
JK1067.Z85 1983   027.6'5   82-18652
ISBN 0-87287-358-7

Libraries Unlimited books are bound with Type II nonwoven material that meets
and exceeds National Association of State Textbook Administrators' Type II
nonwoven material specifications Class A through E.

Preface

This volume is intended to serve as a research guide to the vast amount of information consumed, weighed, and issued by the United States Congress. How information in general, and printed information in particular, is transmitted to, within, and by Congress forms the framework of discussion. To encourage and facilitate the use of such information, its sources and purposes are related to its role in the legislative process, while its content and format are related to its sources and purposes.

If one grants the importance of public policies, then the volume and variety of documents that accompany their formulation, consideration, and enactment must be accorded equal status. Though congressional publications are probably most widely known and used as a means to illuminate and interpret legislative history, they can be profitably consulted for at least as many reasons as there are subjects that receive legislative attention. The opportunity to exploit such material to meet tangible interests and demands need not be limited to those professionally concerned with or engaged in the art of governing.

An exploration of the perceptions and purposes of legislative authors is meant to orient interested individuals to view congressional publications as parts of an organic whole rather than as isolated works. Though this approach may not be necessary for all research needs, it can render their nature more intelligible and their use less arduous. Anyone investigating any aspect of national or international affairs or the response and performance of government is in a position to take advantage of what congressional publications have to offer.

Though the title of this book indicates that its chief purpose is as a specialized research tool, its utility is not limited to specialists. Librarians familiar with the documents discussed may find that the legislative process perspective suggests additional ways to service them. Researchers acquainted with the legislative process may find that the publications perspective suggests additional ways to enhance their product. Students seeking information about a subject are provided with the means to choose or devise a search strategy that best meets their needs.

One may desire information contained in congressional publications either because of or irrespective of its relationship to the legislative process. To focus on the first possibility, there is no conclusive answer to the question of what pertinent information Congress should acquire or convey to establish effective controls over policy formulation and implementation. Thus, one who is generally familiar with the legislative process and methods of locating desired information may still find that many matters regarding its production and functions remain unclear. From this standpoint, the major questions addressed in the following pages are: What types of information are emphasized in each type of publication? How can one identify and fill information gaps? Which entities exercise the greatest control over which publications? How do chronological factors, legislative procedures, and political relationships affect content?

Where subject matter is the only or most significant factor, two major barriers to the use of congressional publications seem to be their relationship to other members of the same family and difficulty in gaining access to particular portions of a text. A discussion of the circumstances under which each is issued offers an approach to understanding the natural links between these publications. An examination of formats that relates them to the dynamics of the legislative process may suggest methods for more expeditiously extracting essential information. Regardless of research viewpoint or needs, one cannot escape the fact that the legislative process definitely conditions the manner in which information is presented.

For those mainly interested in particular documents, whether substantive or bibliographic in nature, a Document Index precedes the Subject Index. The Appendix is a comprehensive tool for identifying committees and locating their publications. The chapter subheadings listed in the Table of Contents enable one to focus on any stage of the legislative process to amplify or clarify matters concerning certain proceedings or publications associated therewith. An outline of the book describes its organization and highlights the main topics or themes of each chapter. These features are designed to aid readers to readily locate information about the relationship between specific documents or developments or both.

OUTLINE OF THE BOOK

A survey of the relationship between congressional publications and the legislative process poses the question of logical order. Difficulties are inherent in the dual nature of bicameral proceedings and discretion about whether and when to print. Most publications may be issued at various points in the process, while different ones may appear at nearly the same time. The unique nature of issues and uncertain chronology of decisions preclude any explanatory scheme from being applicable in all cases. The arrangement corresponds with the legislative agenda as described in chapter 1 and the legislative process as detailed in chapter 2. However, it should be understood that the correspondence between issuance and activity can only be approximate rather than exact.

Chapter 1 examines the nature of congressional authorship and provides a conceptual overview of the flow and control of information in the legislative environment. It explains how the factors and conditions that affect the availability and use of information influence the volume and management of the congressional workload and the nature of legislative output.

Chapter 2 describes the political setting and presents a systematic account of the legislative process. This is to construct the context within which information is accumulated, assimilated, and applied. It also discusses the properties and purposes of public policy as it evolves in legislative form and argues for an integrated view of legislative history as both a given set of publications and a distinct series of decisions.

Chapter 3 explores those background studies prepared by and for congressional committees to aid them in the performance of legislative and oversight functions. It focuses on the characteristics, contents, and calculations associated with this class of publications and the role of congressional support agencies as the primary sources of such information.

Chapters 4 and 5 analyze the key role of committees as workshops and conduits of information. They are coalitions, not teams, whose members have some, but not all, goals in common. The importance of panel proceedings and pronouncements is based on the general acceptance of such action as an accurate political barometer.

Chapters 6 and 7 provide a picture of chamber proceedings and indicate how they are conditioned by committee output. The procedural and political aspects of this stage require that emphasis be placed on parliamentary rules and the sequence of decisions. The impact of debate and voting on the substance of legislation is examined.

Chapters 8 and 9 focus on those proposals addressed in various ways by other congressional publications. Bills are viewed in terms of their status as official documents, and a bibliographic guide, also applicable to resolutions, is included. Resolutions are compared with bills for pursuing policy goals, and different types are described in some detail.

Chapters 10 and 11 cover two other matters that require joint legislative-executive action. Though budgetmaking and treatymaking produce decisions and publications that are outside the formal legislative process, all three activities are interdependent. Presidential initiative and participation are more institutionalized in regard to budgets and treaties. The budget and treaty processes also proceed on schedules separate from that which applies to legislation. Congressional publications derived from the two former activities differ in content and format, though not in name, from their purely legislative counterparts. Budget and treaty proceedings also generate several types of publications unique to their purposes.

Chapter 10 contends that a public budget is a political blueprint and that its formulation reflects competition for limited resources. It analyzes the political, educational, and managerial functions of the budget and the nature of fiscal policy. The opportunities for and obstacles to promoting policy preferences presented by the annual budget cycle are explored.

Chapter 11 describes in detail the treatymaking process as reflected in the roles of the President and the Senate. It focuses on how the aspects of this process affect the nature and timing of treaty publications. Differences between bilateral and multilateral treaties and the effects of decisions of foreign governments are also discussed.

Acknowledgments

Two groups of individuals have significantly contributed to the impetus for and existence of this book. One, which includes faculty, students, librarians, and researchers at several institutions, generated a steady stream of trenchant questions. The other, composed of staff members employed on Capitol Hill, has responded with a generous supply of instructive answers. Should this project be considered to have some merit, it is also because many things fortunately fell or were gently guided into place. In this regard, I particularly appreciate the efforts of Maryellen Trautman, Government Documents Librarian, National Archives; and Heather Cameron, Libraries Unlimited. As for any errors or deficiencies in the following pages, they test the reader's capacity to forgive and the author's to forget. In any event, I accept the obligation to prevent them from becoming orphans.

To my mother and the memory of my father.

Table of Contents

List of Figures

1

The Congressional Agenda

LEGISLATIVE AUTHORSHIP

Congressional publications are not printed primarily for the convenience of legislators or for the information of citizens, though they serve both purposes. Neither are they merely a useful by-product of parliamentary proceedings. They are constituent elements of the legislative process whose value stems from the perceived significance of those political decisions that shape their content and engender their appearance. An examination of the environmental origins of congressional publications clearly reveals them to be strategic vehicles in the effort to forge public policy.

Congress serves as a public forum for continual national debate. Its ability to perform this function only partially depends on its role as a national lawmaking body. More importantly, it is a system of relationships that continually adapt to meet the needs of the polity and its own status. This view provides a starting point from which to explore how Congress keeps itself and interested publics informed of legislative activities and public affairs. For this purpose, it is necessary to reach behind the content of congressional publications to the motives and viewpoints of their authors. To understand why a publication was issued involves more than the fact that it is a formal obligation or an established custom at a certain stage of the legislative process.

Congress is the most accessible and active arbiter of political disputes having national policy implications. Its extensive responsibilities and substantial influence ensure that it will remain the recipient of a continual and voluminous flow of demands from innumerable sources. The quantity and variety of material printed by and for Congress indicates more than a polite acknowledgment of or voracious appetite for such information. It suggests a strenuous effort to weigh the merits of those appeals that reach its chambers and to document that legislators have accorded them reasonable consideration.

Legislative communications are aimed at those in a position to mold or make decisions that affect the enactment or implementation of public policy. Their purposes may be to suggest, urge, or require that new policy be considered, planned, or instituted or that existing policy be evaluated, continued, or revised. The audience may be composed of legislators, the president, administrators, judges, private citizens, officials of local or foreign governments, or some combination thereof. The range of its authority and activity affirms that Congress is an influential and informative author.

These circumstances, coupled with its decentralized organization, account for the fact that Congress is also a prolific author. However, to speak of

Congress as an author obscures its key characteristic in this regard, namely, that it is actually many autonomous authors. Messages are constantly being delivered or exchanged, both internally and externally, in the form of bargains, recommendations, requests, criticisms, warnings, and demands. As a consequence, it can be difficult to discern whose views are being articulated. From this standpoint, Congress may be observed and studied as a communications network and the legislative process as an information medium.

The two principal factors in this information environment concern the internal and external aspects of a communication. The former refers to the relationship between components that are framed to inform and persuade. The educational function of Congress is an inevitable result, rather than a deliberate goal, of its legislative activity. This fact does not impair the informational utility of congressional publications, but means it is necessary to look beyond the printed word if a complete grasp of their import is desired.

The analysis of any congressional publication, in addition to its substance, should also include the relationship between its source and audience. Official sources are both houses of Congress acting jointly, one chamber, or a committee. Unofficial sources are party organs, informal groups of legislators, or individual legislators. The difference between these two types of sources is not due to their potential influence but to the formality of their communications. Those of the former appear as official documents, those of the latter do not, if they are written at all. The mutual impact of both sources, though not always evident, is taken into account by an intended audience.

In a technical sense, communication between a legislative source and an audience is based on the scope of formal jurisdiction. However, while the authority to act may be legally prescribed, the ability to exert influence is not. The levers of influence that may be manipulated by political agents condition the clarity and intensity of the signals communicated. Statements are accorded respect to the degree that they can alter the competitive status of political interests. Despite the force or zeal behind a congressional publication, its content is normally expressed in moderate terms. Legal authority tempered by political prudence serves to avert resistance or hostility that can ultimately produce legislative stalemate or defeat.

THE INFORMATION FRAMEWORK

A legislator desires several types of information about any given issue. Substantive information refers to the means and ends of a proposed policy as well as the effects of past governmental action in a policy area. Political information concerns the relative strength of those who support or oppose a proposal and the probable consequences of alternative actions for a legislator's future. Procedural information relates to the legislative rules and practices that may be used to control a measure's progress. Either or both substantive and political merits tend to govern the choice of procedures.

A discussion of the flow of information in congressional channels centers on the concepts of time and control. The quantity of potentially useful information is too great for a single legislator to absorb without neglecting other responsibilities or priorities. Time is not only needed to collect and collate information, but to explore whether it may be used for purposes other than those for which it was originally created or acquired. Also of importance is that the length of the interval between the receipt of information and the need for action determines the time available to investigate possible options and make political calculations.

Efforts to minimize the costs of obtaining information begin with the wide range of sources that communicate with or are used by members of Congress. A partial listing would include rank and file legislators, party and committee leaders, personal and committee staff members, congressional support agencies, the president and his staff, administrative officials, local government officials, public advisory bodies, constituents, interest groups, nongovernment specialists, the media, and public opinion polls. Legislative organization offers one solution to the difficulties presented by this situation.

The division of labor and subject specialization represented by its committees denote that Congress is a committee-centered information system. Only panel members have the time to thoroughly familiarize themselves with the matters under their jurisdiction. This advantage is reinforced by extensive, poorly indexed and delayed printing of hearings, unanimous committee reports that avoid expressing diverse views, expeditious routing of legislation to the floor, and domination of chamber debate by committee members. Information resources tend to be used to further the purposes of those in a position to control them.

Legislators who possess valuable information know that the manner and timing of its release can significantly shape actions and outcomes. It may be used to challenge or supersede the accuracy of other information. It may be withheld to thwart opponents or may be disclosed to the media, other government officials, or anyone else. When and to whom information is distributed affects both the size of a potential audience and the level of political participation. This is because most policy proposals affect far more people than those aware of their existence.

Limitations imposed by time, capacity, and interest compel legislators to employ search strategies to cope with the volume, validity, and timeliness of vital information. Each legislator applies a combination of values and goals to aid in the selection and synthesis of desired data. Depending on the nature of an issue or subject, the dominant characteristic of legislative perception may be constituency opinion, policy objectives, political competition, or personal ambition. Constituents and colleagues are the sources most relied upon when legislators invest a significant portion of their resources in a public question. Other sources are consulted to the degree that they can provide information compatible with a developed position or firm conviction.

The legislative process is an amalgam of strategies and techniques devised to locate, acquire, assess, organize, retain, and transmit information. Political interests and intentions determine whether to accept, affirm, supplement, ignore, question, or refute circulating information. A vital need for reliable and relevant data is evident since legislators are obliged to state positions and make decisions in public. The extent of efforts devoted to the mobilization and manipulation of information is a sign of political competition and salience. Though information is plentiful, its presentation in a persuasive fashion and on an opportune occasion is an infrequent occurrence.

To demonstrate effectiveness in the access to or control of information enhances the ability to exert political influence. This applies with particular force to the capacity to restructure units of available information so as to form a new product or use an existing one for new goals. The discretion to restrict or grant access provides alternative strategies for achieving the identical purpose. To create resources of value to other political participants places one in a strong position to attain desired objectives. How general information is transformed into political currency and the latter into public policy are underlying themes of this book.

THE LEGISLATIVE AGENDA

The process of forming an agenda involves making choices about which decisions to consider. There are always more matters that merit attention than can be profitably or prudently addressed at any one time. This means that congressional decisions are a scarce resource in the political community. Placement on the agenda is only a first, though crucial, step on the route to a formal response. Because time is equally as valuable a resource for group proceedings as it is for individual action, congressional politics reflects a perennial struggle to control the legislative agenda.

Several enduring conditions guarantee that a large number of questions will be presented as meriting agenda status. The impact and intricacy of the economy entail a continual need to determine whether and what type of legislation is appropriate. Social diversity and competition generate demands and counter demands for redesigned public policy. The interrelationship of society and government requires that the functions and activities of the latter be adapted to changes in the former. The scale and complexity of many issues means that government is the only institution capable of effective action.

Once an item reaches the legislative agenda, it must still survive a winnowing process. Factors that limit the potential number of legislative decisions include the two-year life of a Congress, various obligations and objectives of individual legislators, numerous and competing interests that seek official policy statements, comparative ease of delaying rather than advancing legislation, difficulty in securing timely and reliable information, and persistence necessary to form a favorable consensus. The number of major bills that can clear all such barriers during any congressional cycle is quite limited.

An important distinction for agenda purposes concerns those items subject to discretionary action and those which are not. Recurring business in the latter category includes the budget and appropriations processes and numerous housekeeping chores. Nondiscretionary matters that arise with less regularity are reauthorizations of expiring programs and emergencies or crises. The resources consumed by these affairs control the discretionary agenda, which is more likely to consist of reinstated and familiar, rather than novel and weakly supported, proposals.

There are three phases in the development of the legislative agenda. The first centers on issue salience and involves political initiative, or the ability to make an issue a subject of public and congressional concern and debate. An issue is any matter that generates political controversy over the allocation of or access to public or private resources. External entities actuated by specific events, including elections, tend to predominate during this phase. The president, federal agencies, political parties, judicial opinions, constituencies, and interest groups are the main determinants of congressional business.

The leading actor at this juncture is expected to be the president. His national perspective and constituency, combined with vast informational and communications resources, when skillfully and vigorously used, enable him to promote policy goals by influencing public opinion and building political coalitions. However, the open competition that characterizes this phase precludes any individual or group from consistently dominating it. The interplay of conditions and interests within the confines of the legislative process determines which issues are certified for congressional consideration.

The second phase of agenda activity concerns issue definition and structure. The key agents at this point are congressional committees and subcommittees. These panels are legislative laboratories that test and digest the proposals under their jurisdiction. Should the advantages of or necessity for legislation become apparent, committee responsibilities for issue analysis and consensus formation assure them of several options, which translates into political power. The value of information as negotiations are commenced, alternatives assessed, and bargains concluded cannot be overemphasized.

The basic decisions on the type and level of resources to be committed are made during this period. A consequence of wielding the power of virtual life or death over bills also enables committees to assume an entrepreneurial role. Placing problems on the agenda for which there are no satisfactory solutions creates demands and opportunities for such remedies. An unsatisfactory response may even be advanced as a means of stimulating a search for something better. The ability of committees to control substance and to facilitate legislative transactions places them in a commanding position to influence the form and flow of the legislative agenda.

The final phase of agenda development is issue disposition. Party leaders play the primary role as they endeavor to coordinate the functional areas of the committee system and manage each chamber's legislative workload. Decisions on the arrangement of a legislative schedule reflect efforts to reconcile political demands and institutional efficiency. The results of negotiated agreements and chosen options are brought before the two houses of Congress. Most proposals are ratified due to a combination of committee competence and chamber deference. A sure sense of timing and parliamentary skill are also important.

When action by the parent body is imminent, the different scheduling needs of legislators become a principal problem. Majority party leaders require flexibility to regulate the volume of floor business and to assemble majorities for certain bills. Minority party leaders demand an opportunity to offer legislative alternatives and debate substantive issues. Committee members insist on retaining discretion to control the measures reported by their panels. Individual legislators desire a predictable timetable so that they can plan their activities with certainty. The conditions or procedures that serve the needs of one group often conflict with the needs of others.

The manner in which the agenda evolves significantly affects the legislative output. Minor and routine legislation is usually passed earlier in a session, while major and controversial bills require more time for their content to be refined and support aligned. For these latter proposals, the legislative process progressively narrows the range of available alternatives at each successive stage of action. In informational terms, this involves the segregation of facts and the integration of values.

Because facts are specific and stubborn, their interpretation can easily lead to disagreement and deadlock. Those which cause or have the potential to cause such results must be filtered out for legislation to advance. Because values are general and adaptable, they can be expressed so as to appeal to competing interests. Those which contribute to the necessary degree of political inclusiveness are carefully incorporated into a bill. These two aspects of information management form the foundation of any legislative strategy.

Each phase of the legislative agenda generates information about prerogatives, priorities, and procedures. Certain types of information accrue to certain legislators due to their positions. When and how they communicate this information is as important as its substance. Access to information in the legislative process is a necessary, though not sufficient, condition for favorable legislative action. The drive to reach desired goals provides the incentive to share information, for communication is the essential prerequisite for legislative progress.

Enactment of a law acknowledges that a problem exists and authorizes government to act. However, because statutory language does not necessarily define problems or specify means, a new round of decisionmaking is inaugurated. Though expressed in fixed form, legislation evolves through the interpretation of its provisions, the resources available for its implementation, and the vigor of its enforcement. It is the interplay between legislative authority and administrative discretion that determines the ultimate shape of public policy.

THE OVERSIGHT AGENDA

Since the large majority of congressional publications are generated by the consideration of legislation, most of this volume focuses on the legislative process. Legislative oversight is a related activity that results in a significant amount of material. This is the review by Congress through its committees of the administration of the laws it has enacted. Though the role of oversight in the pursuit and publication of information by legislators receives some attention in other chapters, it is discussed below in the wider context of legislative communications and transactions.

While information practices are similar for both legislative and oversight activity, the significant difference is the absence of a formal oversight process. Without a mandatory timetable for conducting and concluding such action, it is necessarily subordinated to legislative matters. That oversight is entirely a committee prerogative and draws less notice than lawmaking may enhance its appeal to many legislators. These circumstances enable legislators to exercise some influence over the implementation of laws, which can be as politically important as influencing their enactment.

The scope and complexity of contemporary issues means that legislation can no longer directly prescribe the conduct of private individuals, but must govern the activities of public officials. Almost all public laws involve the delegation of policymaking authority by legislators to administrators. Legislators often cannot either foresee or resolve questions that entail the application of general laws to specific situations. As social and economic conditions become increasingly fluid and interrelated, administrators need an opportunity to experiment with and adjust possible courses of action. Lawmakers are justifiably reluctant to enact rigid mandates in the face of political necessity and uncertainty.

Practical reasons for such delegation are that Congress possesses neither the expertise to master many matters which it is induced to address nor the time to cope with the numerous details that arise from its prescriptions. To establish policies that accomplish desired objectives, Congress must do more than enact laws embodying means and ends. Its lawmaking power must be exercised with a degree of flexibility and practicality that enable government to cope with volatile or perplexing conditions.

Political reasons stemming from societal problems that precipitate sharp conflict among competing interests also result in greater administrative discretion. Legislators unable to reach agreement on clear policy statements before public opinion can crystallize are inclined to shift the burden of making concrete decisions to appointed executives. In some instances Congress may find responsibility so politically burdensome or so devoid of political rewards that it assigns a task to an administrative agency.

Both legislators and administrators derive advantages from this situation. The technical and political dilemmas posed by current affairs render it extremely difficult to formulate legislative standards that are specific and feasible. Only by leaving some matters somewhat nebulous can sufficient support be mustered to pass legislation. The deliberate vagueness of statutes provides administrators with the flexibility to translate general policy pronouncements into practical criteria for applying the law in particular cases. This development also enables government to respond in a timely manner to continuously changing conditions that may threaten the welfare of citizens or society. The degree and propriety of delegation are based on the consideration by Congress of such factors as the limits of its competence, size of its workload, need for expeditious action, and locus of political accountability.

The explicit or implicit delegation of policymaking authority to administrators acknowledges their professional capabilities and capacity to concentrate on a matter over an extended period of time. The accumulation of administrative experience may eventually enable Congress to incorporate into statute those policies derived from agency practices. However, delegation also permits legislators to postpone policy decisions and affords them an opportunity to criticize administrative action. The double-edged sword of delegation means that administration cannot be viewed merely in terms of neutrality and efficiency. Each public law is vague to the degree that its provisions can neither clearly specify all the appropriate instances in which it should be applied nor the results it should yield in each such conceivable situation. A newly enacted law is only a policy in embryo that leaves to administrative discretion the task of grappling with further political decisions.

Agencies are frequently entrusted with a policy to execute that has not been clearly defined because a consensus concerning desirable means failed to develop. The general guidelines embodied in legislative language require administrators to interpret its meaning and assign priority to stated objectives. To implement policy, an agency must issue rules and regulations that cover circumstances not addressed or anticipated by authorizing legislation. The formulation and application of these directives involve consultation with all interested parties and continual management decisions. It is political rather than legal factors that place limits on these agency actions. When the administrative process supplements and refines statutory provisions, it is an extension of the legislative process.

Congressional oversight is the authority of legislators to require administrators to explain their actions. Such information is needed to determine what relationship, if any, exists between lawmaking and problem-solving. Attempts to ascertain the effects of legislative decisions on program results meet with two major obstacles. First, though legislative history may record the intent of those responsible for passage of a measure, changes in the political environment over the course of time necessitate policy adaptation. Second, the professional perspectives and political interests that prevail in an administrative agency after a bill becomes law differ from those that resulted in its enactment.

Because neither the substantive nature of problems nor their relative importance remain static, the suitability of a given legislative solution tends to be modified by unfolding developments.

The specific conditions that lead to oversight activity may be grouped under purposes that are primarily legal, political, and administrative, though these categories often overlap. The legal goals of oversight focus on whether programs are meeting statutory objectives and whether existing programs should be reoriented or terminated, holding administrators accountable for their use of public funds and uncovering abuses of authority or neglect of duty. Political motivations include efforts to protect and support favored programs, publicize legislator or committee views, criticize or challenge executive action, or satisfy constituent or clientele demands. Administrative questions relate to whether program benefits justify costs for delivering services, how required procedures affect the delivery of services, conflicting approaches of agencies with similar missions, and the policy impact of certain managerial decisions. Though it is legislators who perform oversight, the initiative may come from administrators who view such action as favorable for their own reputation or purposes.

Executive branch and independent agencies are the main sources of information for legislators about the administration and effectiveness of government programs. When appointed officials are reluctant to divulge information to lawmakers, one means of making them more amenable to oversight inquiries is to introduce or threaten to introduce bills that would curtail the scope of or reduce funds for an agency or program. In such cases the delivery of information may seem to be a reasonable price to pay for maintaining ongoing agency operations. The use of any particular means to obtain information does not necessarily indicate a lack of voluntary cooperation by administrators. Legislators may employ various methods to keep themselves informed of or to publicize agency activities. They may wish to condemn, commend, or otherwise control such action to further either legislative or oversight purposes. The continuing dialogue between legislators and administrators prepares the ground for many, if not most, legislative decisions.

BIBLIOGRAPHY

Anderson, James E. *Public Policy-Making.* New York: Praeger, 1975.

Cobb, Roger W., and Elder, Charles D. *Participation in American Politics: The Dynamics of Agenda-Building.* Boston: Allyn & Bacon, 1972.

Harris, Joseph F. *Congressional Control of Administration.* Washington: The Brookings Institution, 1964.

Jones, Charles O. *An Introduction to the Study of Public Policy.* Belmont, CA: Duxbury Press, 1970.

Kingdon, John W. *Congressmen's Voting Decisions.* New York: Harper & Row, 1973.

Saloma, John S. *Congress and the New Politics.* Boston: Little, Brown, 1969.

U.S. Congress. House. Commission on Administrative Review. *Scheduling the Work of the House.* House Document No. 95-23, 95th Congress, 1st Session. Washington: U.S. Government Printing Office, 1977.

U.S. Congress. Senate. Committee on Government Operations. *Congressional Oversight: Methods and Techniques.* Committee Print, 94th Congress, 2nd Session. Washington: U.S. Government Printing Office, 1976.

Walker, Jack L. "Setting the Agenda in the U.S. Senate," in *Policymaking Role of Leadership in the Senate.* A Compilation of Papers Prepared for the Commission on the Operation of the Senate. Committee Print, 94th Congress, 2nd session. Washington: U.S. Government Printing Office, 1976.

Young, Roland. *The American Congress.* New York: Harper & Brothers, 1958.

2
Dimensions of Legislative History

Decisionmaking is the conversion of information into action. The nature of available information and the diverse aims of legislators are the factual and political data that permeate and delimit legislative proceedings and production. This chapter explores how the decisionmaking process influences the range of political options and the content of policy statements. The first part examines the roots and attributes of legislative language through an overview of Congress' lawmaking function and decisionmaking process. The effort to transform political conflict into expedient agreement is seen as the most significant factor affecting the text of bills. The second part surveys the wide variety of key decisions at each stage of the legislative process. This serves as a guide to the types of information that may be obtained from those congressional publications issued at major decision points in a bill's journey.

Legislative history comprehends three distinct but interrelated factors. First is the totality of actions taken regarding a particular policy proposal. Second is the collection of congressional publications that contain information on which such actions were based, recording the decisions reached and furnishing a justification. Third is the interpretation of the meaning of actions whose causes, qualities, and directions may differ. This last element is the essence of that elusive concept commonly known as legislative intent. A full account of legislative history need not only identify actions that had a substantive impact, but also recognize the ongoing relationship among past, pending, and expected decisions. Construing the final terms of settlement and their implications involves the competition and reconciliation of various versions of legislative intent. It is this continuing campaign that provides public policies with their distinctive texture.

PUBLIC POLICY

Two ways of approaching the legislative process have been combined in the following pages—one is a description of the evolution and ecology of public policy; the other is an explanation of how congressional publications fit into and illuminate the policy process. The term "public policy" does not simply denote a decision made by one or more public officials having the legal authority to exercise judgment. The two key components of public policy are a customary style of decisionmaking and a fairly stable pattern of decisions. Any particular policy is the result of a consistent series and cumulative impact of official actions, which means that a course of inaction is also a policy. In this sense public policy may be defined as a specified set of conditions that officials endeavor to bring about in a given area of concern.

The somewhat elastic nature of this definition reflects the fact that policymaking itself is a process of determining whether certain conditions or concerns are or should be within the purview of policymakers. Most policymaking is routine in that regularized procedures and acceptable outcomes have conferred legitimacy on the vast majority of government programs. Because the values underlying these activities have become basic assumptions of our social and economic environment, they are virtually immune from political assault. Thus, the most common form of policy decision entails marginal changes designed to meet new needs or circumstances.

Controversy arises when differing interpretations of reality cannot be harmoniously settled among political interests. When this prompts determined efforts to initiate a departure from an established policy trend, the existing policy consensus is disturbed. Policymaking is not the sole preserve of legislators, and their inclination to act need not be expressed through the passage of laws. To what extent and at what point along a policy continuum Congress becomes involved are equally important for estimating legislative influence. Despite their value, there is more to the policy process than can be learned from congressional publications alone.

Congress' authority to enact laws is the most familiar and formidable of its powers. Lawmaking is the effort to erect a basic legal order for the various objective classes of people and organized groups that compose society. To establish a pattern of conduct that enables citizens to pursue desired and desirable ends requires that certain rights and duties be defined and sanctioned. The enactment of public policy represents an attempt to integrate and balance personal and group needs so as to promote the achievement of individual and communal goals. This substantive aspect of legislation concerns the formulation of general rules that may be stated for the first time or may combine several existing and possibly inconsistent rules into one comprehensive mandate for action.

Statutes may create programs, confer privileges, impose obligations, or prohibit conduct. Major legislation, which adjusts relationships and allocates resources, usually combines two or more of these functions as it tries to balance the substantive and symbolic gains and losses to be experienced by those to be affected. Public laws are a means to minimize or mitigate societal conflict and encourage or engender communal harmony. They enunciate purposes that are intended to justify the regulation of activities between citizen and government or citizen and citizen. Legislation empowers federal agencies to enter designated policy spheres in response to conditions acute enough to affect the welfare of a significant number of people or of government itself. The apprehension and instability generated by incessant change trigger demands that ensure a continuous cycle of legislative adaptation.

In a narrow sense public policy involves the enactment of legislation that is recognized as binding by virtue of its official promulgation. Though Congress may prescribe or proscribe conduct, the willingness of citizens to obey the law is based as much on access to decisionmakers and a sense of fair play as on constitutional prerogatives and legal forms. The legislative process is designed to diagnose the needs and validate the claims of societal entities in a manner that fosters the equitable distribution of benefits and burdens. All interested parties should have an equal opportunity to express their views to those responsible for making political decisions. The procedural aspect of lawmaking pertains to the prior knowledge and acceptance of the process by which policy is enacted. The authority of law stems from a combined perception of the legality of legislative power and the legitimacy of the legislative process.

DECISIONMAKING

Lawmaking and representation are the two principal functions of Congress. While the former reflects the desire for decisions, the latter denotes the demand for deliberation. Though these functions are not incompatible, their orientations differ. The emphasis of lawmaking is on problem-solving and the effectiveness of the legislative product. The focus of representation is on communication and stresses the responsiveness of legislative proceedings. It is the interaction of lawmaking and representation, or choice and consideration, that mainly accounts for the structure and process of the congressional environment.

Decisionmaking in and the decisions of Congress are shaped by its decentralized character and concomitant diffusion of influence. The key factors responsible for this condition are elections, bicameralism, committees, and rules. Legislators are primarily accountable to their constituents rather than their colleagues. The diversity of geographical localities produces many differences of opinion regarding appropriate policies. That there are two houses of Congress means that the personal and political views and values of senators and representatives can often clash. Different perspectives and practices also lead to legislative competition between the chambers as a whole. The use of committees enables Congress to cope with a large and complex agenda by distributing its workload among specialized panels for study and recommendation. This division of labor along functional lines creates the need to coordinate policy proposals that intersect and overlap the boundaries of committee jurisdiction. The rules and customs of the House and Senate have evolved to promote stability and prevent domination of the legislative process by any internal element or external entity. As a result, procedures may be employed or invoked to impede action and maintain the status quo.

The legislative process is characterized by multiple points of access, fragmentation of power, varying motives of legislators, and lack of central coordination. For a bill to become law requires the approval or acquiescence of different units or alliances at each of the several stages through which it must pass. The chain of decisions that affects the progress of legislation offers many opportunities for delay, modification, or defeat to those able to influence the fashion in which any link is forged. A process of continual bargaining is necessary to aggregate portions of power possessed at each decision point and convert them into successive majority coalitions. Only through a series of negotiated compromises can the various organizational units and diverse political elements within Congress be sufficiently coordinated to produce a major legislative decision.

The nature of legislative decisionmaking significantly affects the movement and content of legislation. That many individuals may participate in the process places some limits on the quality of possible decisions. The support of legislators for a given bill depends on its relationship to their goals and priorities. When compromises regarding the desirability or language of a proposal, which require time and tact, are combined with the complexity of many policies, the most likely result is gradual change. Negotiated settlements tend to be modest in scope because drastic departures are unlikely to secure the support of all legislators who may exercise a veto in their domain of influence.

Agreement on the need for and shape of major policies denotes a temporary accommodation among private and public entities pursuing different objectives. The enactment of public laws entails the consolidation of competing political claims as various concessions are made to garner essential support. Though it may be generally acknowledged that legislation is necessary, commitments to accept or not oppose a specific bill are usually the result, rather than the cause, of legislative action. The results of bargaining may make passage a mere formality, while in other cases the outcome may remain in doubt until the votes are cast. The two inseparable aspects of the legislative process are the evolution of legislative language and the formation of legislative majorities. A consensus on content and a coalition for passage reflect successful efforts to coordinate substance and strategy.

LEGISLATIVE LANGUAGE

In an ideal setting, statutory standards would cover the objectives to be achieved, the extent of administrative discretion, the criteria for making decisions, and the controls to be exercised. Furthermore, new policies would be coordinated and integrated with existing laws and relationships. However, consensus on public policy usually focuses on broad generalities rather than on details that can aggravate political differences of opinion. Modern legislation tends to generate general agreement on ends and disagreement on means. Political conditions conducive to passage of a major bill ensure that it will not be a model statute. Its language will be phrased in terms less than explicit and precise, if not deliberately ambiguous and vague, to maintain the support necessary for its enactment. A major statute is a collective articulation of shared interests that combines facts and values so as to promote its approval rather than clarify its provisions.

Statutory solutions represent the results of competition among numerous values and goals. A consequence of political bargaining is that different groups of legislators will support a measure for different reasons. The translation of compromises into acceptable language is intended to enable entities with differing interests to work together harmoniously. The equivocal nature of legislative terminology signifies that political friction has been moderated or averted. Legislation embodying indefinite or flexible objectives is the means used by Congress to satisfy its many constituencies. Should a major bill be written in plain and clear terms, its content and sponsor would be more likely to invite attack than attract support. Lucid language may cause quarrels, while evasive expressions can facilitate accommodation when all parties with a demonstrable stake in the outcome are afforded the opportunity to have their positions publicly recorded.

Even in the absence of political and technical complexity, limitations of lanuage preclude that clarity of expression which would produce unanimity on the meaning of all provisions of significant public laws. Bills require scrutiny in relation to existing law, technical provisions, potential amendments, and political implications. Their drafting is not simply a technical operation that demands legal skill but is an integral part of the process of policy formulation. Compromise language may be inserted into the text of a bill, into phrases that appear in accompanying documents, or in both. Drafting requires dexterity in the use of language to convey or, when necessary, obscure meaning. An innate feature of the legislative process is that language considered politically astute is not always legally acute.

The printed record for a piece of major legislation, including statutory language, when viewed in its entirety, discloses a political fabric woven with miscellaneous fibers and methods. Controversial measures are in a state of continual development as they advance toward enactment and their contents are subject to revision at each stage of consideration. The meaning of most provisions, or what is construed as such, must be derived from the entire process and cannot be assumed to be limited to a single publication or stage of proceedings. The serial nature of congressional decisionmaking renders it difficult to assign weights to inputs at any one stage or to discern a clear corporate opinion. The expression of legislative intent, which is a blend of the short-term purpose of passage and the long-term purpose of interpretation, is an exercise in the accretion and adaptation of language.

THE PRINTED RECORD

To secure passage of many public bills, it is necessary to avoid alienating or antagonizing certain legislators. This has two notable consequences for the content of congressional publications. First, those parties that fail to have their views incorporated into a measure's legislative history at one stage may succeed at another. Such a development may occur despite, or because of, contrary statements that appear in earlier parts of the printed record. Second, words that do not appear in print may be as important as those that are included. This covers provisions rejected or deleted as well as matters not discussed.

Legislative history may be derived from the meaning of words, the relationship of words, the nature of the subject matter, the historical background of an issue, or some combination of these factors. Because the history of one provision may illuminate the meaning of others, it may be necessary to trace a particular purpose or interpretation as it evolves and emerges at the final stage of the legislative process. As the several stages through which a bill must pass to become law are interdependent, so are each of its major subdivisions. While the latter tends to be explicitly noted in the printed record, the former tends to be only implicitly addressed.

That the volume of the printed record may be large or small does not always reflect the actual importance of a measure. Where a majority is sure of its strength its members may not feel the need to offer a thorough explanation, while those in the minority may not wish to employ their resources in a futile effort. Of course, such conditions do not preclude either camp from engaging in an extended discussion of a proposal for political or other purposes. It is where proponents and opponents are uncertain of the legislative outcome that the use of all available arguments and evidence about an issue ensures that the printed record will be most complete.

In addition to those congressional publications issued during the Congress in which a bill is enacted into law, legislative history also consists of relevant material generated during prior Congresses. Recourse to previous documentation may be necessary to disclose those factors that temporarily delayed passage and those that contributed to eventual enactment. Since most legislation amends existing statutes rather than creates new policies or agencies, a similar search offers the surest clues to the reasons for such revisions. Though the following discussion focuses on the last lap of the legislative process, it is equally applicable to the results of earlier action. The printed record also identifies reports by government agencies or private entities as well as judicial opinions from which statutory or supporting language may be derived or adapted. (See figure 1 for an overview of legislative documentation.)

Figure 1
Checklist of Legislative History Documents

Prologue
1. Committee-sponsored policy research
2. Presidential message (with draft legislation)

First Chamber
3. Introduced print of bill
4. Committee hearings
5. Committee mark-up (amendments)
6. Committee report
7. Reported print of bill
8. Special order or "rule" in the House or Senate Unanimous Consent Agreement
9. Chamber debate on "rule" or Agreement
10. Chamber debate on and amendment of bill
11. Act print of bill

Second Chamber
12. See documents 3-10
13. Bill as passed

Bicameral Documents
14. Chamber debate on and amendment of the two different versions of bill or
15. Conference Report (with Joint Explanatory Statement)
16. Chamber debate on conference report

Enactment
17. Slip law

THE LEGISLATIVE PROCESS

The second part of this chapter approaches the legislative process from the standpoint of its major stages. Efforts preceding enactment cover a variety of strategies, bargains, coalitions, and explanations. Congressional publications directly address only the last of these, while information about other legislative transactions must be derived through inference or deduced from results. Strategic decisions involve such questions as whether to bypass a particular stage, which subjects to raise or avoid, whose support to seek, and when to proceed to the next stage.

The legislative process blends the discretionary nature of its proceedings with the mandatory nature of its output. Participants are continually testing the limits of their influence and are aware that discretion does not imply unconfined choice and that mandates do not imply unavoidable obedience. Successfully retaining options for future contests, whether in the legislative or administrative arena, is the essence of political skill.

An examination of who influences priorities and how alternatives are framed at major decision points is combined with a survey of those publications that originate at each stage, suggesting the manner in which such documents are affected by prior decisions and how they affect later ones. For researchers, the prime drawback of the legislative process is that Congress is rarely able to speak with a single and clear voice. The great advantage is the availability of published material due to the open and inclusive nature of its policy process.

The bound *Daily Digest*, issued at the close of each session of Congress, is the single most complete source of facts on legislative business because it covers both chamber and committee proceedings. It is arranged chronologically, with entries for each day on which any formal congressional activity occurred. Under the heading of Chamber Action, it identifies bills introduced, reported, considered, and passed. For those measures acted on, it describes the amendments adopted and rejected and notes the method of voting and vote totals. References to the appropriate pages of the bound *Congressional Record* are included. Under the heading of Committee Meetings, it distinguishes among full committees, subcommittees, and conference committees. If the meeting was a hearing, the names of witnesses are listed. The subject, bill number, and status of the legislation are given for hearings, mark-ups, and conferences. This information enables one to follow the progress of measures during the all-important stage of committee consideration. A subject index cites bill numbers and separately identifies action on each measure in terms of hearings, mark-up, report, chamber action, conference consideration, and public law or veto. Its concise format and thorough coverage make it an excellent place from which to begin tracing legislative history.

The *Legislative History Annual*, published by Congressional Information Service, identifies all pertinent printed items, while for essential information inadequately covered by legislative material, the indispensable source is Congressional Quarterly *Weekly Reports* or *Almanac*.

ORIGINS AND AVENUES

The period that precedes or immediately follows the introduction of a major bill is one that involves competition to stimulate legislative interest. The key question is whether the substantive or political aspects of an issue are sufficiently compelling to warrant congressional consideration. Should there be an affirmative answer, corollary questions focus on whether a statutory solution is possible, necessary, or desirable, and these may be debated throughout the life of a proposal.

The decision to seek a congressional remedy entails attempts to persuade legislators to commit personal and public resources. The former refers to the time and effort legislators are urged to invest to rectify a given situation. The latter concerns the appropriate level of personnel and funds needed to administer a program. The advantages of traveling the legislative route relate to the binding nature and popular approval of a law. It provides a source of legitimacy on which to draw and build. The disadvantages of the legislative process are its unforeseen contingencies, which may lead to an undesirable statute. The failure to pass legislation may also foreclose the option of successfully pursuing other alternatives.

The most effective strategy for securing legislative action is presidential endorsement and support. The president's access to and coverage by the media enables him to publicize and dramatize the need for legislation. Another vehicle for promoting widespread interest in proposed policy is the congressional investigation. Its focus on societal inequities or exposure of governmental ineptitude can serve to attract attention and generate action. Major bills enacted into law during any given session of Congress have invariably received consideration during earlier sessions. For most societal change to be ratified or hastened by legislation, support must be accumulated gradually over a number of years. A lengthy gestation period is needed to accustom the public and officials to the political and practical feasibility of significant policy innovations. Since the consequences of controversial issues tend to be clearer than their causes, time is also required for a consensus to develop regarding whether and how to address either the consequences or causes, or both.

Once the need for legislative action is conceded or confirmed, efforts are devoted to the political architecture of a bill. This endeavor embraces its components and configuration, which directly affect its scope and strength as well as the committee to which it will be referred. Some preliminary questions are whether to assign a program to a new or an existing agency, the degree of presidential authority or agency autonomy to grant, the amount of resources to allocate, and whether to include provisions for a legislative veto or judicial review. A bill may be written as a virtually finished product or may contain only a few general propositions whose substance is designed to serve as a basis that will enable its supporters to draft a more adequate measure.

An important choice at this point is between an appropriation bill, which is a less visible but still an effective means of action, or an authorization bill, through which more can be gained but which is more difficult to pass. If the latter type of measure is used, there remains the question of amending an existing law or enacting a new one. The former course gives the impression of a routine revision but may introduce complications by attempting to integrate incompatible intentions. The latter approach allows for a unity of purpose that may provoke greater opposition. Another decision is whether to draft an omnibus bill, each of whose parts might be a separate measure in itself, or a less ambitious proposal. The advantages of the former are that it can accomplish a great deal if enacted and can provide ample bargaining room to form the coalitions needed for passage. Its disadvantages are that it may generate endless bickering among interested parties and its scope may be perceived as too threatening to existing relationships. Though more modest bills may be drafted with greater ease, they may be viewed as too narrow to warrant sufficient support.

The prominent publications of this stage are presidential messages and policy research studies. The former appear in the *Congressional Record* and *Weekly Compilation of Presidential Documents*. They may address salient issues, convey general recommendations, or request the passage of specific measures. In this last case, they often contain the text of draft bills. Policy analyses may be prepared by permanent government agencies, temporary study commissions, industrial organizations, research institutions, congressional support agencies, or congressional committees. These reports may appear in any class of congressional, government, or commercial publication. Those issued by support agencies and committees in the form of agency studies or committee prints, due to the importance of their sources, are more likely to signify contemplated legislative action.

INTRODUCTION AND REFERRAL

Most bills are introduced for reasons unrelated to their anticipated enactment and are intended to generate publicity for election campaigns or novel ideas or to demonstrate that a legislator is promoting constituency interests or influencing national policies. Bills may be divided into three categories based on origins and content. There are those with insufficient support to advance beyond referral to a committee. Another class consists of routine measures considered necessary or desirable and whose passage is expedited. Major proposals, primarily drafted by executive branch agencies or influential private organizations, consume most of the resources devoted to legislative business.

A significant factor associated with introduction is the solicitation of a sponsor. This involves either a request submitted to a member of Congress by an external entity or a prearranged selection based on a legislator's participation in the formulation of policy and strategy. Introduction by a committee or subcommittee chairman ensures that a bill will at least receive a hearing. The rules of both houses permit an unlimited number of members to cosponsor bills. Multiple sponsorship, which serves notice of bipartisan or majority support, can encourage committee action on a bill should the chairman not be among its sponsors.

Introduction also involves the question of whether to act at the start of a Congress to maximize the time available for passage or wait until an election year when public attention and partisan factors play a greater role. A further decision is whether to seek introduction and action in both houses simultaneously to demonstrate broad support or else concentrate on one chamber and use its approval as leverage for passage in the other.

Referral of bills to committees is generally a routine practice that is governed by parliamentary precedents, earlier legislation, and panel jurisdiction. Bills are usually drafted so as to ensure their referral to the committee most likely to proceed favorably. The great majority of all bills are referred exclusively to a single panel. Measures whose subject matter overlap the jurisdiction of two or more committees are referred to the appropriate panels concurrently or consecutively. While multiple referral may reduce friction among committees, the practice may also encumber the legislative process, for increased participation does not guarantee agreement or action.

The printed record for this stage comprises introduced prints of bills and brief statements in the *Congressional Record* regarding introduction, referral, and purpose. This relative scarcity of material indicates that the decisions reflected are generally foreseen and routine.

COMMITTEE CONSIDERATION

Committees are the crucibles of survival for bills, where most succumb to neglect. This is the most critical stage in the life of legislation because of a committee's ability to delay, modify, or kill a measure. Though the committee imprimatur is essential for passage, its power to impede exceeds its power to advance bills. The reasons for its position are due to the factors of workload, expertise, negotiation, and coordination. The large volume of bills introduced during each Congress demands that someone decide which should receive attention. The complexity of contemporary policies requires subject matter specialists to master their substance. A forum is needed to facilitate bargaining among constituency, functional, party, and ideological interests. Local control of elections and heterogeneity of membership render political parties incapable of functioning as cohesive national policy organs. Committees are the only agents that can meet all the needs suggested by these conditions.

A committee chairman, upon receipt of a bill, will normally refer it to a subcommittee for study and report. The subcommittee, in turn, refers it for comment to the federal agency having responsibility for its subject matter. The agency reply can decisively affect a subcommittee decision to schedule hearings. If either the political climate necessitates it or committee members desire to sway public opinion, hearings will be held to enable legislators to exert political influence and justify policy decisions. A thorough public hearing open to those with a substantial interest in or knowledge of a proposal is needed to help the committee forge a bill capable of surmounting the obstacles with which the road to enactment is paved. Hearings provide an opportunity to gauge whether the investment of additional legislative resources would be politically profitable. It is through hearings that committees determine which interests will have access to the policy process, a crucial judgment that significantly affects the substantive impact of Congress on the end product. The readjustment of societal relationships entailed in the formation of new programs prompts widespread efforts to participate and persuade. The hearing is a legislative tool designed to elicit information, focus attention, encourage compromise, and foster consensus among competing political elements.

Hearings are followed by one or more mark-up sessions. At these meetings, each line of a bill is open to discussion and analysis. Decisions are reached by consensus when possible and by vote when necessary. The subcommittee must initially determine whether to report the bill to the full committee and, if so, in what form. A measure may be reported as introduced, reported with one or more amendments, or completely rewritten. In this last case the subcommittee can report a substitute, which retains only the number of the introduced version, or a clean bill, which is introduced by a committee member, assigned a new number, and referred to the panel that drafted it. There also remains the option of reporting an original bill, which is a proposal that has not been previously introduced.

Additional decisions necessary for authorization bills address the life span or funding level of programs, which may be established on a permanent basis or for a prescribed period. Legislation may simply state that "such funds as may be necessary are authorized," without specifying a figure. Should a sum be included in the bill, there remains the question of whether to make it available for an indefinite or determinate length of time. This matter relates not only to the immediate measure but is also a factor that will influence the actual allocation of funds granted by a subsequent appropriation bill. The effective administration of programs depends, to a significant extent, upon decisions made by the appropriations committees concerning an agency's financial resources.

The report that accompanies a bill outlines its overall purposes and provides a detailed explanation of each major provision. These documents supplement the legal language of bills through factual and political analysis and argument intended to present the strongest possible case for favorable legislative action. Reports contain the findings and recommendations that stem from the committee's interpretation of an issue and distillation of its evidence. The aim is to elucidate and generate support for the committee's position regarding the political, substantive, and administrative feasibility of the reported measure. The full committee may accept, modify, or reject subcommittee recommendations, or it may proceed with its own consideration of the bill, including hearings and deliberations. In some cases the full committee will examine and evaluate legislation without referring it to a subcommittee, while in other instances a bill may be referred to a subcommittee for hearings with the full committee retaining responsibility for its substance.

The degree of committee unity is one of the key factors that affects a committee decision to report a bill favorably to its parent body. The closer a panel is to unanimity, the greater the possibility its proposal will be approved as reported. It is considered embarrassing and distressing for committee members when their recommendations are rejected, reversed, or revised by floor action—thus, the need and desire for panels to accommodate their members without unnecessarily weakening a bill. This process accounts for language in a committee report that may appear inconsistent with the language of the bill. For controversial proposals, reports serve as handbooks for advocates during floor debate, while their contents enable routine legislation to be accelerated through to enactment with little or no debate.

Committee decisions about the initiation and organization of hearings as well as the reporting and amending of bills are of immeasurable importance. The framework within which further deliberations proceed tends to be firmly set by committee action. Hearings and reports not only emphasize the rigor of committee scrutiny and standards, but it is through these publications that an attempt is made to alter the perceptions and influence the alignment of those legislators yet to act. Though these documents may be neither the first nor last to issue from the legislative process, they serve as the twin cornerstones of any legislative history.

REPORTING AND SCHEDULING

Bills are officially reported when referred to a calendar, which is a list of measures in the chronological order in which they have been submitted for chamber consideration. Referral to one of these legislative dockets constitutes a committee recommendation and does not require action by the parent body. Since there is insufficient time to act on all bills reported by committees, a combination of formal procedures and informal practices is used to determine which will receive priority for floor action. The most important factor at this stage is timing, as proponents endeavor to discover or create a propitious moment for action.

Public bills in the House are referred to either the Union or House Calendar. The former lists measures that directly or indirectly raise revenue or appropriate money, while all other public bills are assigned to the latter. The referral of a bill to its proper calendar is based on its text as it was referred to, not reported by, a committee. Except for general appropriations bills, all major measures must be accorded priority by resolutions reported from the Rules Committee to receive timely floor consideration. These resolutions are privileged business and, when approved on the floor by majority vote, confer a privileged status on the bills to which they apply. The Rules Committee may delay reporting such a resolution because a majority of its members or of the House deem a bill to be politically inexpedient or substantively deficient.

Any member may request that a measure on the Union or House Calendar be placed on the Consent Calendar, which is reserved for uncontroversial bills. The

Speaker may also recognize members to offer motions to suspend the rules. Consent Calendar bills require unanimous approval for passage, while those brought to the floor under suspension of the rules require a two-thirds majority for approval. Both methods enable proposals to become privileged for consideration on specified days, sharply restrict the amending process, and are used to expedite minor or emergency measures. Any bill may also be passed by unanimous consent while still on its original calendar if the majority and minority party leaders agree. Suspension of the rules can also be used by the Speaker as leverage against a committee that impedes legislation with widespread chamber support.

The Senate has a single calendar for legislative business, with almost all routine bills brought to the floor by unanimous consent and passed with little or no debate under an informal clearance procedure that involves all interested senators. The Senate has neither a counterpart to the House Rules Committee nor designated days for the consideration of certain classes of business. Virtually all major legislation is scheduled through the use of unanimous consent agreements negotiated by the majority and minority party leaders. Since these compacts may be thwarted by the objection of a single member, each senator has an opportunity to influence their content. Without a unanimous consent agreement there exists no limitations on debate or amendments that can be conveniently invoked. The prerogative of any senator to propose that a bill be considered by the chamber or to offer it as a nongermane amendment to a measure under consideration means that legislation cannot be impeded by the refusal of a committee to report or an individual to schedule it.

The major developments that affect scheduling are chamber workload, political pressures, adjournment plans, and action by the other house. The earlier a measure is scheduled during a Congress or session, the greater the time available for proponents to negotiate the compromises necessary for passage. Should proponents delay scheduling until later in a session, when members are eager to adjourn, they may be able to pass a bill that could not withstand extensive scrutiny. This strategy also places opponents in a key position to kill a bill through dilatory tactics unless granted concessions. Scheduling in the Senate is a result of cooperation between the majority and minority party leaders, while in the House the majority leadership acts independently of, but informs, the minority.

Information about bills reported, a purely formal matter, is available from the chamber calendars and the *Congressional Record*. Special resolutions from the House Rules Committee and unanimous consent agreements in the Senate appear in the *Record* and the journal of each house. A summary of each chamber's scheduled business for its next daily session is inserted at the end of the *Daily Digest* section of the daily *Record*. A more detailed discussion of the forthcoming legislative program may appear at the end of the proceedings section, particularly in Friday editions, as party leaders announce and reply to questions about the agenda.

CHAMBER CONSIDERATION

Under ideal conditions, this stage provides for retrospective and prospective accountability. The former refers to review of the actions of agents and entails an appraisal of committee recommendations. The latter pertains to the publicity accorded member statements and votes which enable constituents to evaluate their legislative effectiveness. However, the complexity of floor procedure tends to obscure responsibility, and the reality of legislative influence contributes to committee autonomy. Committee expertise regularly enables panel members to lead debate and guide the amending process.

The relatively large size of the House has resulted in reliance on formal procedures and forceful leadership to conduct its business. Its proceedings accentuate the discipline of organization and its decisions are rendered by a preponderance of numbers. The comparatively small size of the Senate has contributed to the employment of informal practices and collegial action to manage its workload. Its deliberations emphasize freedom of expression and its verdicts are reached through a consensus of opinion. That the House is governed by majority rule and the Senate sanctions minority rights means that legislation is the product of complementary modes of parliamentary action.

Most legislators have committed themselves to support or oppose a major bill by the time it reaches the floor. Debate is less an assessment of options than it is a variety of attempts to adopt or avert change. A committee or subcommittee chairman who is designated as floor manager has the primary responsibility for the passage of a measure across the legislative terrain. With occasional exceptions, amendments are offered by those who wish to weaken or kill a bill, while the floor manager engineers efforts to maintain the committee product intact. Since amendments may be designed to refine, as well as undermine, a measure, decisions must also be made about whether to accept or propose alternatives to them. Members may offer amendments to accommodate an external entity, attract public attention, delay proceedings, or test sentiment for a proposal. Floor managers must be tactful when opposing the amendments of those who are not necessarily opposed to the bill.

Since roll-call votes only occur during consideration of controversial measures, they constitute a record of major congressional decisions. Legislators may cast their votes in response to partisan or ideological preferences, electoral or political aspirations, or colleague or presidential expectations. Two key factors that affect votes relate to their visibility and type. Much can depend on whether the vote is to be recorded or unrecorded, as well as whether a vote will be on the merits of a bill or on a procedural action. The latter of each of these pair of possibilities allows more leeway for explanation. A vote on final passage may be relatively routine after the disposition of amendments and other motions intended to defeat, delay, modify, protect, or expedite a bill. The interrelation and variety of parliamentary motions and political maneuvers make floor debate the most complex stage of legislative proceedings.

The chief difference between the chambers at this stage concerns the decision to close debate. The three methods available in the House are special orders reported by the Rules Committee, motions for the previous question, or unanimous consent. The first two are provided for by the rules and are the procedures most commonly employed. Deliberations conclude in the Senate when discussion expires of its own accord, through a unanimous consent agreement, or a motion to invoke cloture. The first two, though beyond the reach of Senate rules, are the means on which it regularly relies. That a majority may terminate debate in the House whenever it is so inclined, and a minority may prolong debate in the Senate for an extended period, has an unmistakable impact on the style of floor action and the strategies available in each chamber.

The restrictive nature of House debate encourages members to be pointed and prompt in their remarks since amendments and other motions are acted upon with relative dispatch. The principal consequence of time limitations is to enhance the influence of standing committees. These panels are vested with the primary responsibility for the content of legislation, and those who would recast a bill must demonstrate the validity of their case. House customs compel sponsors of major amendments to overcome the conviction that bills should be thoroughly considered in committee rather than inexpertly formed on the floor. Because the rules reinforce this view, it is extremely difficult to successfully challenge committees, whose recommendations tend to be ratified by the parent body.

The opportunity for each senator to significantly influence the course of legislative proceedings by taking advantage of the rules militates against the rigid control of time. This condition, combined with many demands on the time of members, means that controversial matters must often await resolution until floor consideration of a bill has commenced. Minimal restrictions on debate permit political bargaining to occur and policy decisions to be made during the amending process. Mutual recognition by senators of the needs and prerogatives of colleagues incline committee members to share their influence with those who are not members of the panel that reported a bill. As a result, Senate committee proposals are always subject to extensive review.

A complete account of legislative debate appears in the *Congressional Record*. The impact of committee decisions underscores the value of its report as an introduction to the substance and strategy of floor proceedings. Explanations offered by floor managers in the course of debate are often considered as supplemental committee reports. Chamber action may also be used to make explicit informal agreements and tacit understandings reached during earlier stages of the legislative process.

SECOND CHAMBER

The Senate and House vary in size, constituencies, tenure, and procedures, the last of which includes dissimilar committee structures and jurisdictions. These differences ensure that political interests will experience different degrees of access and acceptance in each chamber. Those dissatisfied with the results of action in one body will appeal its decisions to the other.

One aspect of legislative strategy concerns the question of which house should act first. It may be decided to initiate action in the chamber that is more likely to pass a bill to generate momentum or employ leverage and establish political legitimacy. Paradoxically, the body more inclined to act may be reluctant to do so if its efforts will be nullified through inaction by the other. To start and succeed in the house where prospects are uncertain almost guarantees that something will be enacted. If both houses are prepared to proceed, it is considered expedient to launch the drive for passage in the chamber that will pass a stronger bill.

A bill passed by one house is normally referred to the appropriate committee in the other. When a bill is amended by the second chamber, the amendments are returned for action to the first and are usually held at the Speaker's table or presiding officer's desk, which are calendars by another name. A bill received by the second chamber that is substantially the same as one reported therein may also be held in the same manner. Because of its privileged status, greater discretion, including more expeditious action, is available to dispose of business that originated in the other house. This condition may persuade one house, or one of its committees, to defer action on a bill until it is reported in the other. A common practice is for the second chamber to revise its own bill and incorporate it as an amendment into the companion measure received from the body of origin. This substitution of text, combined with passage under the bill number of the first house, facilitates the conference process.

It is also at this stage that efforts may be made to bypass committee consideration in the other chamber. House committees may be bypassed by a nongermane Senate amendment to a House-passed bill. In this instance, the Senate amendment is a separate measure that may be held at the Speaker's table for House action. Senate committees may be bypassed by placing a House-passed bill directly on the Senate Calendar, a procedure which any senator may invoke. A Senate-passed bill transmitted to the House and substantially the same as a measure on a House Calendar provides an opportunity to evade the authority of the Rules Committee to grant approval for consideration of the House bill.

Depending on the length of time that elapses between action on a bill in each house and the extent of political differences involved, the publications of the second house tend to serve as an implicit or explicit reply to those of the first. Criticism tends to be muted and indirect and expressed in terms of a discussion of the omission or inclusion of specific provisions and the purposes thereof. Regardless of differences, the nature of legislative language and objectives generally allows ample latitude within which both houses may negotiate satisfactory compromises.

BICAMERAL ACTION

Both houses must adopt legislation in identical form before it can be sent to ..ie president. One method of facilitating bicameral agreement is informal consultation between the party leaders or committee staffs of each chamber. Such an approach is feasible for uncontroversial measures, which tend to pass both houses as introduced or with minor differences. This development leads to amendments between the houses, which are resolved by each chamber acting separately in succession on changes proposed by the other. Action may be deferred temporarily while bicameral negotiations proceed. In the absence of a formal and separate publication, memoranda that explain the text agreed upon may be inserted in the *Congressional Record.*

Controversial bills usually result in the approval of significantly different versions by each body. The instrument used to reconcile these differences is the conference committee. This ad hoc panel is composed of members of the Senate and House committees that have jurisdiction over the legislation. Though a conference meets as one committee, in effect it is two, since decisions can only be made by a majority vote of the conferees of each house. Conferees endeavor to maintain the position of their respective chambers and arrive at a result that will be acceptable to both.

The first step in this process involves the decision to seek a conference. Though one house need only ask and the other agree, the matter is not quite so simple. The chamber that requests a conference customarily acts last on the conference report, which means it has one less option than the body that acts first. The house that considers a report first may approve, reject, or recommit it to conference, while the second chamber to act cannot recommit it since approval by the first terminates the conference. Thus, when one body amends a bill originated by the other, it may return the measure and allow the first house to request a conference or, in anticipation of disagreement, it may ask for a conference prior to returning the bill.

The authority of conferees is limited to amendments in disagreement and does not extend to identical language approved by both houses or to subjects not covered by either body. When the second chamber has passed a substitute, which is an amendment that constitutes a new bill, total disagreement exists and conferees may rewrite the entire measure, though all components must stem from either or both the Senate and House versions. Bills may be reported by a standing committee or passed by one house under the assumption that a conference will be necessary. Amendments that insert or delete certain provisions may be accepted during chamber consideration because it is believed that they can be discarded or restored in conference. The versions of a major bill adopted by each house ordinarily contain some language that is included for the purpose of providing leverage in conference negotiations. This entails political judgments regarding which provisions are of lesser consequence and can be bartered for those of greater importance.

Prior to a conference, the members selected by each house will try to reach agreement on which provisions of their chamber's bill to firmly insist and which of those adopted by the other to resolutely resist. This initially determines which amendments are subject to being traded, compromised, or reported as still in disagreement. Once complete accord has been reached, a conference report containing the language through which differences have been reconciled is filed in each body. When the result is partial agreement, those matters that remain unresolved must be settled through amendments between the houses or another conference.

The prerogatives and prestige of each chamber have as much influence on the results of a conference as the legislation itself. Since the decisions of conferees normally become the decisions of Congress, negotiations can be lengthy and intense as each side perceives a need to claim success, however it may be defined. Two factors contribute to the approval of conference reports by both houses. That they are not subject to amendment means it is necessary to reject the entire product to express dissatisfaction with a portion. Because conference reports usually appear toward the end of a session or Congress, the timing of their consideration creates pressure for passage.

Since the first house to consider a bill usually invests more time and effort, it is prepared to accept some changes adopted by the second rather than lose the measure through an inability to reach agreement. Amendments approved by the second chamber reflect further refinement based upon the views of those disturbed by the legislation as it passed its body of origin. The additional allies secured by such changes, assuming that other support is not alienated, also induces the first house to be receptive.

Two common forms of conference agreement are silence and ambiguity. These devices enable each side to advance a favorable interpretation or preserve its desired options. Though such action may ensure inconsistent efforts in the implementation of law, legislators recognize the uses of political and administrative flexibility. All interested parties gain something with the implicit understanding that the solution is tentative pending actual experience and results. Conference reports embody the ultimate congressional compromise and, despite their occasionally difficult format, exemplify the essence of the legislative process.

PRESIDENTIAL ACTION

In the case of major legislation, the president and his agents will have been active throughout the period of congressional consideration. Presidential influence in the form of a coherent policy and a consistent strategy is normally the primary means for overcoming the decentralized nature of legislative decisionmaking. The entire process is conditioned, to some degree, by the known or presumed preference of the president. In many instances he has publicly committed himself to approve a measure, while in others he implies that a veto is likely if a bill is not framed to his satisfaction. Knowledge of the presidential position may result in legislation that includes provisions which he both approves and disapproves, with the former intended to carry the latter over the final hurdle to enactment. Congress may also pass legislation for which its members can claim credit despite a certain veto, just as a president may wield a veto that is certain to be overridden.

If the president deems certain legislation unnecessary but not objectionable, disapproves of only portions, or opposes enactment but realizes a veto will be overridden, he can allow a bill to become law without his signature. The president has 10 days, Sundays excepted, to act on a measure after it is presented to him. Congress may await an opportune moment to deliver a bill to the White House to minimize the possibility of a veto. The president may feel compelled to accept a bill rather than risk the failure of Congress to pass more suitable legislation within a reasonable period of time or he may have plans for its implementation that can render it more consistent with his views. A presidential decision at this stage may reflect on the proximity of elections as much as on the substance of legislation.

The presidential veto is another means to prevent or postpone governmental action. When the president opposes a bill, his congressional allies will at least attempt to delay it to create the opportunity for a pocket veto. Should the president return a bill to its body of origin with a statement of his objections, an effort to override may be made immediately, deferred, or avoided depending on the prospects of success. The two-thirds majorities needed to override a veto almost always gives the advantage to those who support the president. If a veto is sustained, the bill may be repassed, minus the provisions that prompted presidential disapproval. In this case the veto message, which appears in the *Congressional Record*, becomes part of a measure's legislative history. The *House Calendar* contains the most complete and detailed information on pending and prior presidential action for a session.

SUMMARY

A bill must avoid numerous congressional vetoes well before the possibility of a presidential veto. Greater effort is required to shepherd a bill through the legislative process than to arrest its passage, which can be accomplished at any of several points. Because different entities or perspectives tend to predominate at successive sites of action, earlier decisions reflect efforts to anticipate and affect later ones. This structural feature invites thorough consideration, a result that is generally true of the entire process though it may be precluded at any one stage. (See figure 2 for an overview of the legislative process.)

The bargaining required by a decentralized and fragmented political environment accounts for the relatively slow pace of legislative proceedings, but

Figure 2
Key Steps and Decision Points in the Enactment of a Law

First Chamber
1. Bill introduced and referred to committee
2. Committee hearings planned and held
3. Committee mark-up scheduled and bill analyzed*
4. Committee report drafted and filed*
5. Bill referred to chamber calendar
6. Terms of floor consideration framed
7. Terms of floor consideration approved*
8. Bill debated and amended*
9. Final passage*
10. Bill transmitted to other house

Second Chamber
11. Committee and chamber consideration* (see steps 1-8)
12. Bill approved as received* (to step 20) or
13. Bill approved with amendments*
14. Bill returned to body of origin

Bicameral Action
15. First chamber agrees to amendments* (to step 20) or
16. First chamber disagrees to amendments and requests a conference*
17. Conference negotiations and agreement
18. Conference report drafted and filed
19. Conference report debated and approved by each chamber*
20. Bill delivered to the White House

Presidential Action
21. Bill signed into law

---

*Indicates steps that may or usually involve roll-call votes.

it also permits the adjustment of positions and accommodation of purposes to proceed until agreement is reached. Extensive deliberations facilitate the formation of majority opinion as passage through each stage generates gradually wider acceptance and progressively narrows the scope of contention. Those engaged in this maze of maneuvers require the consent of others to attain any of their objectives. Congress is a preeminently political body where, for each measure that receives sustained attention, a temporary combination of incentives fosters cooperation among autonomous islands of influence.

BIBLIOGRAPHY

Berman, Daniel M. *In Congress Assembled.* New York: Macmillan, 1964.

Folsom, Gwendolyn. *Legislative History: Research for the Interpretation of Laws.* Charlottesville: University of Virginia Press, 1972.

Froman, Lewis A., Jr. *The Congressional Process.* Boston: Little, Brown, 1967.

Gross, Bertram M. *The Legislative Struggle.* New York: McGraw-Hill, 1953.

Jewell, Malcolm E., and Patterson, Samuel C. *The Legislative Process in the United States.* New York: Random House, 1966.

Keefe, William J., and Ogul, Morris S. *The American Legislative Process.* 3rd ed. Englewood Cliffs, NJ: Prentice-Hall, 1973.

Oleszek, Walter J. *Congressional Procedures and the Policy Process.* Washington: Congressional Quarterly Press, 1978.

Rieselbach, Leroy N. *Congressional Politics.* New York: McGraw-Hill, 1973.

Ripley, Randall B. *Congress.* 2nd ed. New York: W. W. Norton, 1978.

Ripley, Randall B., and Franklin, Grace A. *Congress, the Bureaucracy and Public Policy.* Homewood, IL: Dorsey Press, 1976.

U.S. Congress. House. Committee on Science and Technology. *Legislative Manual of the Committee on Science and Technology.* Committee Print, 96th Congress, 1st Session. Washington: U.S. Government Printing Office, 1979.

Wayne, Stephen J. *The Legislative Presidency.* New York: Harper & Row, 1978.

Young, Roland. *The American Congress.* New York: Harper & Brothers, 1958.

3

Policy Research

Policy research is one means by which legislators keep themselves informed of existing and proposed policy developments. Though the theory that underpins this form of information assumes a value-neutral environment, the political context in which it is prepared and applied significantly affects its content and utility. This chapter examines the ideal and practical aspects of policy research, with particular emphasis on the role of the four congressional support agencies: the Congressional Research Service, General Accounting Office, Office of Technology Assessment, and Congressional Budget Office.

Major policy proposals may originate as, or eventuate in, congressional bills. In either instance, they frequently engender prominent studies and analyses that are designed to probe substantive and political premises and purposes. To explore the research background of legislation is to focus on how public policies are initially framed and legislative objectives provisionally formulated. The usefulness and limitations of policy research depend on the degree to which its sponsors or consumers believe it can help to bridge the gap between ideal solutions and political realities.

Policy research covers a variety of material that cannot be succinctly described or readily identified. It may be prepared by a governmental or non-governmental body; it may be issued by an administrative or legislative entity; it may or may not be printed; its availability may be restricted; it may be an original study or a compilation of previously published material; it may be descriptive or analytical, conceptual or practical, objective or subjective. The reasons for this lack of regularity in sources, accessibility, and content relate to chronology and knowledge.

Though policy research generally precedes legislative action, it is not a mandatory part of the legislative process. Its prelegislative origin usually coincides with views on a given issue that are still in a formative stage. The preliminary nature of its issuance and observations account for the discretion and diversity that characterize its authorship, substance, and distribution. Its appearance as or in a congressional publication or its use by legislators can confer a status equivalent to more formal documents.

RESEARCH AND POLITICS

The nature of policy research can be clarified by comparing it with professional research. The latter focuses on the formulation and consequences of public policy, is intended to advance knowledge in a given field of study, and is aimed at members of a profession. It tends to be structured by empirical data, with its content insulated from personal motives or desires and its validity established by objective criteria. Policy research focuses on matters that extend beyond a specific subject area, is intended as a guide to action, and is aimed at a set of political decisionmakers. It is inevitably affected by external factors, with its content subject to the values and goals of particular clients and its validity established by a process of competitive negotiation.

Policy research may simply incorporate professional research in the form of analyses of the original objectives or unintended consequences of existing government programs, studies of the implications of possible policy adjustments or major reforms, and evaluations of the strengths and weaknesses of proposed alternatives. Professional research may also be used as a base to develop original approaches that include novel and analytical techniques that can be applied to societal problems, the integration of concepts from the fields of politics, economics, administration, and law to illuminate the evolution and effects of public policies, or the examination of seemingly unrelated matters that are actually different dimensions of a larger issue.

To enhance the acceptability of a research product, it is necessary to identify the needs and desires of those entities likely to be affected by a proposed policy and to obtain information about and from them. This undertaking is designed to disclose and neutralize the natural biases of various sources and to accommodate the views of interested parties. Policy research combines disciplinary expertise with insights from the sphere of political dynamics to highlight the interactive processes that are an integral part of an issue and its resolution.

A generalization that can be made about policy research concerns its purpose. Whether authorized or adopted by legislators, it is intended to help crystallize opinion on the merits of an idea or appropriate governmental action. Thus, it is one form of political input and influence that may address a proposal from the standpoint of credibility, desirability, feasibility, or necessity. Such efforts reflect an ongoing contest to set the legislative agenda and affect the activities of political participants.

Complexity and competition are the two factors primarily responsible for the decision to undertake policy research. Policymakers are rarely confronted by conditions or problems with obvious causes or solutions. The scope and impact of contemporary issues must be defined and refined before realistic proposals can be devised. Efforts to generate agreement on the existence and nature of a problem are not merely intended to clarify a specific situation. Analyses sponsored by concerned parties also attempt to foster common perspectives so as to influence public debate and the policy climate.

The purposes of policy research may involve efforts to identify an issue or problem, assess whether legislative action is feasible, accumulate factual data and clarify underlying values, ascertain available alternatives, and provide a technical evaluation of the consequences of alternatives and correlate such consequences with desirable goals. Political factors may intrude at any time depending on the strategy or solution favored by groups of legislators. Some may wish to limit the research focus to the exploration of a possible legislative decision; others may seek to facilitate a timely decision, while still others may desire to support chosen positions. In any case, only legislators can undertake a political evaluation of the consequences of alternatives and foster the consensus necessary to adopt a preferred policy.

Though policy research is a legislative tool of acknowledged value, any given situation usually produces at least one barrier to its unreserved acceptance by all parties involved. The competing goals of legislators can prevent a question from being described with the precision necessary before it is assigned to another entity for further study; objective research may not generate information desired to advance a legislator's personal ambitions or a committee's policy preferences; politicians tend to address only those aspects of an issue that can be exploited to their advantage; legislators prefer to commit resources for application to immediate matters rather than invest in an uncertain future when they may no longer be in a position to exert influence.

Even when legislators are receptive to research input, there exist impediments to its use. Many policy decisions are necessitated by fixed timetables or dictated by unforeseen events. The lack of sufficient time to explore an issue thoroughly often means that all relevant information cannot be obtained. A fluid environment that continually affects the ranking of public priorities, combined with time constraints, generally limits research output to partial and tentative proposals. If technical analyses are inconclusive or inconsistent, a political decision remains the only recourse. For complex policy problems the effort to develop criteria needed to isolate and compare costs and benefits is never complete or definitive and always remains subject to challenge regarding data and interpretation. Since contemporary issues are too indefinite and far-reaching for research alone to offer conclusive verdicts about correct choices, disagreement often ensues about the timing of formal statements or the initiation of other legislative actions.

Congress is an arena of advocates in which legislators who have different roles, constituencies, objectives, and abilities endeavor to advance political viewpoints. Since policymaking occurs in an adversary environment, decisions must be the result of negotiations. The process of formulating and adopting policy receives more attention than its consistency or objectivity. In this climate, disinterested analysis is inseparable from legislative advocacy because plain facts affect political fortunes. Thus, all legislators who support a bill rarely do so for the same reasons and just as rarely for reasons compatible with research criteria.

The several stages of the legislative process require bargaining and compromise to form successive majorities regardless of factual or verifiable evidence. The utility of results is determined by parties engaged in the process of conflict and cooperation. The quality of the research product cannot restrict or override the values or interests of potential users. Political participants who disagree about the need for congressional action on a certain subject may be motivated by the substance of factual and analytical inquiries or by the conviction that such a course will produce a favorable outcome.

Since policy research is not always the only or most important kind of information on a given issue, it must compete with other types. The major alternative to such research is the broad range of policy options generated by parties who do not claim to be objective. The vigorous pursuit and direct clash of concrete interests serve to test various assumptions and aims against one another. Research results can encourage the reconsideration of premises and purposes as the legislative process, which accentuates the aggregation of interests rather than the analysis of information, proceeds. Though the legislative and research processes are not natural allies, they can complement each other.

Policy research can facilitate and guide discussion among political competitors who may not be able to agree on fundamental values or policy forecasts. Research material contributes to the success of political negotiations when it establishes contours and focuses arguments so as to increase the intelligibility of policy options and reduce the resistance to possible decisions. That the validity of policy research is based upon its utility to those attempting to achieve desired goals does not nullify its value, for as with legislation itself, its legitimacy is determined by its acceptability.

CONGRESSIONAL SUPPORT AGENCIES

All policymakers need continuous access to sources that can provide timely, accurate, systematic, and comprehensive information and analyses. The availability of data poses the problem of information management rather than its acquisition. The volume of information is too great for legislators and their staffs to examine and organize in a timely and concise manner. Thus, they must often rely on others to process the information upon which legislative decisions will be based. Since policy research entails investing facts with their political significance, the perspective of those units responsible for accumulating and processing information is a key factor.

Though Congress uses the studies of administrative agencies and private organizations, it has chosen to establish research units to exclusively serve its own needs. The main reason it has done so is to redress the balance of policy initiative between the executive and legislative branches. Congress requires a constant flow of factual, descriptive, analytical, and interpretive information. An independent staff capability to analyze and assess issues and legislation reduces congressional dependence on other political entities in deciding upon the feasibility, purposes, methods, and implications of existing and proposed policies.

Congressional committees are the principal consumers of policy research, which is used to aid them in the performance of legislative and oversight functions. These panels play a pivotal role in policy formulation but seek outside assistance only when they are unable or unwilling to meet demands on their resources. Because most committee staffs are comparatively small and preoccupied with pending decisions, they lack the time for extensive research projects. The result is that policy research, though a regular feature of the legislative process, serves an auxiliary role.

The cost of collecting information tends to increase and its value decrease the longer the process continues. By entrusting a project to a capable and responsive unit, a committee conserves its resources and, by avoiding a commitment to act, keeps its options open. The guidelines stipulated by the committee ensure that the research methods used and form of presentation will be adapted to its needs. The desired result would be a disinterested study whose attributes are attuned to the realities of the legislative environment.

Standing committees are the units among which Congress distributes its workload and through which it promotes policy expertise. Committee members are expected to combine subject specialization with political judgment in preparing and submitting recommendations to their parent bodies. Though this arrangement enables nonessential information to be screened and essential information to be processed, it does not foster the ordering of priorities or the consistency of policies. Committee autonomy tends to insulate related areas of policy from one another. The broad and complex issues generated by social and economic conditions do not fit neatly into the jurisdictional compartments of the committee structure.

Legislative policymaking requires the coherent consideration of several different functional policy areas, each of which is the responsibility of a different committee. The integrated and coordinated nature of policy research serves to partially overcome the diverse and divergent elements that comprise the organizational and political environment of Congress. A comprehensive approach that identifies all relevant factors may also function to counterbalance the views of political interests that have access to committee members.

Anticipatory or long-range studies can identify matters likely to require eventual congressional attention. The collection and analysis of information about such potential problems can proceed in advance, unaffected by political controversy and unhurried by urgent need. Developments can be monitored by specialists without consuming legislative resources until the need for action is manifest. When a legislative decision becomes necessary, a foundation will have been laid that provides an opportunity for Congress to address a subject more quickly and confidently. This promotes a more orderly schedule for the legislative consideration of issues and reduces the possibility of immediate action preceding adequate preparation.

A manageable fund of digested data helps to offset the segmented and fitful nature of the legislative process, which inhibits the accumulation and availability of all pertinent information needed for imminent decisions. Major issues can be diagnosed early enough to permit information resources to be fully mobilized and held in readiness for expeditious application. The employment of specialized skills to identify and analyze conditions and alternatives that can be only dimly perceived on the political horizon enables Congress to more precisely address substantive questions.

Congress confronts the difficult task of trying to forge an effective link between policy specialization, as typified by its organizational features, and policy integration, as demanded by the complexity and scope of contemporary issues. One response of Congress to this matter has been to enlarge the responsibilities of two support agencies, the Congressional Research Service (1970) and General Accounting Office (1970; 1974), and to create two others, the Office of Technology Assessment (1972) and Congressional Budget Office (1974), to meet the short-term policy research needs of committee decisions and deadlines as well as the long-range needs of congressional attention and alternatives.

These four research staffs can ensure the equal availability of information and introduce common frames of reference to both houses and all committees, insulate the analytical phase of research from political biases to produce a more credible product, reallocate resources more easily as changing conditions and congressional needs warrant, and apply information generated for one type of response to other types. Legislative support agencies also have access to, and may enlist the aid of, entities or individuals in the academic or industrial communities with expertise in particular methodologies or subjects. They can pursue information originating outside the legislative arena and adapt it to the needs of congressional clients.

When acting as agents for congressional committees, all four support agencies are empowered to obtain information from any federal agency. Most such requests cause no friction or are resolved through committee-agency negotiations. An impasse, which may reflect political conflict between Congress and the president, may lead to committee issuance of a subpoena or passage by one house of a resolution directing that the information be transmitted. Thus, information which agencies may withhold from the public cannot be easily denied to the legislative branch. Its release to legislators may then result in its public dissemination through congressional publications.

All four congressional support agencies confront the situation of providing information within a political context. Despite their nonpolitical modes of operation, their subordination to a political body means that impartial preparation of research material cannot preclude its interpretation and application from being subject to political preconceptions. Since each legislator has geographical as well as functional constituencies, each is more concerned about the specific effects of public policies rather than their overall relation to the national welfare. Policy research will find greater legislative acceptance when the substance of an issue is perceived as highly technical in nature and its impact is viewed as general in nature.

CONGRESSIONAL RESEARCH SERVICE (CRS)

The CRS is an operationally independent unit within the Library of Congress whose primary function is to provide Congress with research assistance on public issues. It responds to committee requests to judge the advisability of enacting particular proposals, to estimate the probable results that would follow enactment, and to assess alternative means of accomplishing intended objectives. Its studies endeavor to provide a systematic and comprehensive investigation of the practical options and potential consequences within a given policy area. These analyses focus on the specific needs or purposes pertinent to approaching decisions. (See figure 3 for an example of a CRS study.)

Congressional committees use the CRS to help them prepare for hearings and analyze legislation. The former activity embraces the review of new policy concepts and their relation to the legislative process, evaluation of reports issued by and about federal agencies, synthesis of technical information in committee jurisdictions, critiques of interest group positions, summary and analysis of court decisions covering particular areas of public policy, and preparation of subject surveys on federal and state legislation. The analysis of legislation encompasses background reports on the evolution of policy issues; legislative histories of bills or subjects under consideration; in-depth analyses of proposals that address national and international problems; pro and con analyses of potential legislative solutions; section-by-section comparisons of related measures; and memoranda that summarize a bill's purpose and effect, describe other bills of similar purpose previously introduced, and recapitulate all prior action taken by Congress on each such proposal.

The CRS serves as a communication channel between the legislative process and various fields of knowledge, including sources in academia, industry, and government, to keep itself and its clients informed of new forms and uses of information. The agency enters into contracts for research projects when it lacks the expertise or time necessary to meet deadlines. The criteria for approving such contracts include knowledge of an institutional viewpoint, competence in the application of a research or analytical technique, and availability of special facilities. For those issues that overlap committee jurisdiction, its projects are interdivisional in preparation and interdisciplinary in content. In these cases, task forces composed of specialists in different but related subject areas pool their efforts to produce more comprehensive studies that cover the mutual impact of various or possible government actions.

Figure 3
A Study Prepared by the Congressional Research Service

97th Congress }
1st Session } **COMMITTEE PRINT**

RESTRUCTURING THE CIVIL SERVICE RETIREMENT SYSTEM: ANALYSIS OF OPTIONS TO CONTROL COSTS AND MAINTAIN RETIREMENT INCOME SECURITY

PREPARED FOR THE

SUBCOMMITTEE ON CIVIL SERVICE, POST OFFICE, AND GENERAL SERVICES

OF THE

COMMITTEE ON GOVERNMENTAL AFFAIRS
UNITED STATES SENATE

BY THE

CONGRESSIONAL RESEARCH SERVICE
LIBRARY OF CONGRESS

JANUARY 1982

Printed for the use of the Committee on Governmental Affairs

U.S. GOVERNMENT PRINTING OFFICE

88-001 O   WASHINGTON : 1982

Not all CRS research products are printed or readily available to the public. One reason is that many requests from congressional committees are confidential. Also, since those analyses known as multilithed reports and issue briefs often require updating, it is not feasible to print them. Lists of these studies are distributed only within the congressional community. A semiannual publication entitled *CRS Studies in the Public Domain* lists all CRS research products that have been issued by Congress as committee prints, House and Senate documents, or inserted into printed hearings or the *Congressional Record*. Researchers who seek access to current unprinted material need to obtain the approval of the congressional client for whom it was originally prepared or of the CRS. For access to noncurrent material that has been transferred to the National Archives, written permission must be granted by either the appropriate Senate committee chairman or the Clerk of the House. While CRS printed studies can also be found in the *Monthly Catalog* and *CIS/Index*, the most accessible source of information about its unprinted material is its Annual Report to Congress, which appears as a committee print of the Joint Library Committee.

GENERAL ACCOUNTING OFFICE (GAO)

The basic research activity performed by the GAO is program review, or the analysis and assessment of agency programs and operations to determine their compliance with applicable laws and regulations, the economy and efficiency with which resources are managed and consumed, and the costs and benefits that stem from the pursuit of statutory objectives. In addition to conducting its own appraisals, the GAO also evaluates program reviews completed by federal agencies. In its role as the principal congressional monitor of federal programs, it seeks to ensure that existing laws are appropriate, effectively administered, and serving to achieve intended purposes.

Regular GAO audits of agency activities enable it to identify overlap and duplication among programs, inadequate coordinating arrangements among interdependent programs, and inconsistent approaches to programs having related goals. This examination of results not only generates recommendations for changes but also largely determines what type of remedial action is most appropriate. The major difficulty associated with program evaluations is that neither authorizing legislation nor agency regulations establish explicit standards or specify clear goals against which administrative performance can be judged. Not only are measurement techniques almost always less definite than desired, but agreement is often absent regarding a program's precise purposes. In addition, differences between the policy goals of Congress as a whole or a congressional committee and those of the president or an executive branch agency impedes agreement on whether objectives have been met.

Though analyses of agency affairs may be undertaken by GAO at the request of congressional committees, in practice most reports are self-initiated and based upon a perception of congressional interests and needs. The criteria used to decide whether to investigate a program are its social and economic impact as measured by actual or potential political controversy, public criticism by professional groups or other levels of government, or the recency of GAO or other evaluations. Studies focus on the reasons for a sudden or sharp increase in program costs, alternatives to existing programs, economic evaluations of proposed programs, or cost-benefit analyses of program inputs and outputs. Though a typical report contains an intensive examination of an identifiable problem or operational area, collectively they can provide a comprehensive view of an entire program, issue, or agency.

One section of the *Annual Report* of the GAO summarizes its recommendations for legislation contained in its studies and is arranged by congressional committee. A biannual booklet entitled *General Accounting Office Publications* is a list of the agency's reports submitted to Congress during the preceding year. A monthly publication entitled *GAO Documents* is a more up-to-date listing that includes abstracts of reports prepared for Congress. All of the titles contained in these three items would also be found in the *Monthly Catalog*. Those reports not issued separately and which may only appear in printed committee hearings can be identified in *CIS/Annual*.

OFFICE OF TECHNOLOGY ASSESSMENT (OTA)

The OTA was created to provide Congress with policy research on subjects principally relating to science and technology, with emphasis on the broader economic, environmental, social, and political implications of scientific and technological developments. Its studies are designed to serve as an early appraisal of the potential applications and probable impact of technological changes and programs. By relating technology to policy and exploring the possible consequences of alternative technological choices, its reports are intended to offer a thorough and balanced analysis that can facilitate the effective social management of such innovations. This prognostic capability is calculated to orient legislative effort in appropriately curbing, counteracting, controlling, or channeling technological trends in the public interest.

The specific informational responsibilities of the OTA are to identify the existing or probable effects of technology or technological programs, establish cause-and-effect relationships where possible, determine alternative technological methods of implementing programs, ascertain feasible programs for achieving desirable goals, estimate and compare the consequences of alternative methods and programs, and identify areas where additional research or data are required to adequately support estimates and comparisons. Such information is needed by legislators to anticipate, understand, debate, and evaluate existing or emerging problems and to formulate viable policies. A systematic effort to identify and project developments, as well as to analyze policy options before the pressure of events requires immediate action, aids in the legislative assessment of matters where the government is considering support for or regulation of technological applications.

To accomplish its purposes, the OTA is authorized to conduct surveys of existing and proposed government programs with a high technology content, to report on the activities or responsibilities of agencies in affecting or being affected by technological change, to monitor the natural and social environments to detect the effects of technological developments, and to recommend or undertake technological assessments. The value of a possible research project is judged by whether the subject already is, or is likely to become, a major national issue, the significance of a policy's effect on the distribution of economic and social resources, whether a technological impact is imminent or irreversible, the availability of sufficient knowledge to assess the technology and its consequences, or a study's potential for reinforcing or supplementing previous assessments.

OTA research appears either as separate office reports or in the form of committee prints issued by those Senate and House panels having responsibility for such subjects as communications, energy, the environment, health, transportation, and weaponry. The OTA periodically issues a *List of Publications*, and the titles of recent studies appear in its *Annual Report* to Congress, which mainly describe technological programs requiring further study and analysis. This material can also be readily identified through the *Monthly Catalog* or *CIS/Index*.

CONGRESSIONAL BUDGET OFFICE (CBO)

The CBO was created to improve the flow and quality of information needed in the discharge of legislative budgetary responsibilities required by the annual consideration and formulation of the federal budget. Such research applies to the content and passage of budget resolutions, appropriation bills, revenue measures, and other authorizing legislation involving budget authority. As a prerequisite to providing such information, the CBO monitors the performance of the economy and estimates its impact on government activities and analyzes the probable effects of alternative budgetary decisions. Its research products are intended to facilitate the establishment of priorities, in terms of spending totals, allocated among major functional areas of government.

The CBO is required to prepare an annual report on fiscal policy and budget priorities. Part I of this document includes a discussion of optional budget levels for the coming fiscal year, alternative allocations of budget authority, and an assessment of the likely impact of such options on national growth and development. Part II, which appears as a separate publication, estimates the results of the continuation of current fiscal policies, as reflected in the second budget resolution, for the following five years. The purpose is to devise a standard against which Congress can consider possible changes as it examines the budget for coming fiscal years. As part of the annual budget process, it also issues an analysis of the recommendations contained in the president's budget and compares executive and legislative economic forecasts.

For public bills under consideration by committees, the CBO prepares cost implementation and financial effect analyses that appear in committee reports. It also issues periodic reports on the status of congressionally approved budget authority, appropriations, revenue, and debt legislation. This information cumulates the amounts and changes for these fiscal categories as the figures appear in separate bills and compares them with the totals in the most recent budget resolution. Through these reports Congress is kept informed about how its individual decisions affect its overall fiscal policy goals.

The priority for claims on CBO resources are first, the Budget committees; second, the Appropriations, House Ways and Means, and Senate Finance committees; and third, other committees. Its reports and analyses are either issued separately by the office or appear, in whole or in part, in publications originating mainly with the Budget committees. The CBO occasionally issues a *List of Publications* and maintains an index of available information to facilitate public access to its material. At this time, the latter is a strictly chronological listing of items which may be examined only by an in-person visit. Thus, the *Monthly Catalog, CIS/Index,* and *American Statistics Index* are the best means of access to its research output.

COMMITTEES AND COMMISSIONS

Either house of Congress may authorize a standing committee to undertake a specific inquiry and grant it additional funds for such a purpose. A committee may decide, on its own initiative, to assign a project to its staff or let a contract for a major study. Committee research is distributed via nonlegislative committee reports, committee prints, printed hearings, and Senate or House documents.

Research studies may also be required or requested of government agencies through legislation, committee reports, hearings, or informal agreements. Legislation may prescribe that a designated official report to Congress on action authorized under a statute. Reports may be required prior or subsequent to administrative action and may be on a regular basis, a single study, or whenever certain executive findings are completed or decisions reached. The utility of such a product for oversight purposes is enhanced when legal provisions contain a clear statement of objectives, a definite due date, and specifications that reports include information about administrative plans, strategy, and resources. Progress reports that address any difficulties in following legislative intent are particularly informative.

An annual publication entitled *Reports to Be Made to Congress* is issued as a House document and lists all such items mandated by law that federal entities, including the president, must submit. (See figure 4, page 56.)Those that result in oversight hearings will usually be inserted into the printed transcript of the proceedings. Since some of these reports may not be printed or, if printed, may be incorporated into various congressional publications, not all of them will be listed or clearly identified in the *Monthly Catalog* or *CIS/Index.* In this case, one would have to contact the originating agency or appropriate congressional committee for further information.

Two sources that are considered more impartial than standing committees, though they owe their existence to legislative action, are select committees and advisory commissions. Both are temporary units formed to investigate an issue or problem and submit recommendations to Congress, the president, or both. They expire after a specified period of time or upon submission of their final report. Common reasons for the creation of these panels are that they enable all major political interests affected by a given situation to be represented by appointment, focus public attention on a matter by publicizing it, and are a means for according priority to the consideration of complex and critical developments. Select committees are especially useful to overcome the difficulty posed by an issue whose subject matter overlaps the jurisdiction of two or more standing committees. Advisory commissions seem most appropriate when the technical nature of a question and the expertise needed to address it are beyond the capabilities of legislators and their staffs.

Since a research product originated by or through a standing committee eliminates the need for an independent legislative evaluation of findings and recommendations, as well as the additional effort required to translate recommendations into legislative proposals, the formation of temporary panels may reflect a desire to postpone or avoid congressional action. This approach may be a dilatory tactic intended to mollify one or more interests by demonstrating that a matter is receiving serious and sustained attention. In the process of gathering and analyzing information, these interim bodies can also serve as a forum for reaching a compromise among numerous parties with various purposes. Their major functions are to conduct investigations of

Figure 4
A House Document Listing Reports Submitted to Congress

96th Congress, 2d Session - - - - - - - - - House Document No. 96–254

REPORTS TO BE MADE TO CONGRESS

———

COMMUNICATION

FROM

THE CLERK,
U.S. HOUSE OF REPRESENTATIVES

TRANSMITTING

A LIST OF REPORTS WHICH IT IS THE DUTY OF ANY
OFFICER OR DEPARTMENT TO MAKE TO CONGRESS,
PURSUANT TO RULE III, CLAUSE 2, OF THE RULES OF
THE HOUSE OF REPRESENTATIVES

JANUARY 22, 1980.—Referred to the Committee on House Administration
and ordered to be printed

———

U.S. GOVERNMENT PRINTING OFFICE

57–662 O　　　　　WASHINGTON : 1980

specified matters, prepare and issue reports, evaluate the performance of agencies or effectiveness of programs, and submit recommendations or alternatives. The *Monthly Catalog* and *CIS/Index* provide the best bibliographic coverage of these publications.

Other sources of policy research include private organizations, such as the Brookings Institution and the American Enterprise Institute, that issue studies aimed at policy makers. Informal groups of legislators, the largest being the Democratic Study Group in the House, have recruited staffs to investigate matters of particular interest to them. Democratic and Republican party policy units provide research assistance to standing committee staffs and members who need supplemental information. Interest groups also furnish material to legislators and, though generated to support a given viewpoint, it can provide information not available elswhere. The absence of any centralized source for this information requires the use of such search strategies as phone calls, newsletters, and mailing lists.

BIBLIOGRAPHY

Coleman, James S. "Policy Research in the Social Sciences," in *Policy Analysis on Major Issues*, A Compilation of Papers Prepared for the Commission on the Operation of the Senate. Committee Print, 94th Congress, 2nd Session. Washington: U.S. Government Printing Office, 1977.

Schick, Allen. "The Supply and Demand for Analysis on Capitol Hill," in *Policymaking Role of Leadership in the Senate*, A Compilation of Papers Prepared for the Commission on the Operation of the Senate. Committee Print, 94th Congress, 2nd Session. Washington: U.S. Government Printing Office, 1976.

U.S. Congress. House. Commission on Administrative Review. *Final Report*. House Document No. 95-272, 95th Congress, 1st Session. Washington: U.S. Government Printing Office, 1977.

U.S. Congress. House. Commission on Information and Facilities. *Congressional Budget Office: A Study of Its Organizational Effectiveness*. House Document No. 95-20, 95th Congress, 1st Session. Washington: U.S. Government Printing Office, 1977.

U.S. Congress. House. Commission on Information and Facilities. *Information Resources and Services Available from the Library of Congress and the Congressional Research Service*. House Document No. 94-527, 94th Congress, 2nd Session. Washington: U.S. Government Printing Office, 1976.

U.S. Congress. House. Commission on Information and Facilities. *Inventory of Information Resources for the U.S. House of Representatives—Part II: Other Resources in the Legislative Branch*. Committee Print, 94th Congress, 2nd Session. Washington: U.S. Government Printing Office, 1976.

U.S. Congress. House. Commission on Information and Facilities. *The Office of Technology Assessment: A Study of Its Organizational Effectiveness*.

House Document No. 94-538, 94th Congress, 2nd Session. Washington: U.S. Government Printing Office, 1976.

U.S. Congress. House. Commission on Information and Facilities. *Organizational Effectiveness of the Congressional Research Service.* House Document No. 95-19, 95th Congress, 1st Session. Washington: U.S. Government Printing Office, 1977.

U.S. Congress. House. Committee on Science and Technology. *Technical Information for Congress.* 3rd ed. Committee Print, 96th Congress, 1st Session. Washington: U.S. Government Printing Office, 1979.

U.S. Congress. House. Select Committee on Congressional Operations. *General Accounting Office Services to Congress: An Assessment.* House Report No. 95-1317, 95th Congress, 2nd Session. Washington: U.S. Government Printing Office, 1978.

U.S. Congress. Joint Committee on Congressional Operations. *Congressional Research Support and Information Services.* Committee Print, 93rd Congress, 2nd Session. Washington: U.S. Government Printing Office, 1974.

U.S. Congress. Senate. Commission on the Operation of the Senate. *Congressional Support Agencies*, A Compilation of Papers Prepared for the Commission on the Operation of the Senate. Committee Print, 94th Congress, 2nd Session. Washington: U.S. Government Printing Office, 1976.

4

Hearings*

Committees are the instruments through which Congress chooses to screen and process proposals to change public policy. A committee decision to hold hearings, except for the annual appropriations and budget process, indicates a matter has crossed the threshold of political salience. These proceedings serve to focus public and political attention and may be a prelude or an alternative to legislation. This chapter explores the multipurpose nature of hearings, examines their structure and procedure, and discusses their contents. The aim is to offer a framework within which to analyze and assess the printed product.

Committee hearings play a crucial role in the life of legislation. The result of these proceedings determine whether a bill will advance beyond committee consideration and, if so, what revisions, if any, the committee deems necessary. Hearings form a bridge between a bill's referral to committee and a committee's recommendation to its parent body for favorable legislative action. Both the House and Senate have rules that apply to hearings and all committees have additional rules that supplement those of each chamber. These stipulations are few in number and narrow in scope. This encourages political participation and informal negotiation before access to committee members becomes more restricted and procedures more formal during later stages of the legislative process.

PURPOSES

To schedule hearings is an option entirely within the discretion of a committee or subcommittee. Since time is one of a legislator's most valuable resources, the decision to invest it in hearings is evidence that an issue will receive serious consideration. Hearings may be held because committee members express much interest in a proposal or subject, great concern is manifested by other major political actors or a combination of both factors. They may reflect the state of public opinion, or of certain interested publics, as perceived by legislators or they may be planned to influence the way in which an issue is perceived by the public.

Hearings are a means of collecting and conveying factual and political information. As a communication medium that provides the opportunity for several goals to be pursued simultaneously, not all of which are necessarily consistent, they serve as a versatile legislative tool. They enable legislators to judge whether further committee or congressional action is necessary or to

*This chapter derives from an article, "Congressional Committee Hearings," by Jerrold Zwirn, in *Government Publications Review*, Vol. 7A, pp. 453-61, © 1980 Pergamon Press Ltd. Reprinted with permission of Pergamon Press.

demonstrate that such action is or is not warranted. This entails preparing a foundation for recommending that legislative action be legally binding, politically compelling, advisory or deferred.

Legislative and oversight proceedings constitute the two basic types of hearings. The latter are mainly retrospective and involve a review of existing laws from the standpoint of policy priorities, program effectiveness or administrative discretion. The former are mainly prospective and may focus on one or more introduced bills, a bill about to be introduced or a subject on which legislation is contemplated. Since most public policies can be modified by either administrative or legislative action, these differences are more a matter of emphasis than substance. It is not unusual for oversight hearings to indicate that a legislative remedy might be appropriate or vice versa.

The ideal function of hearings is to enable legislators to obtain those facts needed to make informed and rational policy decisions. However, technological and political developments have contributed to an environment in which the prevailing condition is a surfeit, rather than a scarcity, of information. Its availability has transformed the hearing process into a central clearinghouse for ideas and opinions needed by all participants in the political arena. Hearings are an integral part of any overall strategy designed to enact a bill into law.

For all significant legislation hearings are a political necessity. Only by subjecting a bill to extensive and intensive scrutiny can a committee produce a measure that can survive the challenges that await it at each stage of the legislative process. Hearings provide one of the earliest opportunities to ascertain whether the compromises that are an indispensable ingredient of all major bills are likely to materialize. They tend to generate agreement on the main outlines and major provisions of a measure while identifying secondary or divisive features whose elimination would facilitate its passage.

Hearings may last one day or several weeks depending upon the nature of the matter addressed or committee purposes. Proceedings may be prolonged to generate public and congressional interest and support or may be brief in an effort to forestall the mobilization of opposition. A large number of witnesses may mean that, rather than giving a proposal thorough consideration or being too lenient in permitting testimony, a committee is engaged in a delaying action. Such a tactic is employed to obstruct legislation by leaving insufficient time for a bill to pass through all stages of the legislative process prior to congressional adjournment.

Though hearings may be held on a measure there always remains the possibility that a committee will conclude that legislation is unnecessary or inappropriate. One of these situations occurs where a hearing provides a forum for viewpoints denied other outlets. This function can be quite important when it serves to ameliorate social or economic tensions by giving aggrieved parties an opportunity to publicly present their case. There are also occasions when the nature of legislation suggested by hearings is viewed with apprehension by the parties that would be affected. This development encourages an extralegislative reconciliation of differences rather than the acceptance of an imposed solution. In both instances the results will often obviate the need for legislation. A similar result ensues where a committee holds hearings on a bill that its members know will not advance any further. The purpose is to attract attention and introduce colleagues, other political actors and the public to a matter so as to place it on the political agenda and prepare the ground for its eventual passage.

Oversight hearings are a means of monitoring the administration and effectiveness of programs that have been enacted into law. Appropriations and budget hearings are held on an annual basis. The latter is review of broad governmental functions that overlap agency jurisdictions. It constitutes an assessment of national priorities and the direction of current or proposed activities considered essential to attain policy objectives. Other than the president's budget message, budget committee hearings provide the only occasion for a regular and comprehensive overview of public business and purposes.

Though appropriations hearings always precede appropriations legislation, their nature corresponds more closely to an oversight proceeding. Their focus is on administrative decisions as these affect the economy and efficiency of agency operations. The chief topics covered are financial administration and the status of specific projects. These are discussed from the standpoint of the agency's budget estimates for the coming fiscal year. Appropriations hearings entail a detailed examination of everyday matters and provide many insights into the nuts and bolts aspects of government.

Legislative oversight is conducted by the same committees that are usually occupied with the consideration of bills. Thus, oversight by these panels tends to be irregular because it rarely generates the interest and publicity that attends new legislation. When these committees are sufficiently motivated they will hold hearings to determine whether the programs under their jurisdiction are achieving intended purposes. Some of the reasons that lead to such hearings include adverse media coverage, constituent or clientele complaints, admission of difficulties by executive branch officials, a program that results in continual litigation, critical reports by private research organizations or leaks by agency personnel about mismanagement or malfeasance. A trend toward more frequent legislative oversight involves placing more programs on an annual authorization basis. Such reauthorization hearings on bills that would extend or amend existing statutes inevitably result in a form of program oversight.

All oversight hearings serve to keep committee members informed of significant administrative developments, provide for an exchange of views to clarify the nature of particular problems and afford an opportunity for legislators to evaluate the capabilities of administrators. An oversight hearing may address the validity of assumptions underlying existing policies or programs. Such an evaluation of the necessity or adequacy of statutes may elicit information that convinces committee members of the need for remedial legislation. However, these proceedings are usually concerned with either legislative intent or the propriety of particular decisions, both of which stem from the discretion conferred on administrators by all important public laws.

Both legislators and administrators continually seek to reconcile legislative intent with administrative discretion. Legislators endeavor to influence decisions that result from the need to delegate authority, while administrators undertake to apply policy in a manner that will enhance their professional or political status. Since personnel changes in both committees and agencies occur with some regularity the interpretation of legislative intent and the use of administrative discretion are likely to vary over time. Thus, oversight hearings may be employed to reinforce or reemphasize committee messages conveyed at prior hearings, by committee reports or through informal channels. The occasion may also be used by legislators to insist upon, or by administrators to explain, the adoption of different criteria or procedures for implementing programs. By emphatically expressing their views committee members attempt, in a public forum, to extract policy oriented commitments from not always reluctant executive branch officials.

When oversight hearings focus on specific agency decisions they may expose questionable or inefficient practices or function as a disciplinary proceeding for an administrator. In this instance a legislator or a committee in its corporate capacity either anticipates or has experienced some political embarrassment due to agency action or inaction. The aim of committee members would be to either reverse a decision or insure that it did not recur. It should be recognized that congressional dissatisfaction with agency performance may reflect disagreement with presidential intentions. This attention to discrete decisions whose affects can be directly linked to the political reputations of elected officials gives these proceedings a somewhat narrower cast than those discussed in the preceding paragraph.

Hearings may represent an effort to expose the weaknesses and sophistries of some plausible proposal being advanced by a narrow or partisan interest. A committee may wish to discredit such a faction so that a constructive search for policy alternatives may proceed without distortions that impede agreement on a viable approach. In this case legislators must communicate with the public to counteract the effects of political oversimplification. This is not to imply that legislators are always impartial judges seeking only to advance the public interest. Hearings may denote a genuine quest for facts and views or a staged proceeding designed to support a previously reached conclusion. They can be a sincere search for a reasonable course of action that commands wide acceptance or an attempt to confer an aura of respectability on a policy decision of questionable efficacy. Hearings also enable undecided legislators to gauge public opinion by noting who supports or opposes a proposal and to calculate the political advantages or disadvantages of their own position.

Hearings are also an occasion for interested groups and knowledgeable individuals to present their views and versions of the facts. The desired result would be the encouragement of mutual understanding and accommodation that promotes development of a consensus. These proceedings are tangible evidence of citizen access to the policy process. By furnishing a forum for all prominent perspectives a committee precludes the allegation of biased judgment and demonstrates that it has discharged its duties in a responsible manner. Balanced and thorough hearings serve as a source of legitimacy for subsequent committee decisions.

Two factors that influence hearings and are vital to an understanding of their effects are climate and content. The former refers to the political environment of an issue and includes such elements as the primary locus of influence in a given policy area and the nature of committee relationships with other political entities. The latter concerns the political complexion of a bill and involves such matters as the degree of controversy engendered by its provisions and the ability of committee members to negotiate satisfactory compromises among competing interests. These considerations often provide a key to explain subsequent committee or congressional action, such as the length and pace of legislative proceedings and the number and nature of proposed amendments.

Committee hearings may be scheduled to transmit technical or political information, to assess the political feasibility of policy proposals, to influence public opinion or administrative action or to promote or impede legislation. They provide a permanent public record of the views advocated by the various parties interested in a given issue and afford evidence of committee diligence and integrity. Though hearings are not the only means that may be used to accomplish each of these purposes, they are the only means that can be used for all of them. The variety of goals that may be pursued via hearings are closely related but sufficiently distinct to allow their results to be interpreted differently by most interested parties. They can consume much time and effort yet yield an uncertain product. Hearings ultimately represent an attempt by legislators to acquire information and exert influence, which confirms the observation that information is power.

STRUCTURE AND PROCEDURE

Considerable committee staff work is a prerequisite to constructive and productive hearings. These activities pertain to subject matter and witnesses. All pertinent printed materials are consulted and concisely summarized. Prospective witnesses, including executive branch officials and representatives of major private organizations, are regularly sent questionnaires regarding the matter under consideration. These individuals often welcome the opportunity to express their views and prepare the ground for their possible testimony. It is then necessary to systematize this information after determining which specific topics will be addressed. After taking into account the views of committee members, staff members formulate questions designed to elicit the responses considered necessary to yield optimal results.

The gathering of information, including synopses of secondary materials, acquisition of official documents, analysis of questionnaires and related correspondence, generally leads to compilation of a briefing book. Along with an introductory memorandum written by staff members, this collection of material is used to familiarize legislators with the details of the bill or subject and enables them to prepare for their participation in the hearings. While hearings are in progress the committee staff usually prepares a digest of each day's testimony to clarify what ground has been covered and what remains to be surveyed.

A coordinate phase of the preparation process involves the number, selection and order of witnesses. Except for government officials, whose testimony is considered essential on matters affecting the jurisdiction of their agencies, key committee and staff members decide who will be invited or permitted to appear. In most cases all organizations with a substantial interest in the issue will be offered the opportunity to testify. Two aspects to the order in which witnesses appear are status and substance. The former pertains to the positions of individuals, who are usually given priority as follows: members of Congress, executive branch officials, private organization representatives, nongovernment specialists, and others. The latter concerns the overall order of witnesses, which should be planned so as to present a logical development of the subject.

While there is no right to testify, all major viewpoints should be represented to meet the criteria of thoroughness and fairness. The rules of each house of Congress also entitle minority party members to invite witnesses to testify on at least one day during hearings held on any proposal. It is not uncommon for committee staff to meet in private with prospective witnesses prior to their public appearance. A review of projected testimony and planned questions minimizes the possibility of surprise or embarrassment and promotes cooperation and communication. This practice is also intended to preclude the possibility of an adversary proceeding.

Since most legislation or oversight covers ground that committees, to at least some extent, have previously tread, it can be anticipated who will wish to testify and what positions will be taken. The combination of staff preparation and member familiarity with the subject of hearings usually averts unexpected developments. However, what cannot be foreseen with equal clarity is the public impact of and response to all testimony, especially when an issue is dramatized by the plight of ordinary citizens or the confrontation of major public figures.

A well-organized hearing involves observance of certain preliminary procedures. These relate to providing adequate advance notice to all interested parties, informing prospective witnesses of the questions or subjects the committee would like them to address and obtainng written copies of statements from those who wish to submit them. The rules of each house stipulate that committees make a public announcement of the date, place and subject matter of any hearing at least one week in advance, unless there is sufficient cause to begin sooner. The rules also urge committees to require submission of written statements by witnesses and to limit oral presentations to a brief summary of such statements.

Despite adequate preparation and sound procedure hearings may be used to either generate support for or opposition to a proposal. This can be done by the manipulation of their timing and length, the selection and order of witnesses and committee member questions. Hearings may constitute an attempt to advance the views of certain witnesses when members, who share such views, ask helpful questions. They may also represent an effort to harm the prospects of other witnesses when members, who disagree with their views, pose hostile questions. Though testimony from various viewpoints may help to bring an issue into sharp focus, much of it can be propagandistic and intended to score political points.

The House has a rule allotting five minutes to each committee member who wishes to question each witness before any member may proceed to use more time. The Senate has an informal ten minute rule. This traditional format, though it can be expedient for some legislators and functional for the entire committee as indicated by the earlier discussion of purposes, does not promote extended exchanges between members and witnesses. Comparative analyses of different viewpoints or intensive exploration of specific concepts or conclusions are unlikely to emerge.

To induce results that are more informative and incisive a committee may organize a panel discussion in lieu of or in additon to hearings held in the customary manner. This approach is similar to a seminar, with the invited participants and committee members jointly discussing prescribed topics while the committee chairman serves as a moderator. For the consideration of complex or controversial economic or social issues this arrangement has some advantages over the usual procedure of witness testimony accompanied by committee member interrogation.

It enables advocates of one view to directly challenge proponents of a competing view. Exposure of each presentation to criticism from diverse perspectives can highlight areas of accord and promote a synthesis of opinions. The invited panelists, as specialists, are in a better position to evaluate proposals advanced by other specialists than are committee and staff members who tend to be generalists. Thus, the committee is relieved of some of the burden of assessing technical testimony and discerning emerging agreement.

These discussions also enhance the educational value of hearings by contributing to an improved grasp of the subject by legislators, staff and other interested parties. Panel members normally submit research papers to the committee which are printed prior to the hearings. This allows all prospective participants to prepare in advance and focus on points in dispute or on those that need elaboration. That this form of hearing is not more widely used can probably be attributed to the fact that it limits the ability of committee members to exercise control of the proceedings. Also, since panels are usually scheduled in addition to regular hearings, there is the matter of being able to fit them into the legislative timetable.

Regardless of the format, all hearings begin with an opening statement from the presiding legislator, who is a committee or subcommittee chairman. These remarks, which are written in advance of the hearings, review the subject to be covered and the questions to be explored. The specific situation or reason that prompted the hearings and an outline of what the committee expects to accomplish are also offered. On occasion the committee press release announcing the hearings and describing the ground rules under which they will be conducted is inserted into the official transcript. Each witness begins his testimony with a brief summary of the major points included in his written statement. The remainder of this chapter is devoted to a description of the contents and uses of the printed record.

THE PRINTED TRANSCRIPT

The original transcript of testimony is usually available for examination in the committee office soon after the conclusion of hearings. Its printing is at the discretion of the committee, but is almost always ordered when legislation is under consideration. Except for appropriations hearings, they are seldom printed prior to floor action on a bill. The time lag between the presentation of testimony and its availability in print may be minimal or it may be months depending upon committee workload or strategy. The length of this interval is relatively unimportant for most legislators, who would not have the time to read the volumes and who primarily rely on the concise committee report for written information they need on proposed legislation.

The printed record is not a verbatim transcript for three reasons. First, committee members and witnesses are routinely given the opportunity to edit their remarks. Second, the presiding legislator may make and permit others to make off-the-record statements. Finally, confidential matters are discussed at sessions closed to the public and this testimony is not included, though it is usually noted, in the record. However, these practices only rarely detract from the value of what does appear in print. (See figure 5, page 66, for an example of a printed hearing.)

The cover page of a hearing will normally note the subject, subcommittee and full committee name, Congress and session, bill number and hearing date. Though hearings are not a formal series, some committees for their own convenience assign alphabetical or numerical serial designations to them throughout each session or Congress. When hearings are extensive they are issued in numbered parts, a practice that apprises readers of the existence and sequence of the other volumes.

Though all hearings contain valuable material, they are not always edited or printed in a form that facilitates access to their contents. All appropriations hearings have running subject headings and subject indexes. Since these proceedings tend to be the most voluminous, such aids are essential to locate

Figure 5
A Committee Hearing

EXTENDED DAYLIGHT SAVING TIME

HEARING

BEFORE THE

SUBCOMMITTEE ON
ENERGY CONSERVATION AND POWER

OF THE

COMMITTEE ON
ENERGY AND COMMERCE
HOUSE OF REPRESENTATIVES

NINETY-SEVENTH CONGRESS

FIRST SESSION

ON

H.R. 3951

A BILL TO PROMOTE ENERGY CONSERVATION BY PROVIDING
FOR DAYLIGHT SAVING TIME ON AN EXPANDED BASIS, AND
FOR OTHER PURPOSES

JUNE 23, 1981

Serial No. 97–61

Printed for the use of the
Committee on Energy and Commerce

U.S. GOVERNMENT PRINTING OFFICE

87-906 O   WASHINGTON : 1982

specific parts of the text. However, their appearance in other hearings is irregular. For most, the only finding aid is the contents, which may be arranged alphabetically or chronologically by organization or individual. While some contents are convenient guides to witnesses, organizations, committee member statements and supplementary material, many are barely adequate and none can substitute for a subject index. It should be recognized that preparation of such an index requires time that cannot always be so invested due to other committee priorities. In many instances the titles of hearings are either inconsistent, even though the subject matter is identical, or they do not adequately describe their contents. Most of the difficulties posed by these shortcomings have been eliminated by *CIS/Index.*

Hearings do not consist of coherent essays that lead to logical conclusions. As a phase of the policy process they routinely reflect the untidy and fortuitous nature of the political environment, including exaggeration and opportunism. Composed of dialogue that frequently shifts between related or unrelated subjects and numerous insertions of supplementary material, hearings exhibit a somewhat disjointed text. Objective information is available from the statements and reports of neutral sources and may be gleaned from the record by comparing and contrasting the views and data presented by parties in disagreement. Even an instructive hearing, due to the form of its proceedings and format of its transcript, tends to yield its substance with some reluctance.

Equally as important as oral testimony is material prepared either in advance of or subsequent to a hearing and inserted into the record. Printed hearings are regularly used as a means of presenting supplementary material that would not otherwise be published or made readily available. Such information may be placed at the rear of the volume, distributed throughout the text or organized by a combination of these methods depending upon its relationship to oral or written testimony. The various types of such material are discussed below.

1.   Prepared statements are submitted by witnesses in advance of the hearings and address questions that were derived from committee staff analysis of the subject under consideration. Since hearings often result in frequent changes of focus due to the fluctuating attendance and varying interests of committee members, it is advisable to read the prepared statement before turning to the discussion that embraces an individual's oral testimony. Witnesses also have the opportunity to submit additional supporting material for the record. Included are the written statements of those who did not have the opportunity to appear in person.

2.   When panel discussions are held the papers submitted by panelists are arranged and printed by topics in the order in which they are scheduled for discussion.

3.   Administrative documents and directives include internal agency papers that describe and analyze decisions and operations. Though presented in support of agency actions, such material offers an inside view of how policies are implemented.

4.   A committee may request the General Accounting Office or contract with a private organization to evaluate an agency's performance. The resulting management analysis or cost-benefit study will usually appear in the record.

5.   Staff studies prepared by committee or agency personnel or by private entities that specialize in a subject or policy area are commonly made part of the record.

6.   Upon the conclusion of hearings there may be several reasons for the insertion of additional questions and answers into the record. During the course of testimony questions raised by legislators, but not addressed by witnesses, are answered afterwards; some legislators unable to attend the hearings have written questions distributed to certain witnesses; some who do attend do not have the time to ask all the questions they have and also submit written ones; and a review of oral testimony by committee members and staff often results in further questions to clarify statements or obtain more data.

7.   Committee correspondence includes exchanges of information or views with agency personnel or with nongovernment representatives regarding agency policies or plans.

8.   Pertinent newspaper or journal articles are regularly collected and incorporated into the record.

9.   Two multiple insertions peculiar to appropriations hearings relate to budget justifications and spending decisions. The former is composed of detailed descriptions of each program administered by an agency and is prospective in nature. This material includes much statistical data and comparative figures of funds expended in the current fiscal year and the amount requested for the coming fiscal year. The latter consists of explanations of the circumstances involved in the commitment of funds for particular purposes and is retrospective in nature. This material includes information that supports the continuation or expansion of programs and discusses their scope and effects. These two insertions provide a comprehensive and itemized accounting of all aspects of an agency's activities and functions. A major portion of each appropriations hearing is comprised of documentation submitted by the agency being scrutinized.

10.   One other type of insertion, as rare as it is valuable, is the contents of a committee briefing book.

For legislative history purposes one would proceed from subsequent committee or congressional action as expressed in committee reports, floor debate or versions of a bill to those pertinent comments or more elaborate explanations that appear in the printed record. Significant components of legislative hearings are: (1) the text of the bill or bills under consideration; (2) a detailed discussion of the implications of a measure's provisions; (3) agency analyses of bills and suggested amendments; and (4) examination of amendments from other sources. Hearings are especially valuable regarding the origins and background of amendments to a bill as it is reported by the committee. It should be noted that in reaching decisions, legislators are free to ignore testimony delivered at hearings or to apply information not presented at such proceedings.

A mark-up session is scheduled when committee members conclude that they have all the information they need or can obtain or that further action cannot be delayed. At this meeting, or series of meetings, the panel frames its final decisions on the content of a bill. The measure is read line by line, possible interpretations are discussed, and proposed amendments are debated and voted upon if necessary. When these proceedings are printed, which is seldom, they may appear in the same volume with hearings or as a separate publication in hearing form.

There are at least three occasions on which a bill or program is considered by more than one committee and is the subject of more than one hearing. A comparison of these separate but related proceedings provides information about the evolution of legislation, which committees emphasize which aspects of a proposal and those parties impelled to press appeals due to dissatisfaction with the results of earlier hearings. One situation arises when hearings are held on the same bill by the corresponding committees in the House and Senate. Another instance occurs where an appropriations committee considers an appropriate allocation of funds for an agency or program after it has been authorized by a legislative committee. A less common development involves those bills whose provisions overlap the jurisdiction of two or more committees in the same chamber, in which case each panel may consider the entire measure or only specified portions.

An investigation is a proceeding that is closely related to a hearing. The major difference between them is that investigations are precipitated by the failure or frustration of the customary communications process. Because their primary purpose is to compel the disclosure of information they tend to be adversary in nature. Investigative procedures are, thus, more numerous and more formal since the committee may issue subpoenas to compel the attendance and testimony of witnesses and the production of papers, an action that can lead to legal proceedings. In regard to the printed record all that applies to hearings is equally applicable to investigations except for the lack of discussion and material directly related to legislation.

Hearings disclose the alignment of and the rationale for positions maintained by political contestants and illuminate the congressional decision-making process. The development and enactment of public policy invariably involves the readjustment of societal relationships. It is in the context of a potentially altered status that many parties design and deliver their testimony. Thus, to strengthen their case, those who would be most affected by congressional action attempt to link their interests to general communal goals and values. The hearing is an institutionalized mechanism employed to regularize and canalize the multilateral bargaining that always accompanies major legislation. An examination of the printed record in conjunction with related materials reveals that, though legislators make the formal decisions, others often make substantial contributions to the ultimate result.

The printed record is a valuable compilation of material on the nature and impact of an issue and testifies to the fact that information is rarely neutral because of the different interests and values that affect how it is perceived. A hearing or its transcript may be viewed from at least three perspectives For committee members it is an instrument used to shape and justify immediate actions and a yardstick for future hearings. For participants in the political process it is a reservoir of argument and an agent for devising strategy concerning the proposal under consideration. For students of government it is a source of the most up-to-date information on a given policy, program or subject and a guide to further research.

BIBLIOGRAPHY

Berman, Daniel M. *In Congress Assembled.* New York: Macmillan, 1964.

Goodwin, George, Jr. *The Little Legislatures.* Amherst: The University of Massachusetts Press, 1970.

Griffith, Ernest S. *Congress: Its Contemporary Role.* 4th ed. New York: New York University Press, 1967.

Gross, Bertram M. *The Legislative Struggle.* New York: McGraw-Hill, 1953.

Jewell, Malcolm E., and Patterson, Samuel C. *The Legislative Process in the United States.* New York: Random House, 1966.

Keefe, William J., and Ogul, Morris S. *The American Legislative Process.* 3rd ed. Englewood Cliffs, NJ: Prentice-Hall, 1973.

Kofmehl, Kenneth. *Professional Staffs of Congress.* West Lafayette, IN: Purdue University Studies, 1962.

Morrow, William L. *Congressional Committees.* New York: Scribner's, 1969.

U.S. Congress. Senate. Committee on Government Operations. *Congressional Oversight: Methods and Techniques.* Committee Print, 94th Congress, 2nd Session. Washington: U.S. Government Printing Office, 1976.

5

Committee Reports*

The importance of committee reports in the legislative process stems from their inseparable link to congressional bills. Reports are agents of action whose contents are historical, factual, analytical and political in nature. As retrospective documents they present a concise pre-legislative history of issues and legislative history of bills. As prospective documents they explain the purposes and provisions of measures so as to maximize potential support. The implicit and explicit political considerations interwoven with the account of facts, events, expectations and intentions that comprise reports are all essential for an understanding of federal legislation.

United States statutes are neither self-explanatory nor self-executing. Their passage normally represents the culmination of a lengthy process that begins with conception and concludes with enactment. During this period of time proposed laws develop a history that elucidates their means and ends. Such information is most cogently and methodically conveyed via committee reports. This chapter presents a detailed examination of reports, focusing on the purposes, content, format and uses of those that accompany public bills. The underlying theme is the relationship between reports and bills and how this relationship affects the nature and status of reports.

TYPES AND PURPOSES

Though reports originate in committees they are officially termed House and Senate Reports. Since bills are of the foremost importance and are treated as official documents of each chamber, the reports filed with them are designated in a corresponding manner. Reports are the formal means employed by committees to communicate with their parent body. Their contents constitute an explanation by an agent of the manner in which it has discharged the responsibilities delegated to it by its principal. They comprise a separate and distinct class of publications through which committees convey information and submit recommendations for the consideration or approval of each house.

Reports can be divided into two major categories—legislative and non-legislative. The latter category includes those which are exclusively housekeeping in nature and those which have policy implications. The housekeeping variety primarily concern the printing of documents or committee expenditures and

---

*This chapter derives from an article, "Congressional Committee Reports," by Jerrold Zwirn, in *Government Publications Review*, Vol. 7A, pp. 319-27, © 1980 Pergamon Press Ltd. Reprinted with permission of Pergamon Press.

include legislative activity reports issued by each committee. Reports that are non-legislative but may affect or lead to legislation include studies or investigations by committees of programs, agencies or subjects within their jurisdiction, those that accompany concurrent resolutions in conjunction with the congressional budget process and those filed with resolutions which realign committee jurisdictions, create new panels or amend the rules of either house. A non-legislative type that is unique to the House is filed by its Rules Committee and invariably consists of a single sentence recommending adoption of a resolution. The resolution prescribes the rules and conditions that will govern floor consideration and debate of bills previously reported by other committees. Also non-legislative in purpose are those in the Senate that accompany treaties and nominations and are designated as Executive Reports.

Special reports may be either legislative or non-legislative in nature and originate in two ways. Either house may instruct a standing committee or create a temporary panel to study or investigate a given situation or subject. Also, certain standing committees are expected to submit recurring reports to keep their parent body informed of developments in an area of continuing interest. These reports may contain specific legislative proposals, general recommendations for legislative action or simply present the results of an inquiry.

The category of legislative reports can be subdivided into those which accompany public bills and those filed with private bills. While public measures embody proposals to establish general policy, private measures provide specific relief for individuals or organizations from the effects or requirements of existing policy. Private bills are usually based entirely on a factual situation, while public bills involve value judgments and the allocation of resources as well as facts.

Public measures take the form of either authorization or appropriation bills. Authorizations create or continue programs or agencies and set the maximum level of funds that may be appropriated therefor. Appropriations, which normally follow authorizations, authorize agencies to expend specified amounts of public funds for specified purposes. Authorization bills, by repealing law, and appropriation bills, by denying funds, may terminate or suspend the operation of an agency or program. This chapter will focus on the reports that accompany authorization and appropriation measures.

A committee may report a bill favorably, unfavorably or without recommendation. The overwhelming majority of measures are reported favorably. Those which cannot attract the support of a majority of committee members rarely receive committee attention. While a bill is a proposal that would mandate a change in public policy, its accompanying report advances the case for favorable legislative action by marshaling arguments to justify the change. Reports are an essential supplement to bills because the latter, as potential law, consist only of commands and do not offer explanations as to why such commands are desirable or how they should be construed.

Reports present findings and recommendations that are derived from and refined through committee hearings and deliberations. If a bill is brief, simple and uncontroversial, its report will reflect such circumstances and will not contain much more than some general comments and the committee's recommendation for passage. Controversial or significant measures will entail the preparation of detailed and lengthy analyses that highlight committee reasoning on all major points.

The factor most responsible for the content and format of a report is its primary audience—the membership of Congress. It is a relatively concise presentation of the political issues involved and decisions reached during a bill's consideration. Reports are designed to provide members of Congress with sufficient information to evaluate a measure by emphasizing the political context within which the committee acted. The purposes of a bill are addressed from both an overall perspective as well as from an analysis of the objectives of each major provision. This explanation of the relationship between the whole and its parts is intended to elucidate the committee's position and to generate support for the proposal. For busy legislators, reports tend to be the main written source of information on bills because they are presented in a politically useful form.

Agency administrators who will be responsible for the execution and enforcement of a bill once it is enacted into law are also a group that reports are meant to influence. Executive branch officials are expected to regard the directives, suggestions, criticisms and general advice included in reports as having almost, if not the full, force of law. Legislators intend such statements to serve as instructions or guidelines for administrative decisions. If ignored the result may be the use of more formal instruments of control, such as investigations, more detailed and restrictive statutes or reduced appropriations. Thus, while reports are not legally binding, they are regularly consulted by administrators when questions arise about the meaning or purpose of particular statutory provisions.

There are two major reasons for placing some committee dicta in reports rather than in legislation. One is that legislators recognize the need for administrative discretion if programs are to be effectively implemented and should report statements prove to be inapplicable or inimical they can simply be disregarded. Another is the greater time and difficulty involved in attempting to draft legal language to cover the various situations that may confront an administrator. When executive branch officials decide to act in disregard of a report, they are expected to seek prior approval of key committee members.

Another audience at which reports are aimed is comprised of members of the judiciary. In litigation that concerns the application and interpretation of statutes, judges require information that can clarify legislative intent. Reports are almost always consulted in such cases.

The rules of each house of Congress stipulate that, for a standing committee report to be valid, a committee majority must be present at the meeting that authorizes it to be filed, though the actual number of members voting to report may be less than a majority of the full committee. The rules of both houses also provide that each report accompanying a public bill, except for appropriation measures, must contain:

1. The total number of votes cast for and against the motion to report when such decision is made by a roll call vote. In the Senate, the vote of each committee member must also be noted.

2. A comparative print of those provisions of the reported bill and any statutes it would amend or repeal, showing by appropriate typographical devices the proposed changes. Where a bill amends a law by adding a provision, the report must quote the section of the law immediately preceding the proposed amendment. In the House this is known as the Ramseyer rule and compliance with it can only be waived by a floor vote. In the Senate it is known as the Cordon rule and a committee may dispense with its requirements by stating in its report that such action was necessary to expedite Senate business.

3. A detailed statement, where applicable, concerning new budget authority or new or increased tax expenditures authorized by the measure.

4.   An estimate prepared by the Congressional Budget Office relating to the costs that would be incurred by implementation of the measure and a comparison of such estimate with any presented by the committee or a federal agency (if submitted in time for inclusion).

5.   Supplemental, additional, or minority views concerning the reported bill when committee members give proper notice of their intention to file such views. The inclusion of these views must be noted on the first page of the report. This requirement also applies to appropriation bills.

House rules require the following information to appear in its reports:

1.   The findings and recommendations of the committee regarding the administration and effectiveness of those laws within its jurisdiction that relate to the reported measure.

2.   A summary of any findings and recommendations made by the Government Operations Committee pertaining to the reported measure (if submitted in time for inclusion).

3.   An estimate prepared by the committee concerning the costs that would be incurred by implementation of the measure and a comparison of such estimate with any submitted by a federal agency.

4.   An inflation impact statement that analyzes the potential effect of the measure on the national economy.

Senate rules provide that its reports must contain an evaluation of the regulatory impact of a measure, consisting of:

1.   An estimate of the numbers of individuals and businesses that would be affected.

2.   A determination of the groups and classes of such individuals and businesses.

3.   The probable effect upon personal privacy.

4.   The anticipated volume of additional paperwork that would result and costs that would be incurred.

In the absence of such information, a statement of the reasons why compliance with the rule was impracticable must be included.

Though both houses have rules that require all reports accompanying public bills to be printed, the Senate permits its committees to dispense with *written* reports to expedite chamber business. However, the force of custom restricts the use of such discretion to very few occasions.

Information required by House and Senate rules amounts to only a limited portion of most reports and reveals nothing about format. Over time, reports have assumed a form which, though not invariable, has consistent features presented in a regular order. The descriptions below represent a group portrait rather than a picture of a typical member. Differences among reports reflect such factors as previous committee or congressional consideration of the subject, the degree of controversy engendered by the issue, the form and content of the bill itself or committee member preferences.

AUTHORIZATION REPORTS

Reports that accompany authorization bills may consist of as many as eight distinctive parts. (See figure 6 for an example of a committee report.)

1.   Introduction: This part always includes the number and session of Congress, body of origin, report number, succinct statement of the bill's subject, date reported, committee member responsible for submitting the report,

Figure 6
A Committee Report

Calendar No. 267

96TH CONGRESS *1st Session*	SENATE	REPORT No. 96–253

EQUAL ACCESS TO JUSTICE ACT

JULY 20 (legislative day, JUNE 21), 1979.—Ordered to be printed

Mr. DECONCINI, from the Committee on the Judiciary,
submitted the following

REPORT

[To accompany S. 265]

The Committee on the Judiciary, to which was referred the bill
(S. 265) to provide for equal access to justice, having considered the
same, reports favorably thereon with amendments and recommends
that the bill, as amended, do pass.

PURPOSE OF THE BILL

The bill rests on the premise that certain individuals, partnerships,
corporations and labor and other organizations may be deterred from
seeking review of, or defending against, unreasonable governmental
action because of the expense involved in securing the vindication
of their rights. The economic deterrents to contesting governmental
action are magnified in these cases by the disparity between the
resources and expertise of these individuals and their government.
The purpose of the bill is to reduce the deterrents and the disparity
by entitling certain prevailing parties to recover an award of attorney
fees, expert witness fees and other costs against the United States,
unless the Government action was substantially justified. Additionally,
the bill ensures that the United States will be subject to the common
law and statutory exceptions to the American rule regarding attorney
fees. This change will allow a court in its discretion to award fees
against the United States to the same extent it may presently award
such fees against private parties.

BACKGROUND

Legislation providing for the shifting of attorney fees in various
situations has been under congressional evaluation for some time.
Comprehensive hearings on the subject of attorney fees were held by

★(Star print)

committee that considered the measure, bill number, brief description of the bill's purposes, a statement as to whether the measure is reported with or without amendments and a recommendation that the bill be passed. When applicable, it will note that supplemental, additional or minority views are included and there may be a table of contents. The introduction is the most standardized portion of any report.

2.   Committee Amendments: When the text of amendments is included it will usually follow the introduction. Such text will most often appear when a committee reports a substitute, which is an amendment in the form of a rewritten bill covering the same subject as the introduced version, with only the original bill number being retained. If separate amendments are adopted, the precise place in which they are to be inserted is specified by reference to the page and line number of the introduced bill. Should amendments not appear here, their text may be derived from part 5 below.

3.   Body: There are several components of this subdivision, whose content and order is subject to greater variation than any other part.

    a.   Summary and Purpose—A brief presentation of the general objectives of the bill.

    b.   Background and Need—A historical survey of the issues involved along with a discussion of existing programs and policy options. Executive branch communications requesting the introduction and consideration of a measure are likely to be quoted. Where a bill primarily proposes amendments to a statute, there may be an analysis of how well its purposes have been fulfilled.

    c.   Major Provisions—An exposition of the bill arranged topically by its principal purposes, including discussion of the rationale for committee decisions. This portion may cite references to hearings, court decisions and government studies.

    d.   Legislative History—An account of committee and congressional action in prior Congresses on the same or similar bills, which will usually be identified by their numbers. Committee actions in regard to the measure being reported would also be discussed, if not presented separately.

Two components that appear with less frequency are:

    e.   Committee Amendments—A discrete treatment of their substance will most often appear when the bill being reported originated in the other house or was initially considered by another committee in the same chamber. A comparison of the significant differences between the two versions is customarily presented. The committee of original jurisdiction may also discuss its amendments under this heading, but such discussion is usually incorporated into the Major Provisions subsection.

    f.   Hearings—A summary of the testimony which notes the issues raised and the positions taken. The main arguments in favor of and in opposition to the bill, as presented by agency and organization spokesmen, as well as a committee analysis of and response to each major point, may be offered. The information contained under this heading is usually incorporated into either or both the Major Provisions and Legislative History subsections.

These components are not always clearly labeled or distinguished and some may be combined in different proportions, but they can be identified by a cursory examination.

4. Section-by-Section Analysis: This is a detailed explanation, in nontechnical language, of the purpose of each section in the order in which it appears in the bill. It is the most authoritative interpretation and forceful presentation of legislative intent. Included are definitions of all important terms and most of the statements aimed at administrators and judges. General committee expectations, which may be communicated under a separate heading immediately preceding or at the very beginning of this part, would serve as additional guidance for executive and judicial officials.

5. Comparative Print: This is the text of the differences between a reported bill and the law it proposes to amend as required by the Ramseyer or Cordon rule. Of course, if the measure would not change existing law this part is omitted.

6. Agency Views (or Executive Communications): Committees almost always solicit the views of those agencies that would be responsible for a proposed law or program as well as agencies that have government-wide responsibilities, such as the Office of Management and Budget and the General Accounting Office. These views may be conveyed in a letter that summarizes the agency viewpoint or by a report that provides an agency analysis of each major provision of the introduced bill. Since agency personnel regularly appear at committee hearings, these views may be incorporated into that part of the committee report which covers such proceedings.

7. Supplemental, Additional and Minority Views: Though the rules of each house provide only for these three views, most committees will approve the use of other headings to distinguish the views of individuals or combinations of individuals from one another when several reasons are advanced for differing with the majority. Other common headings include concurring, separate, individual, dissenting and opposing views. Some of these views can be differentiated as follows:

    —supplemental views reflect an endorsement of the legislation for reasons other than those offered by the majority.

    —additional views indicate general agreement with the majority except for specified provisions.

    —minority views are reserved for use by minority party members who disagree with the aims or methods or both that are embodied in a bill.

    —dissenting views usually express strong disagreement by majority party members.

All views, except those of the majority, are signed by the members expressing them. The body and section-by-section analysis constitute the majority view.

8. Appendix: There are two types of information that would appear in this part. One is either excerpts, or the quotation in full, from government documents that relate to the matter addressed by the bill. The other is statistical or other data compiled by the committee staff to facilitate consideration of the measure by committee members.

All authorization reports will have an introduction, body and section-by-section analysis, with the inclusion of other parts and the length and detail of any part subject to conditions previously mentioned. The content of a report will often depend on whether the same or a similar bill has been previously reported, either in the same or the other house. If a significant amount of time has elapsed since the earlier report, the later one will usually serve as an implicit or explicit reply. In addition, the subsequent one may contain only abbreviated subsections covering background and need and legislative history, if it does not omit them entirely.

Should the subject matter of a bill overlap the jurisdiction of two or more committees it may be simultaneously referred to each for consideration. A report will be filed jointly and if the panels are unable to reach agreement on the substance of the bill to be reported, the report will communicate this fact. It will also state that the alternatives recommended by each committee will be offered as amendments when the bill reaches the floor to allow the parent body to decide which to accept. Such broad-gauged bills may also be referred sequentially to two or more panels, in which case the last to consider it forges the final form of the reported version. In the Senate all reports by different committees on the same bill have different report numbers. In the House all such reports bear the same number, but are designated as different parts of the first report to be filed.

When numerous bills on the same subject are introduced and referred to the appropriate committee the panel may decide to combine the provisions of several into a single measure. A committee member will then introduce this legislation as a new bill, which will be referred to the same committee and reported as a clean bill. This procedure avoids reporting a bill with many amendments, each of which would have to be considered separately by the parent body. The report will mention when this has been done and will identify the numbers of those bills that were amalgamated into the reported version.

APPROPRIATION REPORTS

Reports that accompany appropriation bills differ sufficiently from those filed with authorization bills to warrant separate treatment. The primary reasons for these differences are: (1) Appropriations must be enacted each year if government agencies are to continue to function; (2) By custom, these measures originate in the House and are reported as original bills, which means that they are drafted in committee rather than introduced by a legislator and referred to a committee; and (3) Their text allocates specified sums of money to specified agencies for specified purposes. At present there are thirteen general appropriation bills that provide the spending authority for all except those few agencies that are self-sustaining.

House and Senate rules each contain a similar stipulation relating to reports filed with general appropriation bills. Senate reports must identify each committee amendment that proposes an appropriation not necessary to implement the provisions of an existing law or treaty. House reports must contain a statement describing the effect of any provision in the bill that would change the application of existing law. Both requirements are aimed at the same practice, which is the inclusion in appropriation bills of provisions that impinge upon the jurisdiction of other committees. Since conditions may render this practice necessary or desirable, the rules instruct the appropriations committees to highlight each such provision so that the parent body may consciously pass upon its expediency.

Reports that accompany appropriation bills may consist of as many as six distinctive parts.

1. Introduction: Except for minor differences derived from the fact that the House Appropriations Committee is reporting an original bill, this part is identical to that for authorization bills.

2. Body: There are usually three components of this part, which appear in the following order:

    a. Summary—A brief description of committee recommendations, including a tabular recapitulation.

    b. General Discussion—A Review of significant matters that were elicited at committee hearings and a brief account of the major factors affecting governmental expenditures covered by the bill.

    c. Major Provisions—A commentary arranged by bill title, with the budgets of larger agencies discussed in terms of their subdivisions. The authorizing legislation under which each agency or program operates is usually cited. The extensive annual hearings held by appropriations subcommittees represent the most regular and thorough review by Congress of the administration of the laws it enacts. Report statements that focus on the use of administrative discretion illustrate the committee's attention to detail and concern with economy and efficiency. Senate committee reports normally reflect the results of appeals made by agencies of decisions reached by the House committee and where differences exist between the two figures, they will be specifically addressed.

3. Agency Views: Due to the nature of appropriations hearings, separate written views are infrequently included. Such views are usually incorporated into the body of the report.

4. Limitations and Legislative Provisions: This part notes those provisions, mentioned above as being required by the rules of each house, that would amend existing law.

5. Supplemental, Additional and Minority Views: This section is identical to that for authorization bills.

6. Expenditure Tables: One table compares permanent budget authority for the current fiscal year, which does not depend upon congressional action, with the level of such authority contained in the budget estmates submitted by the President for the coming fiscal year. This table is arranged by agency and by program thereunder. A second table compares new budget authority that was enacted for the current fiscal year with new budget authority recommended in the bill. The Senate committee report has additional columns comparing its figures with those of the House bill. This table is arranged by bill title and corresponds to the Major Provisions subsection. There will occasionally appear a third table showing the proposed allocation of funds by function or organizational unit and geographical area.

Two other types of appropriation measures are supplementals and budget rescissions. The former provides additional budget authority beyond the levels prescribed by the general appropriation bills due to new programs authorized since their passage or an urgent need that cannot be postponed until the next general appropriation act. The latter revokes previously enacted budget authority prior to the time it would lapse. The submission of formal presidential requests initiates the consideration of both types of measures. Reports that accompany supplementals and rescissions identify, by their House and Senate document numbers, the presidential messages that prompted committee action. All reports on appropriation bills will always include an introduction, body and tables.

MODIFICATION

Committees may file supplemental reports any time prior to floor consideration of a bill and these would be designated as successive parts of the original report. One of the reasons that leads to submission of a supplemental report is the need to correct an error that was overlooked during the process of drafting and proofreading. Another reason would be to complete a report whose original version failed to include all information required by the house rules. A final reason stems from a change in the situation a bill is designed to address, which results in a recommended revision of the measure and a corresponding revision of its accompanying report. Should a typographical error appear in a printed report, it will be reprinted with a star in the lower left-hand corner of the first page to indicate it is a corrected copy.

Once a bill reaches the floor it may be recommitted, or returned to committee by the parent body, for one of two reasons. If a bill is ruled out of order on the floor because its accompanying report fails to meet all requirements of the house rules, it is automatically recommitted. The parent body may also express its disapproval of a measure by voting to recommit it. In both cases the reports are nullified and must be filed anew for the bill to be considered. A subsequent report is treated as a new and separate report and is assigned a new number, but it will identify the previous report by number.

Though reports are formal statements whose importance often rivals the bills they accompany, the fact that they consist of argument and explanation and do not have the force of law means that they are not themselves acted upon by the parent body during floor consideration of a bill. Thus, a report cannot be formally amended by legislators who may disagree with some of its contents. However, there are ways in which reports can, in effect, be amended. One method is to amend that portion of a bill to which a particular report statement applies. To the degree that a measure is significantly amended on the floor, the value of a report for construing its provisions decreases. Another approach is to have language included in a subsequent report that neutralizes language contained in an earlier one. This may be accomplished by the insertion of a restrictive or contrary statement or by omission of the disputed words. One other way is to engage in floor debate about the interpretation of specific report comments with the intention of clarifying or limiting their application.

CONFERENCE REPORTS

The final report that would be submitted on a bill is a conference report. Conference committees are ad hoc panels whose members are appointed from among the members of those standing committees that considered a bill in each house. Their purpose is to reconcile the differing versions of a measure as it was passed by each chamber. Authorization and appropriation conference reports will not be differentiated since, except in one particular, their form is identical. For a conference report to be valid a majority of the conferees from each body must sign it.

A conference report is a combined bill and report. The first, or bill, portion is the conference report proper and contains the text of all changes to the measure agreed upon by the conferees. The second part, which is equivalent to a report, is termed the "Joint Explanatory Statement." It describes the legislative effect of the changes adopted. Unless otherwise indicated, further mention of a conference report will refer to the joint statement.

The introduction to a conference report includes a brief statement of the bill's purposes, the bill number and a summary description of the manner in which the conferees resolved their differences. Its body corresponds to the section-by-section analysis of an authorization report or the major provisions subsection of an appropriation report. The precise format of the body depends upon the manner in which the second chamber amended the bill.

Either house may amend a bill that originated in the other by deleting its entire text and inserting the text of a bill on the same subject that has been reported or passed in the second chamber. This form of amendment is termed a substitute. In this case the conference report will usually contain a descriptive summary of the comparable House and Senate provisions and refer to the derivation of each change adopted. By providing an explanation of how differences in language were resolved and stating whether the conference provision is identical to that of the House or Senate version or a combination of both, it is determined whether a standing committee report or the conference report conveys the conclusive interpretation of any particular provision.

Where the second chamber passes a bill of the first with separate amendments, which can number in the hundreds, the conferees normally trade on most of them, with the first house acceding to some and the second receding on others. Those remaining in disagreement will then be compromised. It is these latter changes that are discussed in the conference report. Amendments that are purely technical or clarifying in nature are simply identified as such and not discussed further, even if they involved compromises. Each amendment is identified by a number that is assigned to it based upon the order in which it appears in the bill and each is discussed in numerical sequence.

Conference reports may or may not identify the section numbers of each bill as it was passed by each chamber. To the extent that they differ from or omit statements appearing in either standing committee report, the latter is superseded. Appropriation bills are invariably sent to conference via the second method outlined above. The one way in which appropriation conference reports differ from those on authorization bills is that, at their close, the former present the totals in the bill and compare them with prior fiscal year figures, budget estimates submitted by the President and the House and Senate versions of the bill as it was sent to conference.

Though dissenting views may not be included, a phrase following a signature in a conference report may note exceptions taken by certain conferees. Those conferees who disapprove of the entire report can only decline to sign it. Statements expressing disagreement would be inconsistent with the basic purpose of a conference, which is the resolution of differences between the two houses. Formal expressions of dissent must await floor consideration of the conference report proper.

A substitute amendment that reaches conference results in either complete agreement or disagreement. Separate amendments sent to conference may also produce partial agreement. The number of each amendment remaining in disagreement appears at the end of the bill portion of the report. In this case the report may discuss the reasons for the lack of total accord and recommend actions to each body that would promote agreement. If the conference report proper is approved by each house, the status of the amendments reported in disagreement remains unaffected. The authority of a second conference would be limited to those matters not disposed of by the first.

When the conference report proper is recommitted or rejected by either house the bill reverts to its pre-conference status. A second conference would have authority to consider the measure as if it had not been previously sent to conference. A subsequent conference report on the same bill, whether due to partial agreement, recommitment or rejection of the earlier one, is assigned a new number and treated as a new and separate report. This latter report will identify the previous one by number. A conference that is unable to reach any agreement will file a report consisting of only the joint statement, explaining why differences could not be reconciled. In this instance there also remains the possibility of another conference.

BIBLIOGRAPHY

Kirst, Michael W. *Government without Passing Laws.* Chapel Hill, NC: University of North Carolina Press, 1969.

Kofmehl, Kenneth. *Professional Staffs of Congress.* West Lafayette, IN: Purdue University Studies, 1962.

U.S. Congress. House. *Constitution, Jefferson's Manual and Rules of the House of Representatives.* House Document No. 95-403, 95th Congress, 2nd Session. Washington: U.S. Government Printing Office, 1979.

U.S. Congress. House. *Deschler's Procedure in the U.S. House of Representatives.* 3rd ed. 96th Congress, 1st Session. Washington: U.S. Government Printing Office, 1979.

U.S. Congress. House. Committee on Rules. *Legislative Reorganization Act of 1970.* House Report No. 91-1215, 91st Congress, 2nd Session. Washington: U.S. Government Printing Office, 1970.

U.S. Congress. House. Committee on Science and Technology. *Legislative Manual of the Committee on Science and Technology.* Committee Print, 96th Congress, 1st Session. Washington: U.S. Government Printing Office, 1979.

U.S. Congress. Senate. *Senate Legislative Procedural Flow.* 95th Congress, 2nd Session. Washington: U.S. Government Printing Office, 1978.

U.S. Congress. Senate. *Senate Manual.* Senate Document No. 96-1, 96th Congress, 2nd Session. Washington: U.S. Government Printing Office, 1980.

U.S. Congress. Senate. *Senate Procedure.* Senate Document No. 93-21, 93rd Congress, 1st Session. Washington: U.S. Government Printing Office, 1974.

6

Debate*

Though the *Congressional Record* contains a detailed account of floor proceedings, it does not elucidate the purposes that inform or the procedures that influence the structure and substance of legislative debate. The differences derived from contrasting parliamentary environments are as important for understanding House and Senate deliberations as are their similarities. The core of congressional debate, around which most discussion revolves, is the amending process. This chapter examines the nature of floor debate, describes the distinctive features and consequences of House and Senate proceedings and explains the rules and practices that govern the consideration of amendments.

Congressional debate is the most formal stage of the legislative process. The body of House and Senate rules and customs is intended to assure systematic and comprehensive consideration of legislation. This goal entails the application of numerous and complex procedures to promote orderly deliberations and facilitate reasonable decisions during proceedings in which all members are eligible to participate and which serve as the basis for final disposition of a bill. Debate invariably reflects and reviews all previous congressional action concerning a proposal. A complete picture of the contents of the *Congressional Record* requires an examination of the essential elements that affect the context of debate.

PURPOSES AND PRACTICES

The ideal functions of floor debate are to inform and persuade. Its immediate aim is to enable legislators to arrive at clear and definite legislative decisions. A parallel purpose is to clarify the reasons that underpin these decisions so that citizens may reach sound conclusions regarding rationale and results. From this standpoint debate engenders a spontaneous exchange of views that provides an explanation of the practical and political merits of a bill, with proponents presenting the case for its passage and opponents arguing for its defeat or modification.

In reality, by the time a major bill reaches the floor of either house most members have committed themselves to support or oppose it while others, due to lack of information or interest, are unfamiliar with its provisions. Thus, debate mainly serves to reinforce the conclusions of legislators who have already reached

---

*This chapter derives from an article, "Congressional Debate," by Jerrold Zwirn, in *Government Publications Review*, Vol. 8A, pp. 175-83, © 1981 Pergamon Press Ltd. Reprinted with permission of Pergamon Press.

a decision or to rationalize the positions of those whose vote is based on considerations other than substance. Deliberations tend to reflect solidified sentiments and only occasionally serve to make converts. Floor action represents efforts to resist or strive for change and, in the process, to publicize views for consumption by those whose support is valued. Also, since the complexity of modern legislation virtually precludes the spontaneous discussion of its technical aspects, debate is commonly composed of a series of prepared statements.

Though legislators consider debate more instrumental for public education, they recognize that it can contribute to their own instruction as well. This occurs most often when knowledge about a proposal is not widespread, when a bill does not present partisan or ideological issues or when amendments raise unanticipated questions. In these cases a forceful and factual speech may offer legislators a compelling reason or defensible justification for their vote. Another function of debate is as a medium of communication among allies on a particular measure in regard to the timing of actions or the nature of amendments. Debate may also provide momentum for a bill prior to its consideration in the other house, in conference between the houses or at the stage of presidential action. Finally, an explanation that may appear unimportant at the time it is delivered may eventually be cited as evidence of legislative intent by legislators, administrators or judges.

The nature of debate significantly differs in the House and Senate. The factor most responsible for the difference in floor environments is size. The relatively large membership of the House demands more formal and less flexible procedures and fosters a more hierarchical organization, while the comparatively small number of senators contributes to the use of less formal and more flexible procedures and produces a more collegial structure. The principal means employed to govern legislative debate is the control of time. The larger size of the House had led it to allocate time in equal amounts to proponents and opponents under rules and practices that impose or permit numerous limitations. The smaller size of the Senate has induced it to grant an unfettered opportunity, despite possible abuse, for members to convince or challenge their colleagues.

Floor debate is conditioned by different, but complementary, values in each chamber. The fundamental environmental factor in the House is majority rule, while in the Senate it is minority rights. The relatively expeditious nature of House proceedings means that deliberations are usually confined to one bill at a time and its consideration infrequently extends beyond a single day. The more adaptable nature of Senate proceedings means that debate may alternate from one bill to another and consideration of a measure may extend over days or weeks even without a filibuster. That the House is decision-oriented and the Senate deliberation-oriented does not imply that either parliamentary style is more desirable. The chief consequence of this difference, which will be discussed in more detail later, is that major House committee recommendations tend to be routinely ratified by the parent body, while in the Senate such proposals tend to receive a more thorough review.

One of the two forms of legislative deliberation is general debate, which focuses on the need and purposes of an entire bill. The other, and more important phase, concerns the proposal and disposition of amendments. While the amending process usually involves specific provisions it can also encompass the entire text of a measure. A discussion of those procedures that apply to debate and amendment in both houses precedes an examination of those which are peculiar to each chamber.

For each bill that reaches the floor a member of the committee that considered it is designated as its floor manager. As the principal spokesman for the bill this individual replies to questions, rebuts criticism, accepts or opposes amendments and manages or monitors the time available for debate. The custom that the floor manager be recognized to speak on all key occasions strengthens his role as the primary parliamentary strategist responsible for guiding legislation through to final passage.

During general debate in the House and all debate in the Senate, a member may not, with rare exceptions, be interrupted without his permission. He may yield the floor to another conditionally, though it is usually for the purpose of asking a question, and may refuse or revoke his consent at any time. To yield for the purpose of proposing an amendment or transacting other business results in loss of the floor.

The formal factor of type and the informal one of source are basic elements of the amending process. The four types of amendments embrace the parliamentary motions to insert, to strike out and insert, to strike out and to substitute. The first and second are known as perfecting amendments and their consideration takes precedence over the other two types. The difference between the second and fourth is that the former applies to only a portion of the pending text, while the latter may apply to an entire subdivision or bill. When a substitute for an entire bill is offered, both the bill and the substitute are open to perfecting amendments. Proponents of a measure always have the opportunity to propose modifications to counteract the appeal of amendments offered by opponents. This practice enables each camp to perfect its proposal prior to a final chamber decision.

The three sources pertain to those amendments reported by a committee in its corporate capacity, those offered from the floor by committee members who disagree with their panel's recommendations and those proposed by non-committee members. In deference to committee specialization and effort, committee amendments are accorded a privileged status and must be disposed of prior to any that may be offered from the floor. However, a committee amendment that is a substitute for an entire bill will not be acted on until all floor amendments have been considered, for the approval of the substitute would preclude any other amendments. With this exception, committee amendments are debated in the order in which they appear in the reported version of a bill.

Since committees may be divided when major legislation is reported, those panel members who differ with the majority are often authorized to offer floor amendments as alternatives during consideration of committee proposals. Committee amendments are recommendations that are not officially incorporated into a bill until formally adopted by the parent body, a condition that also applies to amendments accepted by floor managers. The rejection of a committee amendment that deletes or modifies a portion or all of an introduced bill has the effect of restoring the original text.

A common reason advanced by committee members to oppose floor amendments proposed by non-committee members is that such proposals should have been made while the bill was in committee and more time was available for thorough consideration. Proponents of such amendments often argue that committee membership is not representative of the entire chamber and the amending process broadens the range of interests that may exert influence on legislation. Though both contentions are generally valid, it should be noted that most floor amendments are offered by those who wish to weaken or kill a bill.

Amendments originated by those in favor are designed to strengthen it or to neutralize hostile amendments. The amending process customarily involves efforts by floor managers to repulse attempts to defeat or dilute the committee product.

There are several other important rules that govern the amending process. After an amendment is offered to a bill, another or second degree amendment may be proposed to the first, but amendments in the third degree are prohibited. Once an amendment to a portion of a bill has been formally adopted, the approved text is no longer subject to an amendment. This restriction, however, can be circumvented in two ways. First, words may be added to a previously approved amendment or an amendment to a later section of a bill may be adopted even though inconsistent with the provisions of an earlier amendment. Second, an amendment broader in scope than one previously approved and which encompasses the earlier text as well as other provisions may be adopted.

The rules of each house prohibit amendments to general appropriation bills that embody general legislation or unauthorized appropriations. This is to prevent proposals whose merits have not been sufficiently scrutinized in committee from being attached to essential measures. Such amendments are occasionally adopted to remedy routine matters or meet the demands of urgent situations. This is accomplished through a request for unanimous consent, which is used to expedite business where the rules are silent, prescribe a time-consuming procedure or expressly prohibit an action.

HOUSE PROCEEDINGS

Due to the volume of bills reported by committees and the limited amount of time available for debate each house has a mechanism for establishing legislative priorities and regulating the flow of measures to the floor. Bills of an uncontroversial nature are advanced by methods that bypass the following procedure. In the House this function is performed through the Rules Committee for all major proposals except general appropriation bills, which may be brought to the floor by the Appropriations Committee. All other panels must petition the Rules Committee to accord their bills priority for floor debate. In the absence of such action bills would have to be considered in calendar number order, which would prevent much major legislation from reaching the floor before final congressional adjournment.

The Rules Committee must initially schedule hearings at which only members of the requesting committee testify. Following these hearings the panel determines whether to draft a resolution, known as a special order, that provides for floor action on a bill previously recommended by another committee. Special orders have privileged access to the floor and, upon their approval by the House, suspend the standing rules regarding a given bill. In effect they are special rules that prescribe the terms under which a measure will be debated and are formulated to meet the prevailing parliamentary and political circumstances.

The major provisions of special orders cover floor amendments, length of debate and points of order. A special order may prohibit amendments, permit the consideration of only certain amendments, specify the order in which they are to be debated, limit amendments to only specified portions of a bill or not impose any restrictions on possible amendments. Time limits relate to the number of hours or days allotted for general debate or to a particular day or time beyond which debate may not extend. The waiver of points of order involves the prohibition of challenges from the floor to the effect that the contents of a reported bill violate the standing rules of the House. (See figure 7, page 88, for an example of a special order.)

One other standard feature of special orders is that the bills to which they apply be debated in the Committee of the Whole House on the State of the Union, otherwise known as the Committee of the Whole or simply as the Committee. This entity, as are all other committees, is a creature of the House, but unlike other committees, all members are eligible to participate in its proceedings. The Committee of the Whole is the House in a guise that facilitates the consideration of major bills. The significant differences between the House and the Committee are that the latter requires a quorum of only 100, rather than an absolute majority of 218; several motions that can be used to delay business are not in order in the Committee; and amendments in the Committee are debated under a rule that allots five minutes each to a proponent and an opponent, as compared with an hour rule that governs debate in the House. All bills that provide for the expenditure of funds or the raising of revenue must be considered in the Committee of the Whole. In the absence of a special order, a limit on general debate is usually fixed by unanimous consent.

The initial stage of debate on controversial legislation occurs in the House, rather than in the Committee of the Whole, and concerns adoption of a special order. Though ostensibly a procedural action, deliberations focus on the substance of a measure and the amendments that will be in order. Upon approval of the resolution the House resolves itself into the Committee of the Whole. The time available for general debate is almost always equally divided between and controlled by proponents and opponents of a bill. The leaders of each side, namely the floor manager for those who support the measure and the ranking minority party member of the reporting committee for those who oppose it, alternate in their opening remarks and then apportion time in small amounts to others. Custom constrains the presiding officer to recognize these two committee members in preference to other legislators and these leaders parcel out time, at their own discretion, primarily to other committee members. General debate in the Committee of the Whole provides an occasion to explore and explain the major purposes and provisions of legislation. It is characterized by those arguments most likely to receive extensive media coverage and enables floor leaders to assess member sentiment as a prelude to strategic maneuvers. Since the amount of time allotted to general debate is fixed by the House, motions in the Committee of the Whole to limit it are not in order.

At the conclusion of general debate bills are read for amendment under the five-minute rule. During these proceedings the presiding officer alternates recognition between a member who offers and one who opposes each amendment. In the Committee of the Whole authorization bills are read by section and appropriation bills by paragraph. Amendments to each subdivision are not in order until that part of the bill to which they apply has been read by the clerk. This procedure focuses debate and facilitates discussion of complex and lengthy measures. The purpose of pro forma amendments, which are superficial in nature, is to obtain additional time for debate. They can be recognized by motions to "strike the last word" or "to strike the requisite number of words."

The Committee of the Whole may decide to end deliberations on a portion of or an entire bill any time after debate under the five-minute rule has begun, otherwise debate will continue until all the time allotted for consideration of a bill

Figure 7

A Special Order or "Rule" from the Rules Committee

House Calendar No. 37

97TH CONGRESS
1ST SESSION **H. RES. 189**

[Report No. 97–189]

Providing for the consideration of the bill (H.R. 3275) to amend the Civil Rights
Act of 1957 to authorize appropriations for the Civil Rights Commission.

IN THE HOUSE OF REPRESENTATIVES

JULY 21, 1981

Mr. BONIOR of Michigan, from the Committee on Rules, reported the following
resolution; which was referred to the House Calendar and ordered to be printed

---

RESOLUTION

Providing for the consideration of the bill (H.R. 3275) to amend
the Civil Rights Act of 1957 to authorize appropriations for
the Civil Rights Commission.

1   *Resolved,* That upon the adoption of this resolution it

2 shall be in order to move that the House resolve itself into

3 the Committee of the Whole House on the State of the Union

4 for the consideration of the bill (H.R. 3275) to amend the

5 Civil Rights Act of 1957 to authorize appropriations for the

6 Civil Rights Commission, and the first reading of the bill

2

1 shall be dispensed with. After general debate, which shall be

2 confined to the bill and shall continue not to exceed one hour,

3 to be equally divided and controlled by the chairman and

4 ranking minority member of the Committee on the Judiciary,

5 the bill shall be read for amendment under the five-minute

6 rule. At the conclusion of the consideration of the bill for

7 amendment, the Committee shall rise and report the bill to

8 the House with such amendments as may have been adopted

9 and the previous question shall be considered as ordered on

10 the bill and amendments thereto to final passage without in-

11 tervening motion except one motion to recommit.

and amendments thereto has expired. In either of these instances further amendments may be offered but may not be debated. The only information available is from the reading of an amendment or from informal discussion among members on the floor. This situation tends to favor standing committee recommendations since members are reluctant to support amendments without sufficient reason, which is difficult to establish in the absence of debate.

After the final subdivision of a bill has been read a substitute for the entire measure may be offered. This allows for the consideration of a complete alternative to the pending bill. Also, amendments printed in the *Congressional Record* at least one day prior to chamber action on a bill must be debated under the five-minute rule regardless of any time limitations. The purpose of this procedure is to prevent arbitrary attempts to end debate when important amendments are to be proposed. However, these amendments will not be considered unless offered from the floor and may not contain provisions that would not otherwise be in order.

Priority in debate is accorded to amendments reported by the standing committee that recommends the bill. These are frequently discussed and voted upon as a package, making it necessary to vote against all to reject one, a practice that favors the committee version. At the conclusion of the amending process the chairman of the Committee of the Whole delivers an oral report to the House, the Committee is dissolved and a quorum reverts to 218 members. The special order under which a bill is considered regularly proscribes further debate. Only those amendments approved by the Committee are reported and may, on the demand of any member, be voted upon separately. This procedure is another advantage enjoyed by standing committees. Should an amendment opposed by the floor manager be approved in the Committee of the Whole, a separate vote in the House affords a second opportunity to defeat it, while its proponents do not have another chance if they lose in the Committee. When the House rejects an amendment adopted in the Committee of the Whole the effect is to restore the original text of the bill. The usual practice is for all amendments adopted by the Committee to be approved en bloc by the House.

Debate in the House, as opposed to the Committee of the Whole, is reserved for public bills of a less controversial nature. Only general debate is permitted and is normally limited to one hour. The floor manager parcels out time to others, who may offer amendments at any time while in possession of the floor. In the House a bill is read in full rather than by subdivisions, and amendments may be offered to any part of its text. The floor manager may move to close debate at any time after it has begun. However, this prerogative must be exercised with caution both during the debate of amendments in the Committee of the Whole and consideration of bills in the House. For if the motion is rejected, priority in recognition passes to those opposed to the bill.

There are few occasions in the House when debate is not required to be germane to the matter under consideration. The three general criteria of germaneness are subject matter, fundamental purpose and committee jurisdiction. The subject matter test usually pertains to specific portions of a bill, while that of fundamental purpose normally applies to an entire measure. The standard of committee jurisdiction means that a proposal must fall within the purview of the panel that reported the bill. Whenever any doubt exists, it is the responsibility of proponents to demonstrate that an amendment is germane. Though an amendment may meet all three criteria it may still be ruled out of order based upon a complex constellation of parliamentary precedents. In general, amendments that would narrow the scope of a provision or bill are more likely to be considered germane than those that would enlarge its scope.

The key feature of House debate is that it is restricted. Either a standing or a special rule provides for the allocation of a specific amount of time for the consideration of a bill, while parliamentary motions may be adopted that limit debate even further. Extensive deliberation is subordinated to decisions of the majority. Limited debate induces members to make their points succinctly and promptly since most matters, especially amendments, are brought before the House relatively quickly for disposition. The most significant effect of these time limitations is to enhance the influence of standing committees.

The basic form of most legislation is shaped in committee and the burden of proof is on those who would modify the panel's product. The proponents of major amendments in House debate are always at a disadvantage because the conviction exists that a bill ought to be written in committee and not on the floor. The comparatively large size of House committees and the policy specialization of their members fosters the expectation that the key deliberations on a measure should occur prior to floor action. Because House rules and procedures render it extremely difficult to successfully challenge committees, it is seldom that debate results in more than marginal changes in a reported bill. Since it is not feasible to employ the practice of individual consultation as in the Senate, decisions about scheduling and debate are made by party and committee leaders independent of individual member preferences. The combination of committee influence and impersonal arrangements contributes to debate that largely consists of prepared speeches aimed mainly at external audiences.

SENATE PROCEEDINGS

Senate debate is less structured and more spontaneous than in the House. The Senate has neither a standing committee responsible for devising the ground rules under which bills will be considered nor an equivalent to the Committee of the Whole. Its rules do not contain provisions relating to the allocation of time, but provide only that a vote by 60 members can terminate debate of a measure, a majority that is difficult to assemble. To regulate debate to a greater degree than is possible under its rules the Senate has developed an informal mechanism, known as a unanimous consent agreement, that is a counterpart to the special order. These agreements are informally negotiated and drafted outside the chamber and require unanimous approval when offered as binding contracts from the floor. They enable the Senate to expedite its business by avoiding the inconvenience and delay that would attend strict adherence to its rules. By suspending the standing rules unanimous consent agreements assure timely and orderly debate of major bills. The scheduling of legislation is a function of the policy committee of the majority party, while the majority and minority leaders are responsible for negotiating the stipulations that comprise agreements.

Unanimous consent agreements prescribe the procedures to be followed until the Senate finally disposes of a bill. The most common provisions of agreements concern time limitations and permissible amendments. They may either allot a given number of hours for debate or fix the date and time at which consideration is to be concluded. Related restrictions usually provide that not more than a stated period of time be devoted to the discussion of each amendment and that a vote on some amendments be deferred to a time certain. General debate and the amending process are not separate and distinct phases as in the House and amendments may be offered to any portion of a bill at any time during its consideration. Under an agreement providing for a vote on amendments after a certain hour without debate, amendments may still be proposed, but not debated. Agreements also require that amendments be germane. However, since the objection of a single senator can delay or prevent the approval of a unanimous consent agreement, it is occasionally necessary to defer to a senator who wishes to offer a nongermane amendment. This is accomplished by stating in the agreement that a particular amendment is in order, which renders it germane regardless of its actual relationship to a bill.

A provision in a unanimous consent agreement for a vote on the final passage of a measure at a specified time is not affected when its consideration is interrupted by other business. It is common for an agreement to adopt a committee substitute for a bill or all separate panel amendments. Under this procedure the amended bill is then considered as original text for the purposes of floor action, which merely facilitates the amending process. An agreement that controls time and limits debate may only be modified by another such agreement. Senate practices foster reliance on ad hoc arrangements, while the House uses formal procedures to dispense with its rules. Even the most detailed unanimous consent agreements are not as specific about time limitations and authorized amendments as are special orders.

In the absence of a unanimous consent agreement debate can only be restricted by successfully involving cloture and need only be germane during the consideration of general appropriation bills. Otherwise there are no limitations on time, germaneness or amendments. Though the Senate does have a mild germaneness rule it is rarely observed or enforced. This means that any proposal, regardless of whether it has been introduced or considered by a committee or whether it is related to pending business, may be offered as a nongermane amendment. The effect is to immediately bring any legislative proposition to the Senate floor. Though this practice is subject to abuse, it tends to preclude committee action that defies the wishes of senators who have a strong interest in certain legislation but are not members of the committee of jurisdiction.

Though Senate rules are silent about the printing of amendments, most are printed separately prior to floor action on the pertinent bill. As with House amendments printed in the *Congressional Record*, this practice makes the proposals available to other members in advance of debate. Legislators are more likely to approve amendments that they have had the opportunity to consider beforehand. Printed amendments have no official status until offered from the floor.

As members of a smaller body senators have larger and more diverse constituencies to represent and more committee assignments with correspondingly less time to specialize than House members. To a much greater extent than in the House each senator, due to the possibility of unlimited debate and the prerogative to object to unanimous consent agreements, may significantly influence the course of legislative proceedings. The combination of greater demands on the time of senators and the opportunity to affect floor action prompts party leaders to assure members that every effort will be made to accommodate their scheduling needs. Thus, the Senate functions as a more collegial body than the House and this fact has important consequences for debate.

The Senate controls time less rigidly than the House, with the practice of unlimited debate being modified by whatever agreements are necessary to bring deliberations to a close. Since senators also have less time to devote to bills prior to chamber consideration, a greater number of controversial matters have to await resolution until they are debated on the floor. Minimal restrictions on debate encourage senators to explore all implications of a measure. Committee members are also more willing to share their influence with colleagues who are not members of the panel that reported a bill. It is not unusual for political bargaining to occur and policy decisions to be made during the amending process. This is demonstrated by the privilege of senators to modify their own amendments without chamber approval. Because all members have the opportunity to express their views on the floor and to have them considered, Senate debate is more likely than its House counterpart to produce a genuine exchange of ideas.

CONFERENCE PROCEEDINGS

The foregoing discussion of congressional debate applies mainly to instances in which a bill reported by a House or Senate committee is considered in its body of origin or to occasions when a bill passed by one chamber reaches the floor of the other. Two later phases of debate also require attention, not only because they involve distinctive procedures, but because certain actions taken during earlier debate are specifically intended to influence subsequent floor proceedings.

The procedure used for less controversial measures is known as amendments between the houses. This situation arises when the second chamber amends a bill and returns it to the body or origin for further action. During these deliberations only the amendments adopted by the second house are debated and they are treated as original text for the purposes of amendment. Each Senate amendment to a House bill is examined to determine whether it is germane. The question of germaneness is decided based on whether the amendment would conform to House rules if offered in that body. The differences that stem from amendments between the houses are resolved when one chamber approves the amendments of the other or informal negotiation produces a compromise that is accepted by both houses.

Since each house will pass its own version of a controversial bill, such measures are invariably sent to a conference committee composed of members from the House and Senate to reconcile their differences. Many actions that occur during earlier debate can be explained by the fact that legislators often plan floor strategy with the expectation that a conference will be necessary. The key factors concerning debate of conference reports are that they must be considered as a whole and are not subject to amendment in either chamber. They can only be amended by a complex and lengthy process that entails action by both houses and which is avoided for that reason. Conference reports are privileged business and may be brought to the floor at any time. Special orders and unanimous consent agreements, which appear in the *Congressional Record* and the journals of their respective houses, also apply to these proceedings, though neither would contain provisions concerning amendments.

A standing committee may report a bill with language its members realize will not be accepted on the floor, while floor managers are inclined to accept some amendments to assure passage of a bill. In the former instance committee members may endeavor to have certain provisions restored in conference, while in the latter they may attempt to have portions of the text eliminated. In anticipation of a conference each house may modify or delete provisions strongly supported by the other or adopt expendable amendments. Both actions are intended to provide leverage in the conference bargaining process where some amendments can be sacrificed in exchange for retention of those parts of a bill each chamber considers more important. Thus, the judgment of floor managers must often extend beyond immediate considerations to an estimate of what can survive a conference. Amendments may also be adopted to placate a particular constituency, with the tacit understanding that they will be discarded in conference because their substantive effects are inconsistent with constructive legislative objectives. This tactic enables legislators to claim political credit for a popular but deficient proposal without assuming the responsibility for enacting it into law.

A conference appointed to consider separate amendments added by one house to a bill passed by the other may produce only partial agreement. The differences that have been resolved are embodied in a conference report, which is debated as an entity in each chamber. Amendments reported in disagreement by a conference committee may be debated individually or collectively. House rules permit separate consideration of Senate amendments to a House bill embodied in a conference report that would have been ruled out of order as nongermane if offered in the House. The significance of this procedure is the leverage it gives House conferees, who can argue that the inclusion of such amendments will jeopardize the report, since the rejection of a part results in rejection of the whole. Conversely, if Senate language does not include nongermane amendments, Senate conferees can argue that their version should be accepted by their House counterparts because Senate procedures enable a single member to obstruct legislation. In this case there would seem to be less of an obstacle to obtain House approval for concessions to the Senate than vice versa.

The rules of both houses prohibit conferees from including matter in conference reports that is beyond the scope of legislation committed to their consideration. Should conferees find that this restriction impedes their purposes they can try to use debate of the report to circumvent it. This is accomplished by expressly stating an interpretation that cannot be formally incorporated into the bill. The making of legislative history is often deliberately pursued when committee members ask questions of floor managers regarding the meaning of specific provisions at this or earlier stages of debate.

The best introduction to floor consideration of a bill is the accompanying standing or conference committee report. This document contains a discussion of the factual background and political history of legislation and concisely describes its overall objectives and the purpose of each major provision. Reports establish the contours of debate and are keys to understanding the views expressed and amendments proposed. Debate serves to disseminate and elaborate the arguments and explanations of proponents and opponents that appear in the committee report.

BIBLIOGRAPHY

Berman, Daniel M. *In Congress Assembled.* New York: Macmillan, 1964.

Froman, Lewis A., Jr. *The Congressional Process.* Boston: Little, Brown, 1967.

Gross, Bertram M. *The Legislative Struggle.* New York: McGraw-Hill, 1953.

Oleszek, Walter. *Congressional Procedures and the Policy Process*. Washington: Congressional Quarterly Press, 1978.

U.S. Congress. House. *Cannon's Procedure in the House of Representatives*. House Document No. 610, 87th Congress, 2nd Session. Washington: U.S. Government Printing Office, 1963.

U.S. Congress. House. *Constitution, Jefferson's Manual and Rules of the House of Representatives*. House Document No. 95-403, 95th Congress, 2nd Session. Washington: U.S. Government Printing Office, 1979.

U.S. Congress. House. *Deschler's Procedure in the U.S. House of Representatives*. 3rd ed. 96th Congress, 1st Session. Washington: U.S. Government Printing Office, 1979.

U.S. Congress. House. Committee on Science and Technology. *Legislative Manual of the Committee on Science and Technology*. Committee Print, 96th Congress, 1st Session. Washington: U.S. Government Printing Office, 1979.

U.S. Congress. Senate. *Senate Manual*. Senate Document No. 96-1, 96th Congress, 2nd Session. Washington: U.S. Government Printing Office, 1980.

U.S. Congress. Senate. *Senate Procedure*. Senate Document No. 93-21, 93rd Congress, 1st Session. Washington: U.S. Government Printing Office, 1974.

7
Voting

Voting would appear to be one of the clearer and simpler forms of congressional decisionmaking. On both an individual and collective basis, a recorded vote is a conspicuous and concrete fact. However, the structure and strategy of congressional voting, combined with the multiple goals of legislators and legislation, can preclude an obvious or routine verdict. Whether or when to have a vote, on which question, and by which method are decisions that are vital for the progress of a bill. This chapter examines the procedural and political aspects of the voting process and its relationship to legislation.

Though a roll-call vote is the most explicit type of legislative decision, its significance can be subject to varying interpretations. It is not an isolated action and should be viewed in the context of preceding and succeeding votes to be accurately assessed. In addition, voting alternatives are shaped by other decisions in the legislative process that may be more important. The comparative visibility and intelligibility of a congressional vote tend to veil the complexity of its immediate background and ultimate meaning. The parliamentary tactics and political purposes associated with voting affect the passage and form of bills as materially as other legislative proceedings.

The external environment of Congress, including electoral results, presidential action, prominent events, and public opinion, all of which can materialize in a variety of ways, may result in a vote and also determine its outcome. Should a bill reflect partisan or ideological divisions, the party ratio or philosophical cleavage may lead to a predictable result. The continual bargaining that characterizes congressional decisionmaking can contribute to votes that constitute part of the negotiation process. This practice, known as logrolling, involves the exchange of support among those who favor different provisions of the same bill or advocate unrelated bills. Blocs of legislators vote for those portions of or an entire measure important to others in return for reciprocal action. Explanations that focus on the influence of these factors are beyond the scope of this chapter.

PROCEDURAL FACTORS

An examination of congressional voting requires that the stages, types, methods, and forms of voting be distinguished. The initial stage of voting occurs in committee, and each panel must maintain a complete record of all roll-call votes, including the names of those members present but not voting and those using proxies. Proxy voting is the practice of authorizing committee members to cast votes on behalf of absent colleagues. This record is open to public inspection in the committee office, but more accessible sources are transcripts of mark-up sessions printed in hearing form, committee reports, and Congressional Quarterly's *Weekly Reports.* Floor votes during chamber consideration and bicameral action are the two subsequent stages.

The types of votes are quorum calls, which establish that the minimum number of legislators necessary for proceedings to be valid is present; procedural votes, which are decisions on matters other than the merits of a measure; substantive votes, which either adopt or reject amendments to a bill; and final passage, which is a series of votes rather than a single ballot. Each of these types applies to each stage, though the unique nature of each stage means that the types manifest themselves somewhat differently.

A judgment regarding which method of voting to employ during floor proceedings can be as crucial for a bill as a decision to take a vote. There are four methods by which to take unrecorded votes, which do not reveal the name or position of individual legislators. When unanimous consent is used, the presiding officer merely states that "without objection" the motion or measure is adopted or passed. A voice vote is based on the volume of sound of those members responding, and the presiding officer determines whether the chorus of "ayes" or "nays" has prevailed. Since most legislation is minor or routine, these two methods are frequently used to dispose of business. For a division vote, the presiding officer counts the members on each side, who either stand or raise their hands. During an unrecorded teller vote, which occurs only in the House, members cast their votes by walking through the center aisle to be counted by other members, known as tellers; the vote total of those for and against is announced. For a division, the result may be conveyed in the same manner or simply by a statement that one side has a majority.

There are also four methods available for conducting recorded votes. On a recorded teller vote, which is peculiar to the House, members cast votes by depositing cards in a ballot box or by electronic means. When a recorded vote in the House reveals the absence of a quorum, the result is an automatic roll call that combines a quorum call and vote on the pending question. A regular roll call is held whenever demanded and seconded by one-fifth of a quorum. Article I, Section 5, of the Constitution provides for a yea and nay vote on the request of one-fifth of the members present. In the Senate, there is no difference between the last two methods and electronic voting is not used. A legislative call system comprised of bells or buzzers and lights operates to alert legislators in the Capitol and Senate and House office buildings to the type and method of voting in progress on the floor of either chamber.

The forms of voting refer to the manner in which a legislator may communicate or conceal his position. The options are to vote in the affirmative or negative, to be present but not vote, to be absent, to announce at a later time how one would have voted if he had been present, or to be paired. A pair is an unwritten and voluntary agreement between individual legislators that applies to a scheduled roll-call vote. Pairing permits a member to have his position on a given question officially recorded though he is unable to be present. A legislator who will be absent for a floor session may conclude an agreement with a colleague who will attend and vote on the opposite side. The one who is present refrains from voting to redress the imbalance caused by the absence of a colleague who differs with him on an amendment or bill.

A "live" pair occurs when a legislator who is present withholds his vote and pairs with an absent colleague. A simple pair develops when two absent legislators pair with each other. General pairs are used primarily in the House, where members leave their names with the Clerk to be matched with others who have done the same. This indicates only that two legislators would have voted on opposite sides of a question, but does not indicate which side. While pairs are not counted in the vote totals, the names of those paired and their positions, if known, appear in the *Congressional Record*. Though the professed purpose of pairing is to enable legislators to have their positions formally noted in cases of unavoidable absence, it is also a convenient way to avoid a controversial vote. Since pairing is an unofficial practice not recognized by the rules of either house, any errors or misunderstandings that result from the making or breaking of pairs are not matters for chamber notice or action.

When a simple majority vote is necessary to transact business, this means a majority of those present and voting, assuming the existence of a quorum, not a majority of those present or a majority of the entire membership. Legislators present but not voting are counted for the purposes of a quorum. Though a member makes a motion that requires a vote, he may not be familiar with the technicalities of parliamentary procedure and may use improper phraseology. To ensure that the terminology is correct and consistent with the desired action, a vote is taken on a question as it is stated by the presiding officer. Should it be discovered, after a vote has been taken, that a procedural or substantive error was made, the proceedings are vacated by unanimous consent and another vote is scheduled.

POLITICAL FACTORS

Unrecorded votes enable legislators to take ambiguous or contradictory positions during the consideration of a bill. An equivocal stance, though it can be politically expedient, is not necessarily an attempt to deceive or mislead. A roll-call vote compels complete endorsement or disapproval of a proposal even when a legislator may not be that certain of its merits or defects. A member may agree with the aims of a bill, but disagree with its means. Though major bills contain several subdivisions and have multiple purposes, on final passage a legislator cannot vote for some provisions and against others.

The question of whether a vote is to be recorded can be of some political significance. A roll call requires legislators to publicly declare themselves on matters on which they may have taken an unclear position or maintained silence. They prefer to avoid roll calls when their views conflict with those of their constituents. By delaying a vote until after the roll has been called the first time or until most have been electronically recorded, a legislator may join the majority and claim credit with those who favored the proposal while informing those who opposed it that voting with them would not have changed the outcome. When a member personally favors a measure that his constituents oppose, by delaying his vote and determining that it will pass without his support, he can vote against it to please the electorate.

Because of their control of the legislative schedule, party leaders can arrange for votes to occur at those times most likely to produce results consistent with their perception of the party, chamber, or national interest. On less visible votes, mainly procedural or unrecorded ones, party leaders are assured of a higher level of support for the party position. Roll-call votes on the substance of measures are the most visible and tend to attenuate their influence. Leaders closely monitor the tally to determine whether they will need to call upon votes being held in reserve or can release those who would prefer to vote on the other side but have agreed to support the party position if such action would alter the outcome. The presiding officer may exercise some discretion in delaying the announcement of a result to allow time for switches or latecomers to vote. These maneuvers cannot be ascertained from the printed record of a roll call because names are listed in alphabetical order only.

The two major reasons for having an unrecorded vote are to expedite uncontroversial measures or to avoid the publicity of a position. Among the many reasons for desiring a roll-call vote are that advocates of a particular proposal may wish to have those on the other side publicly identified. Also, such a vote may bring more members to the floor and affect the outcome; create a strong chamber position which can be used as leverage during bicameral action; determine the drift of collective sentiment; oblige public demand that a decision be made in the most visible manner; and help gauge the appeal of a proposal as a prelude to further action. Most recorded votes occur on amendments to bills, and all roll calls are assigned numbers in chronological order throughout each session of Congress. In the Senate, roll calls on legislative and executive business are numbered in separate series. Voting procedures in the House are discussed prior to those in the Senate.

HOUSE ACTION

The House may conduct its business either in the Committee of the Whole or in the House. The House, whose quorum is 218, votes to go into the Committee of the Whole, whose quorum is only 100, when it approves a special order reported by the Rules Committee · or adopts a motion to consider an appropriation bill. A quorum call is not in order in the Committee of the Whole once it is determined that a quorum is present, unless the Committee is operating under the five-minute rule and a question is brought to a vote. A motion to rise in the Committee of the Whole is equivalent to a motion to adjourn in the House and, if adopted, the Committee is dissolved and action must proceed in the House.

The primary legislative task of the Committee of the Whole is to consider amendments. Initially the presiding officer, or chairman, puts the question to a voice vote. If he is uncertain of which side prevails, or if a member on the losing side demands it, a division vote is taken. Twenty members, or one-fifth or a quorum, may require an unrecorded teller vote, while twenty-five members may obtain a recorded teller vote. The order of voting in the Committee of the Whole is always voice to division to tellers; the most important is the last, for if a quorum is present it is the final vote on an amendment in the Committee. Teller votes are usually reserved for key amendments or those which were decided by close margins on voice or division votes. Because an amendment may be voted upon more than once, it is possible to lose one vote and win another or vice versa. Since many of the most important votes in the Committee of the Whole may be unrecorded, a legislator may support efforts to weaken a bill favored by his constituents, while on a roll-call vote on final passage in the House, he can vote for its approval.

Once the presence of a quorum has been established in the House, a point of no quorum is in order only when a proposition is put to a vote. The failure of a quorum to respond on a roll-call vote, followed by adjournment, does not affect the pending question, which is voted upon anew when the House reconvenes.

When a quorum fails to vote on any matter and an objection is made for that reason, an automatic roll-call vote by electronic device is ordered. If the number of those voting and those present who decline to vote total at least 218, this procedure simultaneously verifies the presence of a quorum and decides the pending question based upon a majority of those voting.

The demand for yeas and nays under the Constitution must be supported by one-fifth of those present, while a demand for a roll-call vote under House rules must be seconded by one-fifth of a quorum, or 44 members. Which form the demand takes depends upon which is more certain to bring about a roll-call vote. A demand for a roll-call vote may be made following the determination that an insufficient number of members second a request for the yeas and nays. A demand for an unrecorded teller vote, if supported by one-fifth of a quorum, must be granted should a request for a roll-call vote be refused. The Speaker makes a count of members in those cases where a minimum number of legislators is needed to second a demand for a vote. The requirement for such a minimum number to sustain the demand for a vote prevents requests that are dilatory in nature and favored by only a few members. A demand for a division vote is not precluded by the fact that a roll-call or teller vote is denied. If a quorum is absent as indicated by the total number of votes cast on a division or unrecorded teller vote, any member may demand a roll-call vote.

Amendments defeated in the Committee of the Whole are not reported to or voted upon by the House, except for the motion to recommit, which is discussed below. After the Committee reports those amendments it has adopted to the House, the Speaker asks all members to identify those on which a separate vote is desired. The remaining amendments are usually approved as a package by voice vote, after which the contested ones are voted upon individually by roll calls in the order in which they appear in the bill. Votes in the House that reverse decisions made in the Committee of the Whole do so for one of two reasons. If the vote in the Committee was unrecorded, it probably reflected the personal views of members, while a roll call in the House denotes the perception members have of constituent preferences. The larger quorum necessary to transact business in the House means that many members who did not participate in Committee of the Whole proceedings are present for House action. The Speaker or chairman of the Committee usually do not vote, but may do so to make or break a tie since a tie vote defeats a proposal.

There are two motions available to opponents of a bill whose purpose is to test voting strength on a measure. One, the question of consideration, is raised in the House when a bill is initially taken from a calendar. In most cases this will be a vote on a special order reported by the Rules Committee. The other motion is an amendment in the Committee of the Whole to strike the enacting clause, which is debated under the five-minute rule. A vote against consideration keeps a bill on its calendar, while the adoption of a motion to strike the enacting clause, if upheld by the House, kills a bill.

The motion for the previous question, whether incorporated into a resolution reported by the Rules Committee or made by the floor manager of a bill, if adopted, closes debate and brings the House directly to a vote on one or more amendments or all authorized amendments and final passage. Final passage in the House begins with voting on the amendments reported by the Committee of the Whole. Next is engrossment and third reading, a purely formal action that is approved by unanimous consent. This is followed by a motion to recommit, usually with instructions, which is reserved for use by those opposed to the bill. It provides an opportunity to offer a complete alternative to the pending measure and may include amendments defeated in the Committee of the Whole. It is a provileged motion that enables the minority to have a roll-call vote on its proposal; the result may be a more accurate reflection of sentiment than the vote on final passage. Some legislators who vote to recommit will, after the motion is defeated, vote for final passage because they believe the bill to be preferable to none at all or because the latter vote is more intelligible to constituents.

The actual vote on final passage is normally by roll call, but if the outcome is obvious and members are anxious to adjourn or proceed to other business, it may be by voice vote. All votes on amendments or bills, except in the Committee of the Whole, are subject to the motion to reconsider and are not considered final until reconsidered. Should a majority approve the motion, the matter to which it applies is once again before the chamber for action. A prompt motion to reconsider, which is made immediately following the announcement of a vote result, disposes of the matter without jeopardizing a bill. The motion, offered by someone who voted with the majority, invariably fails because all members who participated in the original decision are still on the floor. To delay reconsideration provides opponents of a measure the opportunity to persuade others to change their votes and to bring to the floor those members who were absent.

When several roll-call votes on different measures are likely to occur on the same day, the Speaker may postpone such votes to a designated time on that day or within the next two days. This procedure saves time since a normal voting period is 15 minutes; however, the Speaker is empowered to reduce the voting period to five minutes for all such votes after the first. In addition to promoting efficiency, it is also easier to assemble all members in favor of certain proposals when the exact time of voting can be known in advance. This clustering of votes is also applicable to special orders from the Rules Committee and conference reports.

SENATE ACTION

The Senate has no counterpart to the Committee of the Whole and operates on the assumption that a quorum is always present until a member suggests otherwise or the contrary is revealed by a quorum call or roll-call vote. When less than a quorum responds to a roll call, the results are invalid and the presiding officer orders a quorum call; after a quorum appears, a vote is taken anew on the pending question. A quorum call may be requested by any senator prior to a vote on any motion or measure.

The three methods of voting used in the Senate are voice, division, and roll call, and once a result has been announced no motions for another vote, as in the House, are in order. The presiding officer may request a division vote whenever he is in doubt of the results of a voice vote, or any senator may do the same before the results of a voice vote have been announced. A quorum call or a roll call may be demanded by any senator prior to the announcement of the results of a voice or division vote. Thus, the absence of a quorum does not invalidate a voice or division vote if it is not challenged at the appropriate time. If a senator fails to request a roll-call vote in time, he may still make a motion to reconsider, which, if adopted, nullifies the earlier vote.

A roll-call vote must be taken when demanded and seconded by one-fifth of a quorum, or 11 members, with the number necessary to support such a demand determined by a show of hands. A quorum call may be demanded when a request for a roll-call vote does not have a sufficient number of senators to second it, after which the request for a roll call may be renewed. Though a roll-call vote must technically be demanded by one-fifth of a quorum, in practice it is rarely denied to any senator who desires one, though he may be persuaded to withdraw his request. A roll-call vote is valid when the number of senators voting, plus those present but not voting, constitute a quorum of 51. The Vice-President may vote only in case of a tie, but since a tie vote defeats a proposal, his vote would only be decisive to approve a measure.

Sixteen senators must sign a cloture petition to close debate when the Senate is prevented from proceeding with its business due to a filibuster. This is presented to the presiding officer, who is required to state the motion to the Senate immediately. Two days later the presiding officer submits the matter to the Senate for a roll-call vote. A motion to invoke cloture requires 60 votes to close debate on all questions except those to amend the Senate rules, which requires a two-thirds majority of a quorum. Any Senate rule may be suspended by a two-thirds vote, and this procedure is primarily used to permit legislative amendments to general appropriation bills if unanimous consent cannot be obtained.

Should a unanimous consent agreement specify that a final vote on a bill and all amendments thereto shall occur at or no later than a certain hour, votes may not be taken at times earlier than stated. The first step in final passage is taken when senators no longer have amendments to offer and the presiding officer orders a bill engrossed and read a third time, a formality that requires only a moment. It is not in order to recommit a bill unless a unanimous consent agreement provides for such a motion. The flexibility of the Senate amending process enables members to propose a greater number of substitute or other amendments than in the House. Since substitutes are comprehensive revisions of pending measures, they serve the same purpose as a motion to recommit with instructions offered in the House, while other proposals may be offered to test voting strength.

A roll-call vote on final passage is followed by a motion to reconsider. Voice votes may be taken on final passage though a majority of senators may be absent and, except for a motion to reconsider, the action is final unless challenged before the result is announced. In the absence of a unanimous consent agreement or cloture, a vote on final passage may be delayed as party leaders endeavor to negotiate an end to a filibuster. However, it may not be possible to arrange for such a vote in the presence of determined opposition.

BICAMERAL ACTION

When each house passes different versions of a bill, the differences may be resolved through action by each chamber on the language adopted by the other or through appointment of a conference. In the former case the body of origin may vote separately on each or collectively on all amendments approved by the other house. The decision to seek a conference initiates a series of procedural votes covering a request for and an agreement to a conference and the appointment of conferees by both chambers. Conference committee meetings are open to the public unless a majority of the House membership or of Senate conferees decides by a roll-call vote to hold a closed session. Though a majority of the conferees from each house must vote to endorse any agreements reached and to have a report submitted to their respective chambers, the only equivalent to a roll-call vote taken in conference that appears in print is the names of those who sign the report.

A conference report is filed in each house once conferees reconcile all, or are only able to settle some, of their differences. The first chamber to vote may approve, reject, or recommit the report and, if approved, the second may vote only to accept or reject, since approval by the first dissolves the conference. Should a conference report embody only a partial resolution of differences, the first vote is on the report; if approved, the amendments reported in disagreement may be acted on separately, collectively or through appointment of another conference.

House rules provide for separate votes on those portions of a conference report that are nongermane Senate amendments to a House bill, and if disapproved, the entire report is rejected. Each house may vote to instruct its conferees to insist on retaining language in the chamber's version of a bill or opposing language contained in the other body's version. This procedure, because it cannot influence conferees appointed by the other house and can inhibit the bargaining process, is infrequently employed. All votes that relate to bicameral action are subject to the motion to reconsider.

GENERAL CONSIDERATIONS

Due to occasional errors in the recording of votes and the use of unanimous consent to permit the change of a vote, the most accurate tallies appear in the bound *Record* and the journals rather than in contemporaneous publications. The indexes of these sources cite only the pages on which a given measure received consideration, without specifying where voting data can be found. Thus, use of the journals is more convenient for locating such information since it is not necessary to scan numerous pages of debate, which can easily result in overlooking an unrecorded vote.

Congressional Quarterly issues two annual publications that describe and tabulate several hundred roll-call votes. *CQ Almanac* includes much more than voting-related information while *Congressional Roll Call* contains only such facts. The voting data are identical in each, and both have separate subject indexes for these recorded votes.

Article I, Section 5, of the Constitution stipulates that a majority of each house is the quorum necessary to conduct business, but the House and Senate interpret this provision to meet the practical needs of managing their workloads. All members of Congress have other demands on their time in addition to attending floor sessions of their respective chambers. Senate proceedings foster a greater freuqency of roll-call votes, mainly because of smaller membership and greater collegiality. Also, unlike the House, the Senate does not have a procedure for combining a quorum call with a procedural or substantive vote and has no equivalent to the Committee of the Whole, which facilitates the disposition of amendments through unrecorded votes. The latitude of Senate debate results in a greater number of amendments offered for consideration. Though its rules require a majority of a quorum to demand a roll-call vote, an individual senator is accorded the privilege if insistent. Finally, since the Senate regularly operates without a quorum, any formal notice of this fact leads to a roll-call vote.

When a simple, rather than an extraordinary, majority is necessary to transact business, this means a majority of a quorum. Since a quorum is itself only a bare majority of the entire body, major voting decisions can be made by just over one-quarter of the total membership. In the House, which conducts much of its important business in the Committee of the Whole, where the quorum is 100, only 51 votes are needed to dispose of amendments. A majority vote in either house is sufficient to amend measures that require a two-thirds vote for final passage or to reconsider votes that involved a two-thirds majority. Key votes in the House that affect the substance of a bill are those on special orders, amendments, and recommitment, while Senate decisions on amendments are the crucial votes in that chamber. When procedural votes determine whether a bill will reach final passage, they are of equal significance to substantive ones and constitute basic elements of legislative history.

Though voting is a unique action that is clearly distinguishable from debate, throughout the legislative process the two activities remain closely related. They are two aspects of the same proceeding, with the statements that comprise debate preceding the decisions expressed through voting. The procedural connection is more definite than the relationship between the voting process or a vote result and the content of a bill. The meaning of a negative vote tends to be clearer than an affirmative one, which transforms the multitude of individual views into a corporate expression whose substantive implications are not always evident or consistent. The procedural maneuvers that represent efforts to secure an advantage when the outcome of a vote is uncertain also tend to cloud the meaning of some voting decisions.

It is necessary to mobilize majorities at many points in the legislative process to enact a bill into law. A vote reveals whether a majority exists, what its components are, and suggests other legislative transactions that might be initiated. The strategy for success on floor votes is to have more members present who support one side than the other. This is not necessarily an easy task because of the numerous demands on the time of legislators and the variety of sources that can exert political influence.

Because the order in which votes are taken can have important consequences for the content of a bill, it is a question that can generate some controversy and may be resolved through a special order in the House or a unanimous consent agreement in the Senate. The impact of a vote depends upon its method, margin, and relationship to other votes. The sequence of voting decisions vitally affects the range of options available for successive votes. Thus, the parliamentary and political factors that influence the legislative timetable can be critical for the qualitative and quantitative results of a vote.

Committee consideration of a bill inevitably has a profound effect upon floor votes. Decisions may be made that preclude a floor vote or produce a unanimous or near unanimous verdict. Since a major bill is in a state of continual revision throughout its life, it is possible that an early vote in favor may, due to modifications of the measure or changes in the political environment, develop into a later vote against the bill or vice versa.

The number of voting decisions on a given bill generally reflects the level of controversy generated by an issue. One paradox of the legislative process is that a multiplicity of votes tends to obscure their individual and collective meaning. Another paradox is that though a roll-call vote compels legislators to publicly commit themselves and enables constituents to hold them accountable for their actions, it is just such visible commitments that may impede the negotiation process which is essential to produce compromises that can command wide political support.

BIBLIOGRAPHY

Froman, Lewis A., Jr. *The Congressional Process.* Boston: Little, Brown, 1967.

Gross, Bertram M. *The Legislative Struggle.* New York: McGraw-Hill, 1953.

Jewell, Malcolm E., and Patterson, Samuel C. *The Legislative Process in the United States.* New York: Random House, 1966.

Oleszek, Walter. *Congressional Procedures and the Policy Process.* Washington: Congressional Quarterly Press, 1978.

U.S. Congress. House. *Constitution, Jefferson's Manual and Rules of the House of Representatives.* House Document No. 95-403, 96th Congress, 1st Session. Washington: U.S. Government Printing Office, 1979.

U.S. Congress. House. *Deschler's Procedure in the U.S. House of Representatives.* 3rd ed. 96th Congress, 1st Session. Washington: U.S. Government Printing Office, 1979.

U.S. Congress. House. *How Our Laws Are Made.* House Document No. 96-352, 96th Congress, 2nd Session. Washington: U.S. Government Printing Office, 1980.

U.S. Congress. Senate. *Senate Manual.* Senate Document No. 96-1, 96th Congress, 2nd Session. Washington: U.S. Government Printing Office, 1980.

U.S. Congress. Senate. *Senate Procedure.* Senate Document No. 93-21, 93rd Congress, 1st Session. Washington: U.S. Government Printing Office, 1974.

8

Bills*

Legislative histories usually focus on the political factors and maneuvers that affect the progress of bills or on formal statements that would help to construe their provisions following enactment. A perspective that has received less attention concerns those rules and practices which govern preparation and disposition of legislation. This chapter traces the typical course of a major bill by describing its development and treatment as an official document at each stage of the legislative process. A survey of sources that can be consulted to identify bills and locate their texts concludes the discussion.

Bills are the raw material of congressional business. Considered primarily as political vehicles and potential law, their nature as legislative papers is generally overlooked. The procedures that apply in this latter regard determine when a bill is printed and in which congressional publications it will ultimately appear. For the purposes of what follows, the term "bills" includes joint resolutions, since both are treated in an identical manner and, upon being approved, are law. The only exception is a joint resolution that is a proposed constitutional amendment, which does not require presidential approval upon passage. Otherwise, the major differences between bills and joint resolutions are that the latter are numbered in a separate series and tend to be used for the incidental or subordinate purposes of legislation.

PRE-FLOOR PRACTICES

In the House, printed blank forms on which members have the original draft bill typed are available in the stationery room. All forms must be signed by the legislator whose name appears first thereon before they can be accepted for introduction. Once formally introduced by being dropped into a hopper at the desk of the Clerk of the House, bills are assigned a number, beginning with 1, that they retain for the duration of the Congress. The parliamentarian, under the supervision of the Speaker of the House, then designates the committee to which the bill is referred for consideration. The bill clerk, under the direction of the Clerk of the House, prepares a duplicate copy of the draft and forwards it to the Government Printing Office. Upon delivery of printed copies to the bill clerk, the bills are distributed to the document rooms of both houses and the office of the Secretary of the Senate. One official printed copy is transmitted to the chairman of the committee to which it was referred, for which the bill clerk obtains a receipt. The original draft is retained in the files of the Clerk of the House. (See figure 8, page 106, for an example of an introduced print of a public bill.)

---

*This chapter derives from an article, "Congressional Bills," by Jerrold Zwirn, in *Government Publications Review* Vol. 7A, pp. 17-25, © 1980 Pergamon Press Ltd. Reprinted with permission of Pergamon Press.

Figure 8
An Introduced Print of a Public Bill

97TH CONGRESS
1ST SESSION

S. 709

To require a refund value for certain beverage containers, and for other purposes.

IN THE SENATE OF THE UNITED STATES

MARCH 12 (legislative day, FEBRUARY 16), 1981

Mr. HATFIELD (for himself, Mr. PACKWOOD, Mr. CRANSTON, Mr. LEAHY, Mr. STAFFORD, Mr. INOUYE, and Mr. TSONGAS) introduced the following bill; which was read twice and referred to the Committee on Commerce, Science, and Transportation

---

A BILL

To require a refund value for certain beverage containers, and for other purposes.

1   *Be it enacted by the Senate and House of Representa-*

2   *tives of the United States of America in Congress assembled,*

3   That this Act may be cited as the "Beverage Container

4   Reuse and Recycling Act".

5   FINDINGS AND PURPOSES

6   SEC. 2. Congress finds and declares that—

7   (1) the failure to reuse and recycle empty bever-

8   age containers represents a significant and unnecessary

Printed forms are also available in the Senate, where draft bills are presented for processing to clerks at the presiding officer's desk. They are endorsed at the desk to indicate the author and the committee that has jurisdiction. After referral by the parliamentarian, under the supervision of the presiding officer, the bill is sent to the Secretary of the Senate's office to be numbered and forwarded, by the bill clerk, to the Government Printing Office. Printed copies are usually available the following morning and distributed as in the House. The original copy is filed in the Secretary's records. Bills introduced in either house whose provisions overlap the jurisdiction of two or more committees may be referred simultaneously or sequentially to those panels. In the House only, a bill may be divided into parts for referral to different committees.

Members of either house who introduce private bills may themselves indicate the committee to which the bills will be referred. Private bills apply to identifiable individuals or organizations within a legislator's geographical constituency and do not affect the general public. However, the distinction between public and private bills is not always clear, and bills may contain provisions of both a public and private nature, in which case they are treated as public measures.

Legislators frequently introduce numerous bills that are similar in purpose. Under these circumstances, a committee may choose one bill and incorporate the provisions of others. Another option is to amalgamate the best features of several bills and draft an entirely new version, which is then introduced and assigned a new number. This latter measure is referred to as a clean bill. For particularly complex and significant matters, primarily involving appropriations and revenue, the legislation is regularly drafted in committee, the first print is the reported version, and it is termed an original bill. A committee may also report a substitute, which is an amendment in the form of an entirely new bill, with only the original number being retained. Identical measures introduced in each chamber are known as companion bills.

A bill of some length and complexity often occupies a committee for several months. When extended consideration engenders numerous revisions, the panel will have the bill printed periodically to reflect the changes. These drafts, which serve as working papers, are designated as Committee Print No. 1, Committee Print No. 2, etc. Because they are issued in a limited quantity and their printing is not formally noted, knowledge of and access to these prints tends to be restricted to parties immediately concerned with the legislation. Independent researchers usually do not learn of their existence until granted permission to use committee records after they have been transferred to the National Archives.

The contents of an introduced print are: number and session of Congress, bill number, house and date of introduction, name(s) of legislator(s) who sponsored it, committee to which it was referred, type (bill or joint resolution), and the law(s), if any, it proposes to amend. After the member's name there will occasionally appear in parenthesis the phrase "by request." This denotes that the bill was introduced at the request of a government agency or private organization and that the legislator does not necessarily endorse it. Each line of the text is numbered, beginning with 1, on each page.

The text of a public bill may consist of as many as 12 distinct parts: 1) title — a brief statement of purpose(s); 2) enacting clause — identical for all bills; 3) short title — a descriptive phrase specifying its primary subject; 4) table of contents; 5) declaration of purpose — a statement of conditions the bill is intended to rectify; 6) definition of terms; 7) main body of the text in numbered titles and/or sections; 8) exceptions and provisos; 9) amendments and repeals; 10) savings clause — continues the effectiveness of specified legal obligations to avoid inadvertent lapsing or impairment; 11) separability clause — provides that if any provision of the *act* is declared invalid, the remainder is to be unaffected; and 12) effective and expiration dates. For a joint resolution, (2) is a resolving clause and (5) a preamble. All bills include (1), (2), and (7), though the text, if brief, will not be subdivided.

Printed forms for submitting proposed amendments are available only in the Senate. The key information included is a brief statement of purpose, the Senate or House bill number, name of the member offering it, and the page and line number where it is to be inserted. The bill clerk adds an amendment number. If the bill to be amended is in committee, the amendment is referred there; if not adopted, the sponsor may, after the bill is reported, resubmit it for consideration when the bill reaches the floor. At this time the amendment will be printed with the identical calendar number of the bill. This number signifies the bill's readiness for consideration by the parent body. A senator may receive permission for such a printed amendment to be retained at the presiding officer's desk for submission when the bill reaches the floor. These amendments, as well as unprinted or floor amendments, are numbered separately and serially, beginning with 1, throughout the existence of a Congress. Both printed and unprinted amendments are prepared on an identical form and become part of the official bill file.

When a committee has completed consideration of an introduced bill, its staff drafts a copy that incorporates all amendments adopted. It is delivered to the bill clerk, who transmits it to the Government Printing Office. The reported print, as this version is known, contains, in addition to the information appearing on the introduced print, a calendar number, a report number, date reported, name of member reporting it, and amendments, if any. Amendments are printed in lined-through type if they are deletions and in italics if they are additions. These amendments are committee recommendations only and must be approved by the parent body before being officially incorporated into the bill. A bill referred to two or more committees concurrently is reported only once, either jointly or by one of the panels which considered it. Measures referred to two or more committees consecutively, or those divided for referral in the House, may be reported by each panel.

Introduced bills, printed amendments, and reported bills, both prior to and after being printed, are examined for accuracy by the bill clerk. A printed copy found to contain a typographical or other error is stamped "STAR PRINT," the error is noted on the print, and the correct matter is inserted. It is then returned to the Government Printing Office and, when reprinted, will have a small star in the its lower left-hand corner and the words "STAR PRINT" on the first page to indicate that the original print has been corrected.

FLOOR PROCEDURES

Once a bill reaches the floor, all amendments offered must be in writing and may be printed, typed, or handwritten. If introduced at least one day prior to floor consideration in the House, amendments are printed in the daily edition of the *Congressional Record* in advance of debate. These amendments are deposited in a separate receptable at the rostrum or with the official reporters of debates and must bear the member's original signature. In the Senate they may be printed individually or in the *Record* prior to debate. An amendment must include the name of the legislator, the number of the bill to which it pertains, and the precise place in the bill it is to be inserted. Each amendment adopted in the House is initialed by two reading clerks to certify its approval. The legislative clerk in the Senate notes each amendment passed on the desk, or official, copy of the bill. When a bill under consideration is printed prior to passage to show which amendments have been adopted, the official copy remains at the desk for use as further amendments are proposed.

Upon completion of floor action, the bill clerk transmits to the enrolling clerk (who also serves under either the Clerk of the House or Secretary of the Senate) all papers relating to a bill passed by the chamber. These papers include the official copy of each bill, a separate copy of each amendment adopted, and any supplementary material. The enrolling clerk does not alter the official copy, but prepares a "printer's copy" using cut-outs of the reported print, copies of amendments approved, and any typed instructions regarding the arrangement and format of the text. The "printer's copy" is edited so that amendments appear in their proper place in the bill. Editing, in this instance, refers to the preparation of a "true copy" of the chamber's action on a bill, including the incorporation of technical and clerical changes where authorized. Such changes usually involve punctuation, cross-references, or the renumbering of pages and subdivisions of the text. For particularly lengthy bills, the "printer's copy" is updated on a daily basis. This process is officially known as the engrossment of a bill.

The edited copy is sent to the Government Printing Office and is now technically termed an Act, denoting that it is an act of one house of Congress. Though a bill is redesignated an Act after it has been passed by its body of origin, the designation of a joint resolution remains unchanged. The final copy of such a measure whose passage has been attested by the signature of either the Clerk of the House or Secretary of the Senate on its last page is known as an engrossed bill. An engrossed copy is retained in the files of either the Clerk or Secretary. The official printed copy, prior to being signed and transmitted to the other house, is examined for accuracy by the enrolling clerk. If no errors are found, it is delivered to the presiding officer's desk while the second chamber is in session. An accompanying message contains its number, title, date of passage, and a request for concurrence.

Upon being received by the second chamber, it is referred, but not delivered, to the appropriate committee(s). The bill clerk, after making a copy, transmits the official engrossed bill to the committee and obtains a receipt. The copy is sent to the Government Printing Office, and this version is termed the Act or referred print. It contains number and session of Congress, bill number of the body of origin, house to which it has been transmitted, date it was received, committee to which it has been referred, the law(s) it proposes to amend, and the date it passed the first chamber. This date is normally a calendar day in the House, while in the Senate the legislative day is noted if it differs from the calendar day. A legislative day extends from the time either house meets following an adjournment until it again adjourns. The Senate often decides to recess, which does not end a legislative day.

Engrossed bills may not be altered by the other house. When action by the second chamber results in passage with amendments, the changes must be transcribed on separate paper, stating which words are to be inserted or deleted and where, by reference to page, line, and word of the bill. However, action on the measure proceeds as in the body of origin, and the reported print will incorporate the text of amendments adopted in committee. Upon final passage, all amendments approved are engrossed and, when printed, are numbered consecutively in the order in which they appear in the bill, beginning with 1, unless there is only a single amendment. The engrossed bill and engrossed amendment(s) are then delivered to the body of origin. An accompanying message requests that the first chamber concur in the amendments.

If an identical or substantially similar measure has been reported in either chamber prior to receipt of an engrossed bill, the latter may not be referred to a committee and printed. It may subsequently be referred or substituted for the reported bill depending upon strategic or procedural considerations. A common action is for the second chamber to pass its own bill and then substitute its text under the number of the companion measure received from the other house. This procedure, which technically involves approval of an engrossed bill in lieu of the measure that was reported in the second house, facilitates anticipated bicameral negotiations.

CONFERENCE PROCEDURES

If the body of origin agrees to the amendments, or if amendments are not adopted by the second chamber, legislative action on the bill is completed. However, if there is disagreement that cannot be resolved by the houses acting separately in succession, the house having custody of the official papers on a bill may request a conference with the other to reconcile their differences. The papers, which consist of the original engrossed bill, engrossed amendments, and all messages exchanged between the chambers concerning the measure, are then delivered to the other body, for in conference procedure a house may only act when in possession of the papers. Upon agreement to a conference, the papers are returned to the house that asked for the conference. The bill clerk of the requesting body then gives the papers to its conferees, or managers, and obtains a receipt.

The authority of conferees is confined to choosing between or compromising on the amendments in disagreement. They may neither alter the text approved by both houses in identical form nor add provisions not adopted by either body. These restrictions do not apply when the second chamber has adopted a substitute, which is an amendment in the form of a new bill. In this case there is total disagreement, and conferees are free to write an original bill covering the same subject, though its provisions must be derived from at least one of the two versions under consideration. Though new matter is not permitted in conference reports, clarifying language or changes in phraseology to effect legislative consistency are acceptable as long as they do not broaden the scope of the bill beyond the differences committed to conference.

There are several possible outcomes of a conference. Conferees may trade, accepting the language adopted by the other house for one or more provisions if the other body's conferees will do the same; all amendments in disagreement may be compromised; or there may be some combination of these two possibilities. One other result would be the inability to reach agreement on all or any of their differences. If agreement is reached on some, a report is filed disclosing which matters have been resolved and which remain in disagreement. Approval of such a report by each chamber means that the remaining differences must still be settled before the bill can be enrolled.

When the managers reach agreement they file a report which, to be valid, must be signed by a majority of the conferees of each house. The report is drafted by staff members of the committees that considered the bill in each chamber. It is prepared in duplicate, with House conferees signing first on their copy and Senate conferees first on theirs. The managers of the house that requested the conference now give the official papers to the managers of the house that agreed thereto. The latter deliver them to the presiding officer, following which the bill clerk examines the report for accuracy, assigns a number to it, and forwards a copy to the Government Printing Office. Most conference reports are printed in the House only to avoid unnecessary duplication, but occasionally one is printed by both houses, in which case it will have two separate numbers. Should a typographical error be discovered in a printed conference report, it would be reissued as a star print.

A conference report is, in effect, a bill or an amended portion thereof, containing the text of all changes agreed upon, with an accompanying explanation of actions taken. Where the report refers to pages and line numbers, references are to the engrossed bill and engrossed amendments. The report includes the number and session of Congress, the house in which it was printed, report number, subject of the bill, date reported, name of member reporting it, and bill number. It may not be amended by either house acting independently of the other, but only by a concurrent resolution, which is used to coordinate the internal affairs of both houses on matters of mutual interest.

Upon approval of the report by one house, the papers are transmitted to the other with a message communicating its action. Endorsements noting legislative action taken by each house on the conference report, and the dates thereof, are noted on the engrossed bill by the Clerk of the House or Secretary of the Senate. Rejection of the report by one chamber may lead to another conference, in which case the second report would supersede the first. If both adopt it and, thus, agree upon an identical version of the bill, all papers relating to the measure are delivered to the enrolling clerk of the body of origin.

In the House only, special treatment may be accorded a bill whose subject matter falls within the purview of two or more committees. The Speaker is authorized to appoint an *ad hoc* panel composed of members from those committees with jurisdiction to consider such a measure, which is known as an omnibus bill. Upon passage its subdivisions are engrossed separately and, in the Senate, are referred to the appropriate committees. When the components of an omnibus bill are returned from the Senate with amendments, or when such amendments result in a conference, each component is considered separately, but agreement must be reached on all components for the bill to be enrolled.

ENACTMENT

An enrolled copy is prepared from the engrossed bill, engrossed amendments, the conference report, and all messages exchanged between the chambers concerning a bill. The procedures for enrollment are identical to those for engrossment. An enrolled bill is the final copy of a bill passed in identical form by both houses. It is printed on parchment and endorsed with the signature of either the Clerk of the House or Secretary of the Senate to indicate its body of origin, in whose files the official papers are retained.

Bills that originate in the House are examined for accuracy at the enrollment stage by staff members of the House Administration Committee and in the Senate by members of the Secretary's staff. Immediately preceding enrollment, members of both staffs compare their versions of a bill that has passed both chambers. When the bill is found to be truly enrolled, it is transmitted to the

House parliamentarian, who signs a receipt therefor and secures the signature of the Speaker, who signs the bill first, regardless of its body of origin. The measure is then delivered to the Senate parliamentarian, who also signs a receipt and obtains the signature of the President of the Senate. Following this dual signing, the bill is returned to either the House or Senate parliamentarian, depending upon its house of origin, for presentation to the President of the United States.

If a bill has been enrolled and signed by both presiding officers, or only by the Speaker, and an error is found, the signature(s) are rescinded by a concurrent resolution, after which it is reenrolled. The original enrolled bill is delivered to the White House, for which a receipt is obtained from a presidential staff member. Other than final adjournment, there is no time limit within which an enrolled bill need be presented to the President. Congress may request by concurrent resolution that a bill which is forwarded to the President and found to contain an error be returned for correction and reenrollment. An error in an enrolled bill in the President's posssession may also be corrected by a joint resolution. Should an error not be detected until after a bill has become law, it can only be corrected by passage of another bill.

When the President signs an enrolled bill within 10 days of receipt, Sundays excepted, it becomes law even if Congress has adjourned, and he so informs the body of origin. If the President neither signs nor vetoes it within 10 days, Sundays excepted, and Congress has not adjourned, the bill becomes law and is endorsed by the Administrator of General Services. Should the President return a bill to its house of origin with a statement of his objections and it is repassed by a two-thirds vote, an endorsement is made on the bill by the Clerk of the House or Secretary of the Senate to that effect. It is then transmitted to the other chamber, where, if it passes with a two-thirds majority, it is again endorsed, the President's veto is overridden, and the bill becomes law. A bill without an effective date becomes law the day it is signed by the President, repassed by Congress over a veto, or endorsed by the Administrator of General Services.

If the body of origin fails to override a veto, it notifies the other house by message and refers the original enrolled bill and veto message to the committee that reported the measure. Should the second chamber fail to override, it returns the bill to the body of origin with a message regarding its action. When the President vetoes a bill by withholding his signature following the final adjournment of Congress, the original copy is returned to the house of origin. In these instances, no print is made of the bill in the form in which it reached the President.

The house acting last when a bill is approved over a veto has it delivered to the Administrator of General Services. This official receives copies of all enrolled bills that become law. A copy is sent to the Government Printing Office, which prints it in duplicate for the purpose of final revision. Upon the return by the Administrator of one of the duplicates, the Government Printing Office prints the law in its final form.

The first official print of a statute appears in pamphlet form and is known as a slip law. (See figure 9 for an example of a slip law print of a public bill.) Each print indicates the manner in which the bill became law. Slip laws are published in two series — public and private — each of which is numbered separately, beginning with 1, for each Congress. Where some doubt exists as to whether a statute is a public or private law, the decision is made by editors in the Office of the Federal Register after examining the history, nature, and scope of the legislation.

Figure 9
A Slip Law Print of a Public Bill

95 STAT. 144   PUBLIC LAW 97–25—JULY 27, 1981

Public Law 97–25
97th Congress

An Act

July 27, 1981   To amend the Truth in Lending Act to encourage cash discounts, and for other
[H.R. 31]   purposes.

*Be it enacted by the Senate and House of Representatives of the
United States of America in Congress assembled,* That this Act may be
cited as the "Cash Discount Act"

Cash Discount
Act.
15 USC 1601
note.

TITLE I—CASH DISCOUNTS

SEC. 101. Section 167(b) of the Truth in Lending Act (15 U.S.C.
1666f(b)) is amended to read as follows:
"(b) With respect to any sales transaction, any discount from the
regular price offered by the seller for the purpose of inducing
payment by cash, checks, or other means not involving the use of an
open-end credit plan or a credit card shall not constitute a finance
charge as determined under section 106 if such discount is offered to
all prospective buyers and its availability is disclosed clearly and
conspicuously.".
SEC. 102. (a) Section 103 of the Truth in Lending Act (15 U.S.C. 1602)
is amended by adding at the end thereof the following:
"(z) As used in this section and section 167, the term 'regular price'
means the tag or posted price charged for the property or service if a
single price is tagged or posted, or the price charged for the property
or service when payment is made by use of an open-end credit plan or
a credit card if either (1) no price is tagged or posted, or (2) two prices
are tagged or posted, one of which is charged when payment is made
by use of an open-end credit plan or a credit card and the other when
payment is made by use of cash, check, or similar means. For
purposes of this definition, payment by check, draft, or other negoti-
able instrument which may result in the debiting of an open-end credit
plan or a credit cardholder's open-end account shall not be considered
payment made by use of the plan or the account.".
(b) Effective April 10, 1982—
(1) subsections (x) and (y) of section 103 of the Truth in Lending
Act (as redesignated by section 603(b) of Public Law 96–221) are
redesignated as subsections (y) and (z), respectively; and
(2) subsection (z) of such section (as added by subsection (a)) is
redesignated as subsection (x) and is inserted after subsection (w).
SEC. 103. Any rule or regulation of the Board of Governors of the
Federal Reserve System pursuant to section 167(b) of the Truth in
Lending Act, as such section was in effect on the day before the date
of enactment of this Act, is null and void.

15 USC 1605.

"Regular price."

15 USC 1602
note.
94 Stat. 169.

15 USC 1666f
note.
Supra.

TITLE II—BAN ON CREDIT CARD SURCHARGES

SEC. 201. Section 3(c)(2) of Public Law 94–222 (15 U.S.C. 1666f note)
is amended to read as follows:
"(2) The amendments made by paragraph (1) shall cease to be
effective on February 27, 1984.".

The heading of a slip law includes the public or private law number, the number of the Congress, bill number and date of approval. On the last page of each public slip law is a guide to its legislative history that records the committees that considered it and their report numbers, the number of any companion bill, the dates of action and passage by each house, with reference to the *Congressional Record* by volume, year, and date. Also cited is any presidential statement appearing in the *Weekly Compilation of Presidential Documents*. Editorial information in the margins consists of subject headings; citations of laws amended, repealed, or referred to; references to prior or subsequent pages of the statute when its text mentions other sections of it; page numbers of the *Statutes at Large* on which it will appear; and section of the *United States Code* in which it will be inserted. None of this information is part of the law itself. Once printed, slip laws are delivered to the document rooms of both houses of Congress. They are legal documents and may be used as evidence in any legal proceeding.

BIBLIOGRAPHIC GUIDE

The preceding account applies to the usual route of major and controversial bills which, though few in number during any given session of Congress, generate the bulk of legislative business. Bills are routinely printed upon introduction, when favorably reported from committee and after passage by one house, unless additional printings are specially ordered by either chamber. A routine printing may be omitted if it would unreasonably delay legislative action, a situation that occurs most often during the closing days of a session.

There are numerous exceptions to the usual route that affect the printing of bills, and some of the more common or important ones should be noted. A message from the President requesting enactment of specific legislation will usually contain a draft bill and, when referred to a committee, may serve in lieu of an introduced bill. The initial printing is the reported print for legislation that originates in committee. If a bill is referred from one committee to another, it is reprinted on each such occasion, but there will be only one reported print. An Act print is omitted in the second chamber when one of its committees has reported a bill identical or substantially similar to one subsequently received from the other body. Each house may consider bills passed by the other without referring them to a committee. In this instance, there will not be a reported print in the second chamber, though the bill will be printed with a calendar number.

Most bills enacted into law are not controversial and pass both houses either without amendment or, if amended, are agreed upon without a conference. The vast majority of all bills are, of course, not enacted into law, and most do not progress beyond being referred to a committee following their introduction. The life of all bills expires with the final adjournment of a Congress. Any bill may be reintroduced in a succeeding Congress, but it will be assigned a new number and action on it will begin anew regardless of the stage it reached during its prior consideration. The form in which it is reintroduced will, to some extent, usually reflect any changes it underwent in its earlier life.

The following is intended to serve as a general guide to the more accessible publications that enable one to identify bills and locate their texts. A bill number is its foremost identifying characteristic, but there are several ways to identify the number if not known. Regardless of which source is used, either the number of the Congress or the year needs to be known to narrow the search.

Sources that provide access by subject include the index to the bound *Congressional Record* and that of each chamber's journal, which present information about *all* bills introduced, the Monday and final editions of the *House Calendar*, which contains information about all bills *reported in both houses* and the *Digest of Public General Bills and Resolutions* (DPGBR), which is issued by the Congressional Research Service of the Library of Congress.

Sources that provide access by public law number include the *House Calendar*, DPGBR, the end of the session edition of the *Daily Digest* section of the *Congressional Record, Statutes at Large, CIS/Index*, and *CQ Almanac*. For access by private law number the *House Calendar* or *Statutes at Large* can be consulted, both of which provide subject access to all bills enacted into law.

Sources that provide access by bill sponsor include the index to the bound *Record*, DPGBR, and the House *Journal*.

Legislative history or status tables reveal the stages of the legislative process through which a bill passed or those which it bypassed. Such information indicates the occasions on which a bill was printed. The index to the bound *Record*, though not arranged as a status table, that is, by law number, is the most comprehensive listing, arranged by bill number. Two tables arranged by public law number and which are cumulative throughout a Congress are found in the *House Calendar* and DPGBR. Public law listings that are cumulated at the end of each session appear in the final edition of the *Daily Digest, Statutes at Large, CIS/Index*, and *CQ Almanac*.

Presented below are sources that can be consulted for the different versions of or changes made in a bill as it progresses through Congress.

1) Introduced print: The primary source is hearings held by the committee(s) that considered the bill. To determine whether such hearings have been printed one can use the *Monthly Catalog* or *CIS/Index*. Both provide access by subject, bill title, and committee; the latter also by public law number, bill number, and popular name of the law or bill.

2) Committee amendments rejected: All committee roll-call votes and the text of amendments voted on are recorded in a minute book. Sources that are more accessible would be the printed transcript of a mark-up session; the supplemental, additional, or minority views contained in the committee report; floor amendments proposed by committee members; and the descriptions of committee action that appear in Congressional Quarterly's *Weekly Reports* and other print media.

3) Committee amendments adopted: These are available in printed mark-ups and committee reports. The existence of the former can be determined through use of the sources mentioned in (1) above. Report numbers are listed in the status tables of publications previously discussed. If a committee reports a clean bill, with a new number, in lieu of the introduced version on which hearings were held, this will be noted near the beginning of the report. In the Senate, when more than one report accompanies a bill, each will have a different report number. In the House, all reports on a bill are assigned one number, but are designated as different parts of the same report. In each chamber, all reports on the same bill will have the identical calendar number. The report may also identify by bill number similar or identical measures introduced in prior Congresses. All reports are in the Serial Set but appear in the *Record* only on those infrequent occasions when they are read on the floor or are printed therein by unanimous consent.

4) Floor amendments adopted and rejected: Proceedings section of the *Record*.

5) Act print (engrossed bill): Committee hearings held in the second chamber. See (1) above.

6) Committee amendments rejected and adopted: When a committee amends and reports a bill passed by the other house, its report contains an explanation of its amendment(s) and is most likely to include the text if it reports a substitute. See (2) and (3) above.

7) Floor amendments adopted (engrossed) and rejected: See (4) above.

8) Conference report: The text always appears in the *Record* and in the journal of each house. Also see (3) above, except the number is not given in the *Daily Digest*. When one house has passed a substitute, this report contains the entire text of the bill.

9) Vetoed bill: Measures returned by the President with a veto message are listed in the index to the bound *Record*, the *Monthly Catalog, CIS/Index*, and the *Weekly Compilation of Presidential Documents*. The last includes the text of all messages submitted to Congress concerning legislation and all public statements regarding the same. The text of all veto messages, which includes the bill, also appears in the *Record* and the journal of the house of origin. The text of the bill, along with the message, is printed in the Serial Set as either a House or Senate document, depending upon the body of origin. The text of a bill that is pocket vetoed must be compiled from its latest print, plus any amendments adopted that appear in the *Record*, including any conference report.

10) Laws (enrolled bills): These are published in the *Statutes at Large*.

11) Companion bills: Their number is given in the index to the bound *Record, House Calendar*, DPGBR, *Daily Digest*, and *Statutes at Large*.

12) Concurrent resolutions: These appear in the *Record, Statutes at Large*, and the journal of each house.

Some of the publications noted above have unique features. *CIS/Index* provides information about bills prior to the Congress in which they are enacted into law; otherwise one must use either a subject or sponsor approach to identify such measures if a committee report does not discuss its history. The *House Calendar* and House *Journal* list all vetoed bills, separately identifying those returned with a message and those vetoed when the President withholds his signature following congressional adjournment. A status table for major legislation, including all general appropriation bills, appears on the final pages of the *House Calendar*. The DPGBR is the only source that provides a synopsis of each bill, which is presented in the form of both an abstract and a factual description.

Introduced and reported versions of bills are occasionally printed in the *Record*, but the irregularity of this practice means that it must be consulted in each instance. Their text, as well as that of printed amendments, is more likely to appear under Senate proceedings. The dates of introduction and presidential approval are always given in the *Record*.

A very limited number of multivolume sets of bound bills are issued sometime after the final adjournment of each Congress. These contain all introduced, reported, and Act prints of both houses, as well as printed Senate amendments. They are distributed to the House and Senate libraries and the Law Library of the Library of Congress. The Government Printing Office distributes introduced, reported, and Act prints of all bills and printed Senate amendments, in microfiche only, to those depository libraries that choose to receive them.

BIBLIOGRAPHY

Cummings, Frank. *Capitol Hill Manual.* Washington: The Bureau of National Affairs, 1976.

Thaxter, John H. "Printing of Congressional Bills." *Library Resources and Technical Services* 7 (Summer 1963) 237-43.

U.S. Congress. House. *Constitution, Jefferson's Manual and Rules of the House of Representatives.* House Document No. 95-403, 95th Congress, 2nd Session. Washington: U.S. Government Printing Office, 1979.

U.S. Congress. House. *Deschler's Procedure in the U.S. House of Representatives.* 3rd ed. 96th Congress, 1st Session. Washington: U.S. Government Printing Office, 1979.

U.S. Congress. House. *How Our Laws Are Made.* House Document No. 96-352, 96th Congress, 2nd Session. Washington: U.S. Government Printing Office, 1980.

U.S. Congress. Senate. *Enactment of a Law.* Senate Document No. 96-15, 96th Congress, 1st Session. Washington: U.S. Government Printing Office, 1979.

U.S. Congress. Senate. *Senate Legislative Procedural Flow.* 95th Congress, 2nd Session. Washington: U.S. Government Printing Office, 1978.

U.S. Congress. Senate. *Senate Manual.* Senate Document No. 96-1, 96th Congress, 2nd Session. Washington: U.S. Government Printing Office, 1980.

U.S. Congress. Senate. *Senate Procedure.* Senate Document No. 93-21, 93rd Congress, 1st Session. Washington: U.S. Government Printing Office, 1974.

U.S. Congress. Senate. Committee on Rules and Administration. *Automated Legislative Record Keeping for the United States Senate.* Committee Print, 92nd Congress, 2nd Session. Washington: U.S. Government Printing Office, 1972.

9

Resolutions

Congressional resolutions are an auxiliary means for expressing legislative policy and influencing governmental action. As formal measures, they may precede, supplement, or serve as an alternative to or constitute an ingredient of, legislation. Resolutions may or may not affect public policy, and those that do may have slight or significant consequences. This chapter concentrates on resolutions whose policy implications are both important and intentional. How their uses and results relate to and compare with public bills is a recurring feature of this discussion.

TYPES AND PURPOSES

The three forms of resolutions are joint, concurrent, and simple, but since the first is equivalent to a bill, the term "resolutions" as used below refers only to the latter two forms. Concurrent resolutions result from the combined action of both houses of Congress, while simple resolutions involve one chamber acting independently of the other. The major difference between bills and resolutions is that the latter do not contain legislation and need not be presented to the President for approval. Procedures for the consideration and disposition of concurrent and simple resolutions, which are numbered in separate series, are essentially the same as that for bills. Their course from introduction through adoption differs only in the length rather than in the route of their journey.

The uncontroversial nature of ceremonial or hortatory resolutions usually means expedited action and an absence of related congressional publications. Three relatively routine uses, however, are of more than passing interest. Resolutions are used to authorize the printing of many Senate and House documents that appear in the Serial Set. Concurrent resolutions fix the date of final adjournment for a session or Congress and necessarily affect which measures can be considered before time expires. They also serve to correct the text of bills, as detailed in chapter 8. Some resolutions having policy objectives are examined elsewhere in this volume. Special orders reported by the House Rules Committee are analyzed in chapter 6; budget and impoundment resolutions originating with the Budget and Appropriations Committees, respectively, in chapter 10; and resolutions of ratification from the Senate Foreign Relations Committee in chapter 11. Resolutions that have a substantive impact on public policy usually generate some, if not all, of the same types of congressional publications that are issued in the course of enacting laws.

Resolutions are the formal means by which either or both houses communicate with their members and committees. These housekeeping measures may concern chamber rules, congressional investigations, or select committees. Such statements are compulsory in nature and regularly authorize activities, prescribe procedures, and determine purposes. Their direct and immediate effect on legislative organization, operations, and resources can have as much policy impact as any law. Aims that cannot be achieved directly through legislation may be accomplished indirectly via housekeeping resolutions.

Resolutions also convey advice, appeals, and arguments to officials and organizations outside the halls of Congress. These declaratory measures may prohibit federal administrative action, request information from the executive branch, or suggest proposals on current affairs to independent political agents. Since such statements express opinions and purposes in the form of recommendations, the cooperation of others is necessary to make them effective. They are normally reserved for matters where a statutory solution is considered questionable, inappropriate, or inapplicable.

The distinction between housekeeping and declaratory resolutions does not reflect a difference between those which have policy implications and those which do not. It merely indicates that the former are aimed at members of the congressional community regarding matters exclusively within the authority of either or both houses, while the latter are targeted at external entities whose use of discretion may or may not be limited, but can be influenced by their content. Both types are used by Congress to dispose of nonlegislative business that is an adjunct to its lawmaking power.

Because resolutions may be used in lieu of bills to influence certain policy environments or promote particular policy goals and because few are legally binding, they can be adopted more easily than legislation. Resolutions can conveniently be used when legislators wish to realign their resources, stimulate public debate on a given subject, suspend executive action pending further developments, or issue warnings to other political participants. Whether political aims are pursued by bill or resolution is more of a tactical than a strategic decision and, of course, both means may be used simultaneously.

An examination of three major purposes of housekeeping resolutions is followed by an analysis of an equal number of declaratory ones. The first purpose in each series involves formal procedures that either mandate or prohibit specified actions; the second in each focuses on legislative efforts to obtain information; and the third concerns the nature of guidelines for the use of official authority and public resources, though all three goals may overlap in any particular instance. In terms of exerting influence, the order in which each cluster is discussed represents a progression from a more to a less compelling form of action.

HOUSEKEEPING RESOLUTIONS

The most important housekeeping resolutions are proposals to revise the standing rules of each house. The primary purposes of rules are to allocate authority, confer legitimacy, promote stability, and foster efficiency. Rules designate who is authorized to perform which functions or to act under certain circumstances by establishing positions or units and a corresponding division of labor. Decisions reached in accord with these requirements are considered legitimate institutional actions despite any disagreement with their purposes. The existence of orderly and known procedures means that legislative action can proceed without disputes about the validity of particular decisions. The regularity and predictability afforded by written rules enables legislators to adequately prepare for action and provides mechanisms for legislative coordination.

Because rules prescribe the way things must be done, they often determine what in fact is done. Thus, they are not necessarily neutral statements that affect all parties equally. Rules changes tend to alter the advantages of legislators by making it relatively easier for some political interests, but more difficult for others, to reach their goals. In general, existing rules benefit those who favor the status quo since they can usually prevail at any one of the many points at which a bill may be stifled. Political differences generated by proposed changes in legislative rules reflect contests over the distribution and exercise of power.

Some rules merely enable Congress to cope with a large workload in an orderly manner. They may simply increase or decrease legislative alternatives as a means of facilitating regular and routine business. However, under certain conditions almost any rule may be used to serve policy or partisan purposes. As an integral factor of legislative strategy, they may be wielded by a majority to advance or a minority to impede legislation. Procedures represent power to those in a position to apply or invoke them and thus become ends in themselves. Because the legislature itself has several functions and each member has individual goals, there will often be controversy over rules that affect whose policy views will be realized.

The interrelationship of rules means that several may address the same purpose or one may relate to two or more purposes. Responsibility for the cumulative and unique impact of these politically sensitive stipulations rests with the majority party in each chamber. Such majorities speak through the House Rules Committee and the Senate Rules and Administration Committee in the form of simple resolutions to amend the rules.

Each house has a rule that authorizes its standing committees to undertake investigations of any subject within their jurisdiction. Inquiries initiated under this grant of authority tend to differ only slightly from regular hearings. Though witnesses and records may be summoned and examined for purposes of uncovering illegality or impropriety, the constraints of a committee's budget generally preclude a full-scale investigation. When such a probe is considered necessary, it is authorized by a resolution that states the reasons for and purposes of the inquiry.

The power of Congress to conduct investigations is derived from its power to gather information and educate its members as a vital aid for intelligent lawmaking. These proceedings increase the capacity of legislators to examine and obtain a firmer grasp of social conditions or governmental problems that may warrant legislative solutions. Other matters on which investigations may focus include the effectiveness of existing legislation and its implementation, along with efforts to inform the public or influence the opinion of certain political entities or to protect legislative integrity from the alleged misconduct of members of Congress or against the assumed prerogatives of executive branch officials. Investigations are a tool that enables Congress to better compete with the presidential establishment for public attention and political influence.

Simple resolutions authorizing investigations are reported from the Senate Rules and Administration Committee or the House Administration Committee. These panels have jurisdiction over the contingent fund of each house. This is an appropriated sum upon which each chamber may draw to cover the expenses of unforeseen legislative activities. In addition to providing the authority and defining the scope of an investigation, a resolution may assign the responsibility to a standing or a temporary committee.

Situations arise when it is impractical or inappropriate to commit matters requiring congressional attention to standing committees. Some of the reasons these permanent panels may fail to consider significant issues are a heavy workload, lack of staff resources, lack of member interest, or uncertain political consequences. Also, jurisdiction over a given subject may be so fragmented that no single committee can claim or be acknowledged to have the authority and expertise to thoroughly explore it. Select, or temporary, panels are a flexible instrument that can overcome the inconvenience or reluctance engendered by these conditions.

The basic purposes of a select committee may be to analyze particular conditions or events to discover causes or clarify consequences, to study designated matters and prepare a comprehensive legislative package for action by standing committees, to evaluate the merits of specific legislative proposals, to encourage coordinated legislative decisionmaking by providing balanced representation among all geographical and other interests, to explore the adequacy of existing laws or administration of certain programs, or to give priority to issues of a compelling nature.

Resolutions creating select committees serve as charters that stipulate the functions to be performed and the matters to be examined, confer authority to obtain information, provide for the selection of members, furnish the needed resources and prescribe its life span. The form its recommendations are to take, whether public law, revision of federal regulations, agency reorganization or informal administrative action, is usually included. Since the formation of select committees entails expenditures from the contingent fund, the same House and Senate panels responsible for investigations are also the committees of jurisdiction in this matter.

DECLARATORY RESOLUTIONS

The most frequent and forceful type of declaratory resolution is a resolution of disapproval, more commonly known as a legislative veto. This is a statutory device by which Congress retains authority to review specific decisions of administrative officials. Though most public laws confer considerable discretion on agency executives, legislators are unwilling to relinquish all their prerogatives in politically sensitive areas. The legislative veto ensures formal congressional notice and a binding decision should conditions persuade legislators to invoke their authority to act. This mechanism enables Congress to pass judgment on proposed administrative actions prior to their implementation.

The procedure requires that certain executive decisions be submitted to Congress for a specified waiting period before taking effect. During this interval, Congress may express its approval or disapproval by a concurrent or simple resolution or through committee action. The proposal becomes effective if Congress fails to act before the period expires, though some legislative veto provisions require affirmative legislative action. This process may apply to agency regulations, program options, or presidential initiatives. Its most prominent use occurs when the president formulates and submits reorganization plans for federal agencies, a matter under the jurisdiction of the Senate Governmental Affairs and House Government Operations committees.

The executive communication or presidential message transmitted to Congress under this requirement is printed as a House or Senate document and includes the text of the proposal and a discussion of its background and desirability. The variety and volume of congressional publications generated by the stipulation for a legislative veto depend on the level of political controversy, which legislative entities are authorized to act, and the extent of such action. Any standing committee may have the authority to report a resolution of disapproval, and a list of all laws that contain legislative veto provisions, along with the text of such provisions, appears in the House Manual.

Resolutions of inquiry may be directed at either the President or an agency administrator and may be answered by the latter directly or through the President. They may call for facts or documents in the possession of any executive branch official or agency. These measures are usually reserved for situations in which desired information cannot be obtained through routine channels. Such requests or demands are based on the constitutional duty of Congress to keep itself informed of the need for new or revised public policy. This course also implies that adverse or more compelling legislative action may follow a failure to comply.

The most common types of questions concern the factual basis for having undertaken or refrained from pursuing certain actions, authority under which specific decisions were enforced, the results of administering a particular program, or the agency directives affecting implementation of a law. Resolutions of inquiry are privileged matters in the House only and may be introduced by any legislator. This means that a committee with jurisdiction is obliged to consider the measure even though it disapproves of its purpose. Failure to act would result in loss of committee control of the proposal. As a result of this procedure, a panel is as likely to recommend that such a resolution be rejected as adopted.

Resolutions of opinion or advice contain recommendations to public officials or private entities over which Congress either lacks or chooses not to exercise legislative authority. The former case covers matters of a traditionally local concern or international situations within the purview of other nations. Though these measures may reach further than bills, they are also less authoritative because aimed at conditions not considered susceptible to statutory remedies. As the least binding type of legislative policy statement they may be used to placate interests unable to engineer passage of more forceful measures or to bring policy views to the attention of other groups that may be inclined to consider their merits.

The more important resolutions of opinion adopted in lieu of a recourse to bills are aimed at the President or a subordinate executive branch official. Those addressed to the President relate to matters in which he is authorized or expected to exercise discretion. They may urge that a specific situation be given attention, express support for or opposition to contemplated executive action, or request that plans for meeting certain conditions be submitted to Congress for its consideration. Those directed at administrative appointees may clarify the legislative intent of a statute regarding the legal authority of a federal agency under specified circumstances. These measures may emerge from any committee as concurrent or simple resolutions.

COMPARISONS

Resolutions amending the rules and exercising the legislative veto are much more common than other types. This is because they are the only alternative to legislation for reaching the intended objective. The purposes for which other resolutions are available may also be realized through hearings, advisory commissions, consultant contracts, congressional support agencies, or informal communications with executive branch officials. Despite being a legally milder form of congressional action than legislation, resolutions can arouse or accompany as much controversy as any bill. This is the key factor affecting the quantity and diversity of congressional publications that may be issued in conjunction with legislative consideration of a resolution.

As with most bills, the text of resolutions appears in printed hearings and is more likely than bills to be included in a committee report. Unlike most bills, all resolutions acted on by either house appear in the *Congressional Record* and its journal. The finding aids section of the preceding chapter on bills is equally applicable to resolutions, with the obvious exception of those comments concerning laws and vetoes. Where a legislative goal is being pursued by both bill and resolution, these companion measures are noted in the *Record, House Calendar*, and *Digest of Public General Bills and Resolutions*.

BIBLIOGRAPHY

Froman, Lewis A., Jr. *The Congressional Process.* Boston: Little, Brown, 1967.

Harris, Joseph P. *Congressional Control of Administration.* Washington: The Brookings Institution, 1964.

Oleskek, Walter. *Congressional Procedures and the Policy Process.* Washington: Congressional Quarterly Press, 1978.

U.S. Congress. House. *Constitution, Jefferson's Manual and Rules of the House of Representatives.* House Document No. 95-403, 95th Congress, 2nd Session. Washington: U.S. Government Printing Office, 1979.

U.S. Congress. House. *Deschler's Procedure in the U.S. House of Representatives.* 3rd ed. 96th Congress, 1st Session. Washington: U.S. Government Printing Office, 1979.

U.S. Congress. House. Committee on Rules. *Guidelines for the Establishment of Select Committees.* Subcommittee Print, 95th Congress, 1st Session. Washington: U.S. Government Printing Office, 1977.

U.S. Congress. Senate. *Senate Manual.* Senate Document No. 96-1, 96th Congress, 2nd Session. Washington: U.S. Government Printing Office, 1980.

U.S. Congress. Senate. *Senate Procedure.* Senate Document No. 93-21, 93rd Congress, 1st Session. Washington: U.S. Government Printing Office, 1974.

U.S. Congress. Senate. Committee on Government Operations. *Congressional Oversight: Methods and Techniques.* Committee Print, 94th Congress, 2nd Session. Washington: U.S. Government Printing Office, 1976.

10
The Federal Budget

A public budget is a political blueprint. Its formulation and adoption is the most comprehensive political enterprise in which government engages in any given year. Budgeting involves competition between and within the executive and legislative branches as well as between and among public and private entities. In essence, the budget earmarks specified amounts of money for certain government agencies to achieve stated purposes. Since funds are limited, choices must be made about potential sources and among possible expenditures. These decisions reflect an effort to balance conflicting objectives and satisfy competing claims. The management of public funds requires the exercise of political judgment.

The federal budget is neither established by a single act of government nor contained in a single government document. It is the outcome of a continuous process and is comprised of several series of publications. Budget materials are not merely compilations and descriptions of statistical data, though they are replete with tables and graphs. This form of information serves to translate the text into figures that can illustrate or substantiate, emphasize or summarize, the narrative portions of the budget. This chapter examines budget policy and combines a description of the budget process with a survey of budget publications.

BUDGET POLICY

To distinguish the terms "budget, fiscal, economic and social policy" serves as a useful preface to further discussion. Budget policy refers to decisions made and goals pursued in the context of the annual budget cycle. Since all public activities, whether planned in advance or dictated by events, affect federal finances, budgeting is the most inclusive of governmental functions. The size, composition, and structure of a budget reflect views concerning the proper role and scope of government. The result is to establish and organize priorities so as to form a public agenda.

Budgetary decisions are influenced by national and international conditions, numerous demands and limited resources, and prior commitments and political purposes. They explicitly or implicitly address such questions as the direction and pace of governmental activities, the appropriate level of government involvement in given policy spheres, the relative merits of government programs, who should pay to support and who should benefit from these programs, the nature of the relationship between the public and private sectors of society, and whether to stress fiscal or social policy to achieve desirable goals.

Fiscal policy, which is a combination of revenue and spending measures, is designed to implement the budget. It allocates resources within the federal sector and between the federal and nonfederal sectors of the economy. Revenue laws that cover individual and corporate income, social insurance taxes, and excise levies account for over 95% of all budget receipts. The payment of salaries, the purchase of goods and services, and transfer payments constitute the vast bulk of government expenditures. Transfer payments are funds distributed to individuals for which goods or services are not required in return.

Economic policy consists of fiscal and monetary policy. The latter concerns decisions about the money supply, interest rates, and credit availability. Such matters are the responsibility of the Board of Governors of the Federal Reserve System. The independent authority of this agency means that its judgment may not always be consistent with the views of the executive and legislature as expressed through fiscal policy. The primary targets of economic policy are inflation, employment, investment, and productivity, while its aims are to counteract economic weaknesses, stabilize economic activity, and foster economic growth.

Social policy includes domestic and foreign policy and is intended to promote the public interest through the welfare of specific groups or the enhancement of national security. Its aims are to provide services or benefits to designated classes of individuals and resolve issues of general concern. The main goal in the former case is equity; in the latter, effectiveness. Concrete interests are significantly affected whether government pursues economic or social policies. Public budgeting is an endeavor to combine sound fiscal calculations with desirable social objectives.

The purposes of the federal budget can be described as educational, political, and managerial. It is as an agenda for public debate that the budget serves an educational function. Despite or because of the controversy it may generate, a budget promotes discussion and understanding of government capabilities. As a political instrument, the budget is used to discharge political debts, acquire political credits, and record the results of political compromises. These actions are meant to maintain a balance of support over opposition that can be mobilized for budgetary or other aims. Managerial objectives focus on the efficient use of public resources and guidance for the use of private resources. This is an attempt to coordinate the financial administration of government programs and the contemplated impact of policy decisions. Though these three goals may occasionally conflict, when adroitly blended the budget becomes a formidable vehicle for advancing certain proposals even though all potential effects cannot be discerned.

While the budget is a prominent means of promoting particular policies, the budgetary process also has some inherent limitations, one of which relates to the art of economic forecasting. Predictions regarding the magnitude and direction of the effect of a given policy involve relationships that cannot be charted with a great degree of certainty. Budget estimates are based on assumptions about the performance of the economy, conditions in financial markets, and past experience with tax receipts and spending rates, all of which may be and usually are affected by unanticipated developments. Another factor in the equation is congressional action, which may occur later than expected, be substantially different than expected, or not occur. Different economic forecasts also reflect different estimating procedures and political perspectives.

A second limitation stems from the nature and effect of fiscal policy. The need to prepare a budget well in advance of the situation to which it is to be applied entails a significant time lag between its formulation and adoption. Additional time elapses between its enactment and intended results. Thus, not only is it impossible to time fiscal policy for maximum effectiveness, but such intervals may aggravate an economic deficiency or remedy one weakness by creating another. Other uncertainties are whether to stress tax legislation, which is more difficult to pass and whose effects are more long lasting, rather than spending proposals and the potency of policies intended to stimulate or retard economic activity. Since the broad scope of fiscal policy activates all major political interests, intense conflict accompanies the need to make difficult choices.

The time frame of an annual budget cycle unavoidably introduces some distortion into the ordering of priorities and perception of events. Budgeting involves trade-offs among current policies and between long-term and short-term policies. Because long-term policies to improve economic conditions usually have short-term political costs, immediate concerns tend to receive attention at the expense of underlying economic weaknesses. Even when fiscal policy is considered well balanced and farsighted, it remains only one of several factors that can affect the economic climate. The impact of unforeseen and uncontrollable events can easily frustrate budget plans. While a long-run perspective might reveal that any adverse consequences will be relatively mild, the annual focus prods officials to resort to prompt efforts to offset fiscal aberrations.

An ideal budget document should enable a reader to differentiate between those economic conditions or factors over which government can exercise some control and those beyond its ability to regulate; to identify matters that policies can affect immediately and those that can vary only gradually over time; to ascertain the major policy options available to government, the implications of each, and their relationship to existing programs; to distinguish among proposed actions, the goals to be achieved by such actions, the reasons and justification for them, and the factual data related to each; and to assess the possible indirect effects of proposals. However, the lack of time and tools precludes an integrated review of all budget items and the formulation of an explicit value and expenditure hierarchy each year.

General agreement exists on the fact that there is a relationship between the federal budget and the national economy. However, disagreement on the precise nature of this relationship inhibits formation of a consensus on the specifics of a prudent budget. Though such concepts as growth rate, price stability, and personal consumption have been uniformly defined, this has not led to a comparable accord on their proper level, relationship to one another, or methods of measuring their impact. Which budget policies would most contribute to economic health and which programs would be consistent with such policies cannot be definitively determined. Though economists may offer advice on the anticipated consequences of these choices, the inadequacy of economic analysis inevitably leads to the use of political criteria.

Because fiscal decisions have political implications and social decisions have economic ramifications, a sharp distinction often cannot be made between the economic and political factors that shape budgetary decisions. Economic conditions change much more gradually than political ones, and elected officials are much more familiar with and sensitive to the latter. Accordingly, budgetary actions reflect the primacy of political over economic judgment. Since either the results of a preceding, or the constraints of an approaching, election influence major government decisions, politicians tend to be more flexible than economists regarding the means and ends of budget policy. Even if economics were more of an exact science, it would still remain subordinate to the political incentives and intentions that guide the decisions of elected officials.

Budgeting may be viewed as the central phase of governmental action. It is preceded by planning, which involves assumptions and projections about political, economic, social, and technological developments and their impact on public business and priorities. It is succeeded by an assessment of how well programs are operating and the degree to which they are achieving intended objectives. The budget is one part forecast, as represented by the contemplated results of proposals, and one part feedback, as reflected by the recommended revision of policies. The wide range of decisions and interests involved in efforts to reconcile an existing with an expected state of affairs creates both opportunities and obstacles for budgetmakers.

BUDGET CONCEPTS

Several terms and issues are particularly important for understanding federal budget policy. Government expenditures involve a four-step process: authorization, appropriation, obligation, and outlay. Authorizing legislation establishes the purposes for which public funds may be used. Most budget authority is in the form of appropriations, which is the legal authorization to enter into obligations that entail immediate or eventual expenditures. Obligations are commitments which are made by federal agencies during a given period and that require outlays. Outlays or expenditures are actual payments by a federal entity.

Two other types of budget authority are contract and borrowing authority. These are also known as backdoor authority because they either bypass the appropriations process or preclude the exercise of any legislative discretion in the allocation of funds. The regular funding sequence for most spending measures, an appropriation followed by an obligation, is reversed for backdoor spending. Such authority is granted through authorizing legislation that exempts it from the annual budget cycle to facilitate certain forms of government activity.

Contract authority enables agencies to incur obligations based on agreements whose provisions cannot be resolved in advance or which require an indefinite period of time to fulfill. This approach has the advantage of providing the necessary lead time for construction and other long-term projects. Borrowing authority empowers agencies to incur obligations by using funds borrowed from the Treasury or the public. This method finances commercial-type transactions that make it possible for the agency to refund the money to the Treasury or repay the holders of agency notes. An appropriation would only be necessary when an agency was unable to cover its debts.

The budget consists of two major types of funds. Federal funds are derived mainly from taxation and borrowing and are used as needed for the general purposes and daily expenses of government. Trust funds are accumulated principally from compulsory social insurance programs and must be used for stipulated purposes. This legal restriction or preference means that trust fund programs need not compete with other governmental functions for public funds and ensures beneficiaries that financial assistance will be available as prescribed by law.

Perhaps the key concept in the realm of budgeting is controllability. One of the two major aspects of controllability concerns the proportion of budget authority or outlays that is subject to definite limits for a given fiscal year. A relatively uncontrollable amount refers to spending levels mandated by existing law or prior obligations and which can only be altered by changes in authorizing legislation. A relatively controllable figure denotes expenditures whose magnitude can be determined by current appropriations legislation.

An expenditure will tend to be less controllable if it is not subject to annual action by Congress, if the amount to be spent is open-ended and not set by law, if it has its own source of revenue that can be used without recourse to an authorization, and if it is subject to only one, rather than all three, of the authorization, appropriations, and budget processes. It is not necessarily more difficult to reduce an uncontrollable than a controllable amount. These terms do not describe what Congress can or may do, but merely distinguish between what has already been done by law and what remains to be done in providing budget authority for a fiscal year.

Uncontrollable outlays constitute approximately three-fourths of the budget, with the largest category composed of entitlement programs. These programs are open-ended commitments to designated classes of individuals where payments are guaranteed by law if certain eligibility requirements are met. Expenditures are limited only by the number of those who satisfy the legal criteria for receiving benefits, which usually depends on economic and demographic developments beyond the control of government. Entitlements include Social Security, federal retirement, disability, unemployment compensation, food stamps, public assistance, Medicare, Medicaid and veterans' benefits. Other uncontrollable items are interest on the national debt, loans, contracts, and long-term projects.

Some entitlements are funded by permanent appropriations that do not require current action by Congress, while others have independent sources of revenue, such as trust funds. Though there are entitlements that entail annual appropriations, the disbursement of funds is mandated by statutory formulas. To place these programs under direct, short-term budgetary control would engender uncertainty that might raise questions about their financial integrity. Such action, though legally unchallengeable, would be morally incompatible with the contractual nature of these programs since many beneficiaries depend on them for their subsistence.

A second major aspect of controllability relates to the timing of obligations and outlays. The level of budget authority enacted by Congress limits the amount of money that can be obligated in a particular year. However, funds appropriated one year might not be obligated until the next, with expenditures occurring a year or two later. This results in carryover balances, or the amount of budget authority not used during a fiscal year and which remains available for conversion into outlays at some time in the future.

Since outlays may not occur until after a fiscal year has ended, the lack of congressional control over the timing of expenditures precludes control over the spending totals for any given year. The amount of funds spent in a fiscal year depends on congressional decisions made for the current year as well as prior years. A significant consequence is that a reduction in appropriations does not necessarily produce an equivalent decrease in outlays. Though appropriations and obligations are controlled by law, statements of outlays in a current budget document are only estimates of cash flow.

Though the accrual of carryover balances mainly account for this lack of control over outlays, the reasons for their existence may be either inadvertent or intentional. Inaccurate budget estimates for program needs, or the inability to spend funds as rapidly as anticipated due to unforeseen conditions, result in unplanned carryover balances. Some funding methods enacted by Congress, especially the use of trust funds, where reserves are necessary to meet payments, require such balances. Another deliberate reason involves the practice of appropriating funds on a multiyear or indefinite basis, which provides for necessary executive flexibility and reduces the congressional workload.

While about three-fourths of the annual budget is legally uncontrollable, most of the remainder is politically uncontrollable. In addition, the budget increment, or the amount by which outlays increase each year, is also uncontrollable. Thus, by the time the budget process for a given fiscal year is begun, most of the options have been foreclosed by earlier decisions. Though uncontrollable expenditures are mandatory under prior action and controllable ones discretionary through current choices, this distinction does not imply that the latter are always more desirable than the former.

Congress has consciously created funding arrangements that limit its ability to control all budget items because of the undesirable effects such control would entail. Complete control of all budget funds would vastly increase the workload of Congress, deny discretion to administrative agencies, and negate commitments represented by prior decisions. It would preclude countless public and private entities from making long-range plans, increase costs because of stop-and-go financing, and contribute to social instability. Congress has willingly accepted a loss of budget control to pursue other values, such as efficiency, stability, and financial certainty. Perfect budget control is inconsistent with other goals that are as important, if not more so, from the standpoint of effective government.

The question of controllability is one of degree and the activities to which control is most appropriately applicable. Investments in ongoing programs and projects are sunken costs that can neither be recovered nor discontinued without wasting resources. They also represent moral commitments and generate political momentum which increase their immunity to reduction or dismantling. For reasons of both sound economics and policy effectiveness, expenditures should remain fairly stable in the short run. Fiscal discretion, though limited in any given year, can be applied to less controllable as well as more controllable policy areas if political and economic conditions foster cooperation between the executive and legislative branches.

Though the budget as a whole does not change substantially from year to year, significant variations can and do occur within categories where flexibility exists. While all decisions are made in the context of the annual budget cycle, many important choices which introduce gradual changes in priorities will affect the budget for several or an indefinite number of years. Examples of these multiyear budget decisions include changes in tax laws, program authorizations, entitlement programs, and capital projects.

There exists no single reliable indicator that accurately measures or reflects the net effect of fiscal policy on the national economy. The budget deficit, or the amount by which federal outlays exceed budget receipts for a given year, is the best known numerical summary of fiscal policy. While it is an essential figure for gauging the impact of taxes and expenditures, it is misleading to the degree that the actual results of fiscal policy are due to changes in the economy unrelated to federal action.

During a decline in economic activity, the budget responds automatically to increase the deficit and ameliorate personal hardship through increased outlays for unemployment compensation, while receipts are reduced due to fewer people paying taxes. In periods of inflation, entitlement programs that are linked to the Consumer Price Index result in larger-than-expected expenditures, which also serves to increase the deficit. Benefit payment programs that are adjusted for inflation constitute nearly 50% of the federal budget.

The size of the federal deficit is influenced by national fiscal policy, monetary policy, state and local government fiscal policies, net exports, economic contingencies, and private sector activities. Despite these factors, controversy over the deficit often occurs between those who want to reduce it through less spending to lower inflation and those who are willing to enlarge it through more spending to lower unemployment. The underlying question is less an economic than a political one about whether the government should provide relief and to whom.

BUDGET DOCUMENTS OVERVIEW

The following discussion of the budget process and its publications is organized into three parts: the executive budget, the congressional budget, and budget implementation. This entails a basically, but not strictly, chronological approach. Deviations from strict chronology are due to the fact that some documents are issued within a given time period rather than on a specific date, while others may appear at any time. A survey of budget texts is also affected by three overlapping phases of activity: that of budget formulation for the coming fiscal year and budget implementation for the current fiscal year; that of presidential and congressional actions concerning budget formulation or implementation; and that of the authorization, appropriation, and budget processes within Congress. The entire process for a single fiscal year actually extends over three years from the time agencies formulate their initial requests until final audits are completed.

Budget structure can be organized by function or agency. For the federal budget, the predominant scheme is that of function. Functional categories array budgetary information according to major governmental purposes. (See figure 10.) Each federal activity is classified only under the function that corresponds to its paramount objective, though it may apply to others. Functional totals, which aggregate authorized expenditures by principal policy area irrespective of agency jurisdiction, provide officials with a useful survey of federal activities as a means of assessing current priorities. An agency breakdown of budget composition is printed and for some participants is of equal or greater interest than the functional presentation.

Budget figures denote either of two levels of decision. Priority decisions cover the sum total of expenditures, the allocation of funds among functional areas of governmental activity, the amount of revenue needed to finance all federal programs, and the level of surplus or deficit consistent with sound fiscal policy. Program decisions affect agency resources and operations as they relate to prior and projected achievements. These choices are directly linked to the welfare of clientele groups whose action and vision concern a small portion of the budget.

Figure 10
Functional Categories of the Federal Budget Correlated with Major Federal Agencies

Budget Functions	Agencies
National Defense	Defense Department
International Affairs	Defense, State and Treasury Departments
General Science, Space and Technology	Energy Department, National Aeronautics and Space Administration
Energy	Energy Department, Tennessee Valley Authority
Natural Resources and Environment	Agriculture and Interior Departments, Environmental Protection Agency
Agriculture	Agriculture Department
Commerce and Housing Credit	Commerce Department, Postal Service, Federal Trade Commission
Transportation	Transportation Department, Interstate Commerce Commission
Community and Regional Development	Housing and Urban Development Department, Small Business Administration
Education, Training, Employment and Social Services	Education, Health and Human Services and Labor Departments
Health	Health and Human Services and Labor Departments
Income Security	Health and Human Services and Labor Departments
Veterans Benefits	Veterans Administration
Administration of Justice	Justice Department, Court System
General Government	Congress, General Services Administration, Office of Personnel Management
General Purpose Fiscal Assistance	Treasury Department
Interest	Treasury Department
Allowances (contingency funds)	
Undistributed Offsetting Receipts (miscellaneous transactions)	

The responsibility for priority decisions in the executive branch rests with the President, who relies on advice from his Council of Economic Advisers and top officials of the Office of Management and Budget (OMB) and Treasury Department. Congress as a whole, acting on the advice of the House and Senate Budget committees and the Joint Economic Committee, also makes priority decisions. The budget process is designed to identify and clarify the factors and relationships that affect or flow from these policy choices. The role of President and Congress is to aggregate the demands and integrate the goals of agencies and committees, respectively. However, immediate responsibility to mediate budget claims and maintain the budget process is assumed by the OMB and the Budget committees.

Program decisions concern funding levels for existing and proposed governmental activities. These judgments are made in accordance with congressional committee and federal agency jurisdictions. The actions of the executive branch and independent federal entities, the OMB in the absence of presidential direction, along with the authorization and appropriations committees, focus on program needs and results. Overall budgetary implications and comprehensive fiscal policy are of less importance to these participants. Another aim of the budget process is to disclose the mutual impact of and coordinate the strategies embodied in priority and program decisions.

Differences between the executive budget and congressional budget are due mainly to the factors of visibility and structure. Budget preparation within the executive branch proceeds almost entirely out of public view, with widespread publicity limited to the final results. The desires of political elements whose support the President concludes cannot be gained or is not needed are unlikely to be accorded favorable budget treatment. His position at the apex of the executive hierarchy inclines a president to order his priorities by redistributing funds among governmental programs through the authorization process.

The congressional budget, in contrast, is formulated in the glare of considerable media coverage. The access offered by a legislature of 535 members is more likely to result in the accommodation of all interests able to exert some political leverage at any one of many decision points. As a consequence, congressional priorities are usually expressed by controlling program growth rates through the appropriations process. The unity of the presidency and diversity of Congress produce different approaches to budgeting whose effects permeate the process and its major documents.

The compulsory aspects of federal budgetmaking are intended to elicit practical criteria for reaching reasonable and acceptable conclusions. For the major budget documents, the key questions are what information to include, which points to emphasize, the validity of assumptions, and the credibility of projections. The descriptions of publications below include their author, frequency, content, and relationship to other material.

THE EXECUTIVE BUDGET PROCESS

A proposed budget is submitted to Congress each January by the President for the fiscal year that begins the following October. The fiscal year is an accounting period which, for the federal government, extends from October 1 through September 30 and is designated by the calendar year in which it ends. The most active participant in the preparation of the executive budget is the OMB. Through its authority to supervise the administration of the federal budget for executive branch agencies and evaluate the effectiveness of federal programs, it collects and digests most of the data used to formulate the executive budget.

The executive budget process begins approximately nine months before the document is transmitted to Congress and 18 months before the start of the fiscal year. The OMB, in cooperation with the Treasury Department and Council of Economic Advisers, prepares tentative economic assumptions, forecasts of national and international developments, and fiscal projections. After a presidential review, the OMB issues policy guidelines to agencies for their spring budget survey. The agencies draft reports on the resources consumed and results produced by existing programs and include a set of proposals that present their program goals and financial needs. These analyses focus on major issues and explore alternatives for addressing them.

Upon compiling and evaluating this material, the OMB compares total estimated outlays with total estimated revenues and develops practical options for the President on fiscal policy, program issues, and budget levels. The emphasis here is on important program innovations or modifications, alternative long-range program plans, and budgetary projections. Following a second presidential review in June, general fiscal and social goals are established in regard to total budget size, program initiatives, and policy priorities. The OMB conveys these decisions to agencies, along with planning ceilings to govern the preparation of formal agency budget requests.

In September agencies submit their formal estimates and supporting documents to the OMB. This material is thoroughly analyzed, and agency representatives attend hearings held by budget examiners. After re-examining economic assumptions and fiscal policy from the standpoint of the economic outlook and presidential priorities, the OMB prepares detailed recommendations for presidential action. Final decisions are reached on agency budget figures and overall budget policy during this third presidential review in December. The OMB notifies agencies of these determinations, and unit heads revise their estimates to conform to presidential judgments.

The executive budget is shaped primarily by the OMB in consultation with the President, other officials with economic responsibilities, and agency managers. The OMB assesses agency budget estimates based upon its knowledge of agency performance to arrive at the resource needs of individual programs. Discussion with Treasury Department officials and members of the Council of Economic Advisers about economic conditions and trends results in figures for total outlays and receipts consistent with the fiscal diagnosis. The President provides political input through choices concerning policy commitments, the range of governmental activity, and public priorities. The OMB is expected to integrate the information and balance the objectives of all participants, a coordinating role that invests it with considerable influence.

Formulation and presentation of the executive budget enables the President to publicize his requests to Congress for new programs, changes in existing ones, appropriation of funds, and changes in revenue legislation. It contains a proposed allocation of resources that would establish priorities and attain objectives within the federal sector and facilitate presidential direction of the administrative activities of the federal government. The budget document is also intended to aid and persuade the general public and particular publics to gauge national economic developments and view proposed policies from the presidential perspective.

The executive budget is a comprehensive statement through which the President expresses his judgment about the relative merits of governmental activities in the context of a fiscal policy designed to stabilize the economy and meet societal needs. It also provides Congress with an overall budget program that can be examined in parts, yet remain a general plan. Though it contains only estimates and recommendations, the executive budget offers an unusually favorable opportunity for the President to marshal support behind his programmatic preferences.

EXECUTIVE BUDGET PUBLICATIONS

The executive budget submitted to Congress each January consists of the first four volumes described below. (For fiscal 1983, a fifth volume entitled *Major Themes and Additional Budget Details*, which highlights presidential initiatives, has been added to the executive budget. Also, the chapters for volume three have been issued as separate documents.)

1. *The Budget of the United States Government.* This document contains the President's budget message and an exposition of the proposals that form his budget policy. The budget message offers an overview of purposes and programs in the context of existing constraints and commitments. The executive budget proper presents aggregate estimates for appropriate levels of budget authority, outlays, revenues, surplus or deficit, and public debt. These figures are accompanied by detailed explanations and supporting data. Information on revenues and debt also includes recommendations for changes in existing law.

The heart of the budget is composed of 19 functional categories covering almost all programs and activities of the federal government. Loan guarantees and certain transactions excluded from the budget by law are not discussed in this volume. The figures for requested budget authority and estimated outlays for each function are presented in terms of national needs, agency missions, and major programs. National needs are the ultimate purposes for which funds are expended regardless of the means used. Agency missions are those responsibilities for meeting national needs assigned to particular agencies. Major programs are the legislative and executive means for accomplishing agency missions. The figures for each function reflect budget estimates for each federal agency as approved by the President and his advisers. This is the spending authority the executive considers necessary to administer the programs already authorized plus any additional activities recommended for legislative approval. Information on the legislative and judicial branches, though included in the executive budget, is simply incorporated by the OMB to present a complete statement of budget policy and is not subject to presidential discretion.

This volume also includes final budget figures for the last completed fiscal year and a discussion of the differences between the actual and estimated uncontrollable outlays by major program and revenues by major sources. In addition to the review of an earlier budget, there is a preview of future budgets. The economic assumptions and demographic trends that affect the long-range budget outlook are described and analyzed. Five-year projections of budget authority and outlays covering the coming fiscal year and the four following years are part of this forecast. Tables at the end of this volume summarize the different aspects of the budget and highlight the relationships among different classes of figures. The historical budget data is especially valuable for comparative purposes. A complete list of programs by agency complements the functional classification, to which it is cross-referenced, and serves as an introduction to the second volume of the executive budget.

2. *The Budget of the United States Government—Appendix.* This document presents detailed budget estimates arranged by agency and appropriation account, which is a designated fund established in the Treasury for authorized financial transactions. Included for each agency are budget data for each account, the proposed text of appropriation language, explanations of the work to be performed and the funds needed, and descriptions of new legislative proposals. Combined with schedules of permanent positions for each agency, this information provides the most elaborate survey of governmental activities that exists in a single volume. The authorizing legislation for each program is cited, and the last three digits of the OMB identification code for each program refer to its functional category.

An inventory of supplemental appropriations, budget rescissions, and budget amendments transmitted to Congress for the current fiscal year also appears. These presidential proposals are organized and presented as are the detailed budget estimates. They are also identified by House and Senate document number for those who wish to consult their complete text. These messages cover unanticipated developments that affect the budget and matters on which there may be a divergence between executive and legislative priorities. They also furnish background information on current budget evolution and why budgeting is a continuous process. This mass of data, when used selectively, can supplement or clarify narrative or numerical statements in other budget documents. Both the *Budget* and *Appendix* have an extensive subject index.

Executive budget information presented in terms of functional classification is used by Congress for developing the First Concurrent Resolution on the Budget. The organization of data in the *Appendix* facilitates the preparation of appropriation bills and the exercise of funding control. Since the number of accounts exceeds 1,000 and the number of programs exceeds the number of accounts, most appropriations cover several programs. This format subdivides the budget into more manageable units that enable political participants and other interested parties to more clearly focus on particular areas of responsibility or concern.

3. *Special Analyses — Budget of the United States Government.* This document focuses on matters that cannot be adequately covered under either the functional or agency scheme. A separate volume that consolidates such information is of much value because many topics that are important for understanding budget policy embrace several subjects or agencies.

Two alternative views of the federal budget are included. The Current Services Budget presents budget authority and outlays for the coming fiscal year based on the assumption that all programs and activities will continue at the same level as for the fiscal year in progress. These estimates do not reflect increases or decreases due to policy changes and provide a basis for identifying and analyzing such changes as recommended in *The Budget of the United States Government.* Budget policy changes include proposed legislation and appropriations for uncontrollable expenditures and augmented or reduced outlays for controllable programs. The national income and product accounts (NIA) of the United States is an attempt to fashion a purely economic document that reflects the impact of federal sector transactions on aggregate economic activity. The NIA, in contrast to *The Budget of the United States Government*, uses gross rather than net figures and covers matters excluded by law from the federal budget.

Other parts of this volume present analyses of certain financial activities of the federal government that affect the economy. Among the more important of these are borrowing, credit programs, tax expenditures and aid to state and local governments. The perspectives on the federal budget in this publication highlight the numerous ways in which public finance interacts with private enterprise and underscores the complexity of the relationship.

4. *The United States Budget in Brief.* This is an abridged version of *The Budget of the United States Government.* Its concise format and nontechnical explanations are designed to inform members of the general public about the financial performance of the federal government.

5. The executive budget is updated twice — no later than April 10 and July 15 — to incorporate all revisions recommended by the President since January. These two documents provide an opportunity to explain and justify changes to

his original proposals in view of evolving economic or other conditions. The figures in these publications supersede earlier estimates and are discussed in terms of the overall budget outlook and functional categories. The dates of issuance are timed to correspond with key points in the congressional budget process.

6.   Budget amendments may be submitted to Congress by the President at any time prior to completion of legislative action on the budget for the coming fiscal year. These proposals may either raise or reduce the original estimates, and those which are pending are incorporated into the budget updates. When budget amendments are transmitted or identified separately, they are cross-referenced to the pertinent page of the *Appendix*. The reasons for an amendment and its amount are always included.

7.   *Economic Report of the President*. This document, also forwarded to Congress each January, complements the executive budget. It discusses economic factors from a perspective that transcends the annual budget cycle and examines matters that the budget can influence only marginally, if at all. The *Report* describes the current state of the economy more comprehensively than does the executive budget and more closely relates the implications of proposed fiscal policies to economic conditions and trends. It also contains recommendations for the Federal Reserve Board on the monetary policy that would reinforce the administration's fiscal initiatives. The focus is on economic growth as measured by the annual rate of increase in the Gross National Product.

The issuance of all executive budget publications is noted in the *Weekly Compilation of Presidential Documents* and all are indexed in the *Monthly Catalog*.

THE CONGRESSIONAL BUDGET PROCESS: AUTHORIZATIONS AND APPROPRIATIONS

An authorization is substantive legislation that creates or continues an agency or program for an indefinite or specified period of time. It may prescribe funding methods, sanction a particular type of expenditure, or limit the level of budget authority. The most important type of authorization for budget purposes is taxation, which provides the government with revenue to be allocated among various public activities. Tax laws also influence decisions on the use of private resources through their impact on the distribution of income among population groups. Though changes in tax rates might have a negligible overall effect on revenues, certain categories of taxpayers may be prompted to alter their economic behavior significantly.

Budget status and policy is substantially affected by a form of revenue legislation known as tax expenditures. Many provisions in the tax code grant preferential treatment to particular classes of taxpayers through cancelled, reduced, or deferred levies that result in revenue losses to the Treasury. Such losses are termed tax expenditures because they are equivalent to direct payments by the federal government to designated taxpayers. Tax expenditures are designed to encourage certain kinds of activities or to provide relief to individuals or corporations in specified circumstances by lowering their tax liability. In one respect such special provisions are similar to entitlement programs, where all those who meet stipulated requirements are eligible for them. In another respect they resemble direct spending programs since tax subsidies provide real economic benefits to those who receive them.

A government loan is another type of authorization with consequences for the federal budget. Direct loans to businesses, nonprofit corporations, and local governments serve to finance activities that are intended to foster economic competition and growth, prevent or relieve economic distress and ensure the continuation of essential services or desirable programs. Guaranteed loans obligate the United States to protect the financial interests of lenders through a federal pledge to repay principal and interest should borrowers default. These do not appear in the federal budget, regardless of the extent of federal liability, unless a default occurs.

Tax expenditures and government loans may be used to promote policy goals other than those related to aggregate economic growth. In lieu of federal spending, either approach may create incentives for certain economic or social activities. Because both are embodied in permanent legislation, the annual budget process cannot modify their impact. The key issue is not the total amount of tax expenditures or government loans that should be authorized each year, but proposed changes in substantive law that would increase or decrease the funds available to specified taxpayers.

The authorization process focuses on the practical and political merits of governmental action and programs. It involves an evaluation of socioeconomic conditions and the needs of concrete interests. Authorizing legislation establishes policy goals and designates areas in which government may appropriately act to alleviate societal problems or benefit certain individuals. Such statutes embody value judgments about what government should do to remedy a given situation or promote a particular purpose.

An appropriation is an act of Congress that authorizes one or more agencies to incur obligations and make payments from the general fund or various special funds of the Treasury. It enables agencies to commit approved levels of expenditures for certain types of financial transactions and to fulfill such commitments for specified purposes. Appropriations do not represent funds available in the Treasury, but are limitations on the amounts that agencies may obligate during the time period stated in the law.

Within the limits prescribed by authorizing legislation and the guidelines set by the most recent budget resolution, the appropriations committees review the specifics of agency budget requests as printed in the executive budget. The panels primarily focus on significant changes from the previous year as reflected by increased costs, new programs, innovations in program implementation, and reallocation of expenditures. These changes are examined in the context of the prior year's appropriation and accomplishments as well as the current year's estimate and justification.

Appropriations committees employ several types of statutory controls. Among the most common are limits on the purposes for or conditions under which funds may be spent, restrictions on the amounts that may be used for an authorized purpose, and prohibitions on spending for objects not specifically mentioned in substantive legislation. An appropriation act may also designate the administrative official who is to exercise discretion regarding the amounts to be spent or the units to be assigned responsibility for expenditures.

Though annual appropriations allow agencies to incur obligations for only one fiscal year, the funds to discharge such obligations remain indefinitely available until expended. This type of appropriation is mainly used for salaries and other operating expenses. Multiyear appropriations cover a specified period of time in excess of one year and are usually devoted to special activities of a one-time nature or programs subject to unique conditions. No-year appropriations provide for obligations and outlays until the purpose for which they are granted has been accomplished. These acts primarily finance benefit payments and construction projects where a time limit would not significantly contribute to the control of expenditures.

Permanent appropriations permit funds to become available each year under existing law without annual congressional action. These are enacted through authorizations that limit congressional discretion so as to ensure future benefits. This type of legislation protects certain programs against potentially adverse political developments. Permanent authorizations and appropriations eliminate uncertainty concerning the future availability of funds to meet governmental commitments or obligations.

The appropriations process emphasizes fiscal responsibility and the prudent use of public funds. It entails an assessment of financial resources and the administration of federal programs. Appropriations legislation grants specified levels of budget authority to particular agencies for stipulated purposes and reconciles governmental action with existing budgetary and political constraints. An appropriation act expresses value judgments about what government can do to address certain matters.

Authorization decisions are made by advocates of the public welfare and reflect the needs of citizens. Appropriation decisions are made by guardians of the public purse and reflect the limits of government. There is a natural tension between the investment that is an authorization and the vigilance that is an appropriation. The amount of the latter rarely reaches the level sanctioned by the former. Thus, Congress endeavors to meet demands for both liberality and economy.

THE CONGRESSIONAL BUDGET PROCESS: BUDGET RESOLUTIONS

The congressional budget process begins with the transmittal of the executive budget to Congress in January. The House Appropriations Committee holds special hearings at which the Director of the OMB, Secretary of the Treasury, and Chairman of the Council of Economic Advisers testify. These proceedings present an overview of budget policy through discussion of economic conditions, fiscal options, and national priorities. The Budget committees in each chamber commence more extended and detailed hearings that cover such matters as economic indicators and assumptions, the course and pace of economic trends, economic weaknesses and key issues, budgetary recommendations and alternatives, the fiscal impact of current and proposed policies, and allocation of funds among governmental functions.

By March 15 all standing committees are required to submit views and estimates on their legislative plans for the coming fiscal year to the Senate or House Budget Committee. These reports contain a concise discussion of all the programs for which each panel is responsible and focus on the proposed levels of new budget authority that each committee anticipates it will approve. Authorizing and appropriations committees are obliged to organize their agenda early enough to give the budget panels a comprehensive picture of proposed congressional action for the year.

Both Budget committees are required to report a First Concurrent Resolution on the Budget to their respective houses by April 15. Concurrent resolutions do not have the force of law but are expressions of congressional policy. Budget resolutions are an exercise in legislative self-discipline intended to regulate the budgetary actions of Congress, though they cannot control actual expenditures in terms of amounts, rates, or types. This first budget resolution should be adopted by May 15.

The decisions reflected by the resolution are based on the current and projected state of the economy, recommendations contained in the executive budget, information provided by other congressional committees to the Budget panels, Congressional Budget Office analyses and reports, prior governmental actions, and the political impact of certain issues. Figures that appear in this measure are considered to be targets formed to guide Congress in its subsequent budgetary efforts rather than mandates that preclude discretion. (See figure 11, page 140, for an exmaple of a House-passed budget resolution.)

Authorizing committees are required to report all bills recommending new budget authority by May 15; until this time, neither chamber may consider any revenue, spending, or debt legislation. Though the Appropriations committees will have held hearings and drafted bills before May 15, such legislation may not be brought to the floor until this date. All congressional action on spending and revenue bills should be completed no later than one week after Labor Day. The legislative schedule calls for Congress to adopt a Second Concurrent Resolution on the Budget by September 15 that may retain or revise, in whole or in part, the contents of the first budget resolution. Due to a variety of reasons, Congress may not always adhere to all the dates in the budget timetable.

Major budget battles tend to occur during consideration of the first resolution and usually center on the budget increment, or the amount by which the spending total for the coming fiscal year exceeds that of the current fiscal year. This is because the Budget committees are able to exert more influence over new than continuing programs and over spending than revenue measures. Proposed programs cannot attract the solid political support that protects existing ones from being curtailed. The Ways and Means and Finance panels are subject to fewer constraints under the budget process than are the Appropriations committees, whose actions are more comprehensible than decisions on the intricacies of the Internal Revenue Code. Action on the second resolution constitutes a review to update figures rather than an occasion to reargue issues decided earlier.

The second resolution is based upon recent congressional fiscal decisions and any change in economic conditions or projections. Its figures are binding on Congress and govern all legislative budgetary actions undertaken after its adoption. Upon approval of this measure, neither house may consider legislation that would exceed the spending or reduce the revenue levels contained therein, except through passage of another budget resolution. Once all appropriation and tax bills have been passed, the aggregate totals of these individual measures must conform to the priorities stipulated in the second resolution.

If the fiscal directions that result from legislation differ from the judgments expressed by the resolution, the Budget committees are authorized to initiate a reconciliation process. They may report a resolution to modify the figures in the second budget resolution, instruct other committees to amend previously enacted legislation, or both. This action reconciles spending, revenue, and debt totals with the provisions of the second resolution. It enables Congress to reach all or any components of the budget to establish a comprehensive and consistent policy.

Figure 11
House-Passed Budget Resolution Referred to the Senate

96TH CONGRESS
1ST SESSION

H. CON. RES. 107

IN THE SENATE OF THE UNITED STATES

MAY 15 (legislative day, APRIL 9), 1979
Received

CONCURRENT RESOLUTION

Setting forth the congressional budget for the United States
Government for the fiscal year 1980 and revising the congressional budget for the United States Government for the
fiscal year 1979.

1   *Resolved by the House of Representatives (the Senate*

2   *concurring),* That the Congress hereby determines and de-

3   clares, pursuant to section 301(a) of the Congressional

4   Budget Act of 1974, that for the fiscal year beginning on

5   October 1, 1979—

6   (1) the recommended level of Federal revenues is

7          $509,000,000,000, and the amount by which the ag-

8   gregate level of Federal revenues should be decreased

9   is zero;

The congressional budget process is designed to achieve parity with the President for setting national priorities. Specifically, it enables Congress to correlate total federal revenues and expenditures for the fiscal year in view of existing conditions and commitments; obtain the data necessary to reach rational and feasible decisions on how to balance and integrate fiscal and social policies; coordinate the authorization and appropriations processes; and recognize the implications that separate legislative actions have for the entire budget.

CONGRESSIONAL BUDGET PUBLICATIONS

The large number of congressional budget publications can be more conveniently discussed by dividing the congressional budget process into four stages.

A.   Information gathering and analysis. The House and Senate Budget committees predominate at this stage. Information from the executive, in addition to the executive budget and *Economic Report*, includes the testimony of administration officials at budget hearings.

    1.   The *Annual Report* of the Congressional Budget Office is issued in at least two parts. The first part discusses current economic trends, recent policy developments, short-and long-term economic forecasts, and fiscal policy options. It offers an overview of the relationship between public policy and economic conditions. The second part focuses directly on the budget and contains five-year projections for the entire budget and for each functional category. Its perspective is the relationship between economic assumptions and budgetary decisions and their impact on spending and revenue.

    2.   The Congressional Budget Office also prepares an analysis of *The Budget of the United States Government*. This publication examines the economic implications of the President's fiscal policy, revenue and spending estimates and proposals, and the budget by function and the budget outlook. It explicitly contrasts executive assumptions and projections with those of the Congressional Budget Office and assesses the administration's policy proposals in light of any legislative debate or action on similar or related measures.

    3.   Views and estimates submitted to the Budget committees by the authorizing and appropriations panels are in the form of committee prints. These reports review the impact of executive budget proposals on programs within each committee's jurisdiction, provide early indications of likely committee action on major legislation and its effect on the total budget, and contain estimates of budget authority to be legislated for the coming fiscal year. This information corresponds to the discussion of major programs in *The Budget of the United States Government*, though panel jurisdiction overlaps the functional categories.

B.   First Concurrent Resolution on the Budget. The Budget committees and their respective chambers share influence during this phase.

    1.   The committee reports of the House and Senate Budget panels are the congressional response and counterparts to *The Budget of the*

United States Government. Each report presents the text of its proposed resolution; compares the committee's revenue, budget authority, and outlay estimates with those in the executive budget; contains five-year budget projections; proposes an allocation of the recommended level of revenues by major source and includes tax expenditure estimates by function; explains the economic assumptions and objectives that underlie the resolution; and discusses the information on which the amounts in the resolution were based and the relationship of such figures to other budget components. If the provisions of the most recently adopted budget resolution have been rendered impractical by economic developments, the reports serve as a means to submit revised versions for approval.

Both Budget committee reports also include a discussion of figures for each functional category. Under each function, the House report reviews the Budget panel's recommendations, the views and estimates of other House committees, and the President's request. The Senate report presents an overview of each function and then examines it in terms of major missions. The Senate document incorporates an explanation of principal budget issues within its chapters, while the House publication uses separate appendices for this purpose, two of which are particularly informative. One is a thorough exploration of controllability and discusses reasons for the differences between executive and legislative definitions of the concept. Another is a concise account of each budget function that includes a narrative description, notes all subfunctions, and identifies major programs and agencies. The Senate report contains a record of all roll-call votes taken in committee, including the motion voted on, by whom proposed, and the names of those for and against.

2. Congressional debate in each house proceeds basically as described in chapter 6, though there are some special rules that apply to the budget resolutions.

3. The conference report that reconciles the House and Senate versions gives the full text of the First Concurrent Resolution on the Budget. In addition to explaining how differences were resolved, this document contains target figures for the five budget aggregates of budget authority, outlays, revenues, deficit or surplus, and accrued public debt, as well as budget authority and outlay totals for each functional category. The resolution is also used to convey instructions to other congressional committees necessary to attain the stated sums and recommendations to the President regarding his budgetary responsibilities. Finally, this report allocates expenditure totals among the authorizing and appropriations panels in each house because the functional categories of the budget overlap the jurisdictions of the standing committees.

C. Spending and Revenue Bills. The Appropriations, House Ways and Means, and Senate Finance committees play the leading role in considering these measures.

1. Appropriations and revenue committee hearings and reports are covered in chapters 4 and 5, while floor debate is treated in chapter 6. Appropriations hearings usually include much of the internal

executive branch budgetary documents that were prepared for use during formulation of the executive budget.

    2. The appropriations and revenue panels also issue nonlegislative committee reports that subdivide among their subcommittees the totals allocated to them by the most recent budget resolution. The purpose of these reports is to clarify responsibilities and thus facilitate action.

    3. Following passage of the first budget resolution, the Congressional Budget Office periodically issues Scorekeeping Reports. These publications tabulate congressional budget actions for a given fiscal year. They inform Congress of the status of its budget and of the estimated effects of enacted and pending legislation on the budget authority and outlay levels set in the most recent budget resolution. The two major parts of these reports array data by functional category and congressional committee. The final issue for a fiscal year includes a list of major changes in the executive budget, by program, affected by legislative action. This document provides the same data following passage of the second budget resolution.

D.   Second Concurrent Resolution on the Budget and Reconciliation. The Budget committees and both houses again share responsibilities at this juncture.

    1. The publications relating to the second budget resolution are identical to those issued in conjunction with adoption of the first, though the Budget committees may not hold hearings at this point. Since the second resolution may be the final statement on public finance for the new fiscal year, it is the closest that any single document comes to being considered as *the* federal budget. After taking into account the appropriation bills that have been enacted or are pending, Congress establishes binding aggregate spending totals and binding ceilings on budget authority for each functional category. After reviewing the status of tax legislation, Congress also sets binding levels on budget receipts. The expenditure limits may not be exceeded, or the revenue amounts reduced, without congressional revision of the second resolution.

    2. If the sum of separate legislative decisions on spending and revenue bills is inconsistent with the totals stated in the second resolution, reconciliation of these figures is necessary. The reconciliation process may be initiated by the first or second budget resolution and may involve the revision of an earlier budget resolution, the amendment of enacted legislation, or both. A reconciliation proposal as reported by either Budget panel may apply to one or more standing committees in each chamber. This action would require a search of such finding aids as *CIS/Index*, the *Monthly Catalog*, or *House Calendar* to identify resulting publications.

    3. Should Congress fail to complete action on its budget prior to the start of the fiscal year on October 1, it resorts to continuing resolutions. These are joint resolutions reported by the Appropriations committees that authorize agencies to continue their financial operations through a certain date. Until Congress concludes its

budgetary labors, such measures usually limit agency spending to the same levels as existed for the previous fiscal year. The reports of the Appropriations committees and floor debate provide the information on these proceedings.

E. Background Material.
    1. Studies by both Budget committees and the Congressional Budget Office are continuously in progress and may be issued at any time. They may focus on the budget under consideration, the impact of earlier budgetary decisions, the prospects for certain budget options, or the analysis of budgetary procedures and techniques. Committee publications appear as committee prints, while Congressional Budget Office reports are designated as background papers or staff working papers.
    2. The Joint Economic Committee prepares a *Joint Economic Report* that is issued as a House or Senate report and constitutes a direct reply to the *Economic Report of the President.* Since the *Joint Economic Report* appears within approximately two months of the *Economic Report*, these publications provide an opportunity to compare executive and legislative perspectives and priorities in regard to the economic basis of the first budget resolution. The Joint Committee on Taxation serves as a research arm of the Ways and Means and Finance committees and its studies regularly appear as committee prints.
    3. A massive volume entitled *Appropriations, Budget Estimates, Etc.* is issued as a Senate or House document at the end of each session of Congress. Most of it is devoted to the text of legislation passed during the session that granted budget authority. One section contains a detailed comparison of executive budget estimates, as presented in the *Appendix*, with the appropriations enacted by Congress. It also includes status reports on all rescissions and deferrals, though this information relates to the following stage of the budget process.

All congressional budget publications, except budget and continuing resolutions, floor debate, and the last one discussed, are indexed in *CIS/Index.* All appropriations, budget, and revenue measures are listed in the status table at the end of the *House Calendar* and may also be readily identified in the *Congressional Record, Daily Digest,* or *Digest of Public General Bills and Resolutions.* The *Monthly Catalog* would have to be consulted for the final document.

THE BUDGET IMPLEMENTATION PROCESS

Once congressional action on the budget for the coming fiscal year is completed, most budget authority is apportioned among agencies by the OMB. This distribution is based on appropriation accounts and time periods, usually quarters, and is intended to ensure the orderly use of available funds. The responsibilities of the OMB at this stage, which include determinations of whether appropriations are in excess of or insufficient to meet program needs, give it the same key role it played during formulation of the executive budget.

Where the amount of money available is more than desirable, there are two main reasons for the President to ask Congress for authority to impound a stated sum. An impoundment is an action that prevents funds from being obligated. One reason relates to efficient management. This arises when it is not necessary to spend the total amount appropriated to achieve a specified purpose, when changed conditions render an expenditure unnecessary, or when it is prudent to establish reserves to provide for contingencies. The other reason concerns policy preferences. This occurs when the President seeks to terminate unwanted programs, combat inflation, or otherwise reorient public priorities.

The two types of impoundments are rescissions and deferrals. A rescission is a presidential recommendation that previously enacted budget authority be permanently rescinded. Unless both houses of Congress pass a rescission bill within 45 days of continuous session, the budget authority must be made available for obligation. A deferral is a presidential request to delay the obligation of budget authority temporarily. Only if either house adopts an impoundment resolution disapproving a deferral at any time after receipt of such a proposal must the executive branch make the budget authority available for obligation. The authority to defer, if approved by legislative inaction, may not extend beyond the fiscal year in which the message requesting it is transmitted to Congress.

Many deferrals are necessary due to the clear intention of Congress that funds not be used until some other specific actions are taken or certain conditions become evident. The OMB on its own initiative or at the request of an agency may defer funds through the apportionment process to meet unanticipated developments. Deferrals must be submitted to Congress whenever any executive action or inaction effectively precludes the obligation of budget authority for a limited period of time. Most impoundments are deferrals that represent management decisions which are routinely approved by congressional inaction. Should it be determined that a deferred amount will not be necessary to fulfill the purposes of an appropriation, it can be resubmitted to Congress as a rescission.

The primary purpose of these procedures is to identify those areas or actions where major fiscal or programmatic differences exist between the legislative and executive branches. This is accomplished by Comptroller General review at the second stage of the impoundment process, which follows presidential recommendations and precedes congressional decisions. A copy of each impoundment proposal must be sent to the Comptroller General who, after examining it, informs Congress of its validity and probable effect. Should the executive either submit an invalid message or fail to proceed in accordance with congressional action on a valid one, the Comptroller General is authorized to file suit to make the budget authority available for obligation. It is also the Comptroller General's responsibility to report undisclosed rescissions and deferrals as well as notify Congress when an impoundment has been misclassified. In the former case, such a communication is treated as if submitted by the executive, and in the latter, it nullifies the process initiated by the prior presidential message and triggers the appropriate congressional review mechanism.

A request for supplemental appropriations is submitted to Congress when the executive determines that the level of funds available is inadequate to meet program needs. Additional budget authority is usually sought to meet emergency or unforeseen conditions that threaten life or property, to reimburse individuals or organizations for losses suffered, to compensate for some budget estimates that did not contemplate an increased governmental workload, to finance new programs enacted after completion of the most recent budget cycle, or to discharge a liability that would continue to accrue under the law. A common occasion for supplementals is that existing law requires payments to be made within the current fiscal year. (See figure 12 for an overview of the budget process.)

Figure 12
Key Steps and Decision Points in the Formation of a Budget

Executive Action
1. Data collected from agencies
2. Economic conditions analyzed
3. Overall fiscal policy formulated
4. Specific spending levels established
5. Budget documents prepared
6. Executive budget transmitted to Congress 15 days after it convenes

Congressional Action
7. Budget committees review executive budget in hearings and deliberations
8. Budget committees collect information from other committees by March 15
9. Budget committees report First Concurrent Resolution on the Budget by April 15*
10. First budget resolution debated and amended*
11. Resolution approved by each chamber and sent to conference*
12. Conference report debated and approved by each chamber by May 15*
13. Appropriations and revenue bills enacted by seventh day after Labor Day*
14. Second Concurrent Resolution on the Budget approved by September 15* (see steps 9-12)
15. Reconciliation process completed by September 25*
16. Continuing resolution enacted if congressional budget is incomplete by October 1*

Subsequent Action
17. Supplemental appropriations*
18. Impoundment proposals*

---

*Indicates steps that may or usually involve roll-call votes.

BUDGET IMPLEMENTATION PUBLICATIONS

Budget implementation is a relatively routine process, and of the four presidential messages that stem from this stage, two reflect unanticipated contingencies (1 & 3) and two denote policy differences with Congress (2 & 6).

1.   Supplemental appropriation messages include the reason for the request, the amount requested for each agency, proposed appropriation language, and a cross-reference to the appropriate page of the *Appendix*. Consideration of these proposals by the Appropriations committees may involve hearings.

2.   Rescission messages include the amount of budget authority involved, the agency affected, a discussion of the factors that justify such action, the estimated budgetary and programmatic effects, and a statement of whether it was proposed as an earlier deferral. The OMB identification code enables this information to be correlated with its relevant functional category and appropriation account.

3.   Deferral messages, which are frequently combined with rescission recommendations, contain the same types of information. Any revisions of proposed rescissions or deferrals are submitted to Congress in supplementary messages. Impoundment resolutions disapproving deferrals appear in the *Congressional Record* and journals of each house. Impoundment messages occasionally identify the amount of funds appropriated for programs in excess of executive requests. This indicates the President is attempting to revive fiscal policy that Congress, through the appropriations process, has rejected.

4.   The OMB transmits a cumulative report of rescissions and deferrals for the current fiscal year to Congress by the tenth of each month. This communication notes the status of all proposed impoundments, including the date and description of legislative actions.

5.   Reports from the Comptroller General to Congress review the accuracy of presidential impoundment messages and executive compliance with legislative action on such proposals. The cover page of these publications identifies the House or Senate document number assigned to the message being reviewed. Except where executive action is deemed improper or statements incomplete, the Comptroller General merely describes the proposed impoundment and verifies the validity of the message without commenting on its substance.

6.   The President may veto appropriation and revenue bills on either fiscal or programmatic grounds. If Congress is still in session a message stating his reasons for disapproval is sent to the body of origin. Should the veto not be overridden, another bill modified to meet presidential objections may be passed. See chapter 8 for information on vetoed bills and accompanying messages.

7.   The Bureau of Government Financial Operations of the Treasury Department issues an annual report entitled *Combined Statement of Receipts, Expenditures and Balances of the United States Government*. Part III of this volume, "Details of Appropriations, Outlays and Balances," is arranged by agency and by appropriation account thereunder. The following figures are recorded for each account: the balance of funds available at the beginning of the fiscal year, the new budget authority granted and net outlays for that fiscal year, and the balance at the end of the fiscal year. This publication reveals, through its subject index, the financial status of all agencies and programs, and this information would at least partially explain the treatment of each in the budget for the next fiscal year.

Congressional action on 1, 2, and 6 involves the entire legislative process. Publications 1-6 are issued as Senate or House documents; 1-4 and 6 also appear in the *Weekly Compilation of Presidential Documents,* while the information in 2-4 is also printed in the *Federal Register.* Numbers 1-5 are referred to the House or Senate Appropriations Committee for information or action. Number 4 identifies those issues of the *Federal Register* in which the information conveyed by 2 and 3 is included. Committee reports of the Appropriations committees on 1-3 identify the Senate or House document number assigned to the message that prompted legislative action. This also applies to committee reports that accompany bills reported in response to 6. All budget implementation publications, except for the last, which is printed by the Treasury Department, are indexed in the *Monthly Catalog.*

BIBLIOGRAPHY

Fisher, Louis. *Presidential Spending Power.* Princeton, NJ: Princeton University Press, 1975.

LeLoup, Lance T. *Budgetary Politics.* Brunswick, OH: King's Court Communications, 1977.

Schick, Allen. *Congress and Money.* Washington: The Urban Institute, 1980.

U.S. Congress. House. Committee on the Budget. *Budget Act Review.* Hearings before the Task Force on Budget Process. 96th Congress, 1st Session, December 11 and 12, 1979. Washington: U.S. Government Printing Office, 1980.

U.S. Congress. House. Committee on the Budget. *Congressional Budget and Impoundment Control Act of 1974 — Legislative History.* Committee Print, 96th Congress, 1st Session. Washington: U.S. Government Printing Office, 1979.

U.S. Congress. House. Committee on the Budget. *Congressional Control of Expenditures.* Committee Print, 95th Congress, 1st Session. Washington: U.S. Government Printing Office, 1977.

U.S. Congress. House. Committee on the Budget. *Performance and Promise — Four Years of the Congressional Budget Process.* Committee Print, 95th Congress, 2nd Session. Washington: U.S. Government Printing Office, 1978.

U.S. Congress. Joint Economic Committee. *The Federal Budget as an Economic Document.* Committee Print, 87th Congress, 2nd Session. Washington: U.S. Government Printing Office, 1962.

U.S. General Accounting Office. *Terms Used in the Budgetary Process.* Washington: General Accounting Office, July 1977.

U.S. Office of Management and Budget. *Instructions on Budget Execution.* Circular No. A-34. Washington: Office of Management and Budget, July 1976.

U.S. Office of Management and Budget. *Preparation and Submission of Budget Estimates.* Circular No. A-11. Washington: Office of Management and Budget, June 1980.

Wildavsky, Aaron. *The Politics of the Budgetary Process.* 3rd ed. Boston: Little, Brown, 1979.

11

United States Treaties

This chapter presents a detailed description of the treatymaking process as reflected in the roles of the President and the Senate. Though treaties are a form of domestic law, their international aspect affords greater latitude for official discretion than does the legislative process. The absence of prescribed time limits and unsettled standing of governmental procedents significantly affect treaty publications. The impact of these factors is noted at various points throughout the discussion and is more thoroughly treated in reference to sources that can be consulted to determine the status of treaties.

In general terms, a treaty is an international agreement concluded between nations in written form and governed by certain standards of international law. For the United States, any international compact submitted by the President to the Senate for its approval, whether designated a treaty, protocol, convention, agreement, accord, articles, or otherwise, is a treaty. Other parties to such covenants do not necessarily recognize the difference between those formally considered as treaties under the United States Constitution and those that are not. This is because they assume that the international obligation, regardless of the form, will be fulfilled.

PRACTICES AND OPTIONS

Most international agreements are not concluded through the treaty process but by the President cooperating with Congress to enact a law or else independently exercising the powers of his office to enter into an executive agreement. If legislation should not embody a complete compact, it may authorize the President to negotiate a treaty or other type of accord. A statute that grants the President authority to proceed with such arrangements may state the goals to be pursued and the terms considered acceptable. When the President acts under his sole constitutional authority, the results may be protocols that constitute a stage in the negotiation of a treaty or a *modus vivendi*, which is intended to serve as a temporary substitute for one. Treaties may be preliminary or procedural documents that contain principles or guidelines upon which substantive treaties are to be based, or they may empower the President to conclude executive agreements.

The fluidity of international conditions, including those situations considered emergencies, technological means of global communication, interdependence among nations, and the multilateral nature of much international action combined with the occasional need for secrecy, all contribute to a presidential preference for use of the executive agreement, which excludes congressional participation. Treaties may entail greater formality and incur a more binding obligation than is deemed desirable. United States requirements for approving treaties make both the duration and outcome of the process uncertain. The needs of practicing diplomats are often in conflict with the treaty clause of the Constitution.

The choice of method for concluding an international compact is at the discretion of the President, who may seek or shun congressional advice. These options exist because the subjects that may be addressed by each approach tend to overlap and the different forms have been used interchangeably, though they are not interchangeable in all cases. The inability to command a two-thirds Senate majority may lead to the use of legislation, while lack of majority support in one or both houses of Congress may prompt the negotiation of an executive agreement. The decision regarding which form is most appropriate is less a constitutional or legal than a political and practical matter.

Such factors as the type of commitment, substance of provisions, actual or likely effects, and the context of negotiation and implementation do not provide clear criteria for distinguishing treaties from other types of international agreements or for determining when which form should be used. Treaties are usually considered necessary or desirable when the subject matter has been traditionally embodied in a treaty or is not entirely within the constitutional powers of either Congress or the President, the force of law without legislation is desired or implementing legislation will be needed, major commitments affecting national security or international stability are involved, or maximum formality is preferred to emphasize the long-term and binding nature of the compact.

A survey of international precedent and United States practice indicates that procedure is the only consistent and definite difference between treaties and other international acts. Treaties require Senate approval and supersede earlier conflicting statutes; otherwise their content and effect do not offer concrete grounds for legally differentiating them from other international agreements. The following discussion, except when otherwise noted, pertains to bilateral treaties.

Senatorial advice and consent refers to action on a treaty transmitted by the President after it has been negotiated and signed. Senate approval authorizes the President to ratify it, though the Constitution makes no mention of ratification. Since the authority to make treaties is accorded to both the Senate and the President, such compacts can only be ratified by the last party to act. Thus, it is the President's signature concurring in the Senate's action that constitutes formal ratification. Though the act of ratification is a presidential prerogative, it cannot be executed unless the Senate consents by a two-thirds majority.

EXECUTIVE INITIATIVE

The Department of State has not established definite guidelines specifying when consultation with senators is necessary regarding the desirability or substance of a treaty. The nature and extent of consultation may take several forms, including the appointment of legislators to international delegations, discussion with Senate leaders and members of the Foreign Relations Committee, or a request for adoption of a resolution endorsing contemplated executive action. Neither these nor any other mode of communication or collaboration is required. Though the negotiation of treaties may be pursued without consulting legislators, the interdependence of domestic and foreign affairs creates the need to obtain informal senatorial advice to cultivate legislative understanding and support. A decison to solicit congressional counsel is one that depends upon political rather than legal factors, with key legislators usually kept advised of negotiation developments.

An action memorandum prepared by the Department of State and approved by the Secretary of State formally authorizes United States officials to negotiate a treaty. However, statements by the President, Secretary of State, or their subordinates may serve to initiate the process. The customary method of negotiating a bilateral treaty begins when the government proposing the compact presents a complete draft to the other. Upon the conclusion of negotiations, a treaty is signed by an official of the Department of State and approved or signed by the Secretary. After signature, a report on the treaty, tracing its background and explaining its provisions, is prepared for transmittal by the Secretary to the President. This report is accompanied by a covering letter, the original copy of the treaty, pertinent diplomatic correspondence, any supplementary agreements or additional legal analysis, and a draft message from the President to the Senate. If the President approves, he signs the message and forwards the papers to the Senate.

Initial United States printing of a treaty is in the form of a Department of State press release following its signing and prior to its submission to the Senate. Its text is preceded by a statement outlining its history. A notice concerning its signing and purpose then appears in the Department of State *Bulletin*. The practice of postponing publication of treaties until the Senate removes its injunction of secrecy has been discontinued.

SENATE ACTION

Through the Ninety-Sixth Congress (1980), upon receipt of a treaty by the Senate, the papers were assigned a letter designation by the executive clerk. The official designation of the first set of such papers received during each session was Executive A, Congress and session, while subsequent treaties were assigned letters in alphabetical order. If more than 26 treaties were submitted during a session, double lettering was used to identify them. Beginning with the Ninety-Seventh Congress (1981), these executive documents have been superseded by treaty documents, which are numbered in the same manner as Senate documents. A treaty retains its designation for as long as it remains in the Senate. The Senate next adopts an order removing its injunction of secrecy; the papers are ordered to be printed as a treaty document; and they are referred to the Foreign Relations Committee. The *Executive Journal* and *Congressional Record* contain the text of all treaty messages as of the date they are received by the Senate. (See figure 13 for an example of a treaty submitted to the Senate.)

Though Senate rules do not require the Foreign Relations Committee to schedule hearings or issue a report, such action is customary. The committee holds each treaty for a reasonable period of time to permit public scrutiny and comment, after which most are promptly and favorably acted on by the Senate. Testimony at hearings is given by those familiar with the subject matter of the treaty and the manner in which it was concluded. These individuals are primarily, if not exclusively, Department of State officials. The views of those who will be affected by its terms, mainly representatives of other federal agencies and private organizations, are also presented. Printed hearings normally include the text of a treaty.

Figure 13
A Treaty Submitted to the Senate

97TH CONGRESS *1st Session*	SENATE	TREATY DOC. No. 97–3

CONSULAR CONVENTION WITH THE PEOPLE'S REPUBLIC OF CHINA

MESSAGE

FROM

THE PRESIDENT OF THE UNITED STATES

TRANSMITTING

THE CONSULAR CONVENTION BETWEEN THE UNITED STATES OF AMERICA AND THE PEOPLE'S REPUBLIC OF CHINA, SIGNED AT WASHINGTON ON SEPTEMBER 17, 1980

JANUARY 19, 1981.—Convention was read the first time and, together with the accompanying papers, referred to the Committee on Foreign Relations and ordered to be printed for the use of the Senate

U.S. GOVERNMENT PRINTING OFFICE
WASHINGTON : 1981

79–118 O

When the Foreign Relations Committee reports amendments, a resolution of ratification, or both, the report is placed on the Executive Calendar and assigned a number based on its chronolgoical order. These executive reports are numbered sequentially throughout a Congress and convey the panel's recommendations and its reasons therefor. They may contain the President's message, Secretary of State's report, text of the treaty, and an article-by-article analysis. If hearings are not held or held but not printed, the report will usually include statements delivered to the Committee in lieu of or during such proceedings. (See figure 14 for an example of a Senate executive report.)

Treaties are considered by the Senate in executive session. This means that the Senate meets to transact business that originated with the President, not that such meetings are closed to the public. Treaties are printed in the *Congressional Record* under the date that their consideration commences on the floor of the Senate.

Once a treaty is submitted to the Senate, the Foreign Relations Committee may take no action, choose not to proceed beyond hearings, or report a resolution of ratification. If a report is made, the Senate may unconditionally approve or approve with qualifications, while disapproval may be expressed through inaction, no final action, or rejection by anything less than a two-thirds majority vote. Though a treaty may remain pending in the Senate indefinitely, all proceedings on a treaty terminate with the expiration of a Congress, at which time it is returned to the Foreign Relations Committee. A treaty that is voted upon, but fails to secure a two-thirds majority, is immediately returned to the Committee. Consideration of treaties that were neither approved nor rejected would have to begin anew during the next or a subsequent Congress.

If the Foreign Relations Committee decides against further action either before it reports to the Senate or after the return of a treaty to the panel by the chamber, it will await a presidential request to withdraw the treaty. Should the executive anticipate incomplete action, extensive modification, or outright rejection by the Senate based upon the hearings, the President or Secretary of State may request the Committee to suspend consideration pending the negotiation of a supplementary protocol to render the treaty acceptable. Such an agreement would be submitted to the Senate as a separate compact and treated in the same manner as the original treaty.

Conditions to United States ratification may be proposed at any time during Foreign Relations Committee or Senate consideration of a treaty. The Senate has several options for expressing its views or qualifying its consent to ratification. It may advise and consent to ratification while communicating its sentiments through an executive report. This would have the same effect on a treaty as statements of legislative intent that apply to public laws. Such views will be taken into account by the executive but will not necessarily be followed in implementing a treaty. The President need not take further action in response to these remarks.

A Senate amendment to the text of a treaty is a major substantive modification that requires renegotiation by both parties to the compact. The result may be acceptance by the other party, a revised version of the treaty that would have to be submitted to the Senate, or an inability to reach agreement. An amendment that is ultimately incorporated into a treaty alters the obligations of each government.

A Senate reservation modifies or limits the substantive scope of one or more treaty provisions and constitutes an adjustment of the contractual relationship. It gives notice that the treaty will not be accepted or implemented except under

Figure 14
A Senate Executive Report

97TH CONGRESS *1st Session*	SENATE	EXECUTIVE REPT. No. 97–14

CONSULAR CONVENTION WITH THE PEOPLE'S REPUBLIC OF CHINA

JUNE 17, 1981.—Ordered to be printed

Mr. PERCY, from the Committee on Foreign Relations, submitted the following

REPORT

[To accompany Treaty Doc. No. 97–3]

The Committee on Foreign Relations, to which was referred the Consular Convention between the United States of America and the People's Republic of China, signed at Washington on September 17, 1980 (Treaty Doc. No. 97–3) having considered the same, reports favorably thereon without reservation and recommends that the Senate give its advice and consent to ratification thereof.

PURPOSE

Previously consular relationships between the United States and the People's Republic of China have not been subject to formal agreement. This Consular Convention will establish firm obligations in such important matters as free communication between a citizen and his consul, notification to consular officers of the arrest and detention of their citizens, and permission for visits by consuls of those detained. The consuls of both countries will also be authorized to perform the customary wide variety of other consular services which contribute to the improvement of both governmental and commercial interaction between countries.

BACKGROUND

The Consular Convention between the United States of America and the People's Republic of China, along with a separate exchange of letters, was signed at Washington on September 17, 1980. The new Administration has reviewed the Consular Convention, endorses its provisions and recommends that the Senate consent to its ratification.

MAJOR PROVISIONS

The bilateral consular convention between the United States and the PRC was negotiated for two primary purposes: (1) to secure the

79–119 O

specified conditions. The most common type of reservation is a brief statement that the United States does not agree to a particular article or clause. Its effect is to annul the obligation stated in the provision as it applies to the United States. Reservations are adopted as amendments to the resolution of ratification rather than to the treaty itself.

A reservation may also modify rather than nullify a stipulation contained in a specific article or clause. It may construe one or more treaty provisions in a manner that is inconsistent with the intent agreed upon by the parties when the compact was signed. If the President accepts a reservation, he communicates its terms to the other party prior to his ratification. The other signatory may accept it, in which case the original provision is not binding on either party or is given a revised meaning, file its own reservation, request renegotiation, or reject it and refuse to proceed with ratification. A reservation accepted by the other party becomes an integral part of the treaty.

An understanding or interpretation incorporated into a Senate resolution of ratification is not intended to affect the substantive terms or international obligations of a treaty. It applies to matters incidental to the operation of a treaty or relates solely to domestic action and does not have any legal effect. Such a proviso merely clarifies or explains one or more provisions or contains a statement of policy or procedure. Under existing practice the President informs the other party of these qualifications, though they need not be accepted for a treaty to be ratified. If agreed to by the President and the other signatory, they are considered a valid component of the treaty relationship. Other terms used to express an equivalent senatorial view of matters that are not substantive in nature are declaration, statement, clarification, and explanation.

The designation of a qualification by the Senate is not conclusive. Irrespective of which term is used, its content or effect is of prime importance. The legal significance of a Senate statement depends entirely on its substance. One that alters or restricts the meaning or purpose of a treaty is an actual reservation, while one that addresses an incidental or procedural matter is not. Whether renegotiation is necessary is a political decision that involves the perceived implications of the Senate's action. If, despite the terminology, it is considered a matter that requires further negotiation, the other party retains the right to determine if a statement modifies or interprets the treaty relationship in an unacceptable manner.

Though Senate rules stipulate that treaties be debated and amended article by article in the Committee of the Whole, after which reservations and understandings to the resolution of ratification are in order, this procedure is regularly dispensed with by unanimous consent. Present practice involves the use of motions to accelerate action on uncontroversial treaties and to consider proposed conditions to others without recourse to the Committee of the Whole. Senate adoption of any amendments or qualifications is effected by a majority vote, while consent to the resolution of ratification requires a two-thirds margin. There is usually a separate roll-call vote on each treaty. However, when a number of similar and routine ones are pending, they may be approved by a single vote to expedite Senate business, though the *Congressional Record* will show that they were voted upon individually.

An unperfected treaty is one that has been signed by representatives of the United States but has, for whatever reasons, failed to go into effect within a prescribed or practicable period of time. This is to distinguish such agreements from pending treaties on which further action is anticipated. Unperfected treaties include those never submitted to the Senate, withdrawn by the President, modified by the Senate or the other party in a manner that precluded ratification or disapproved by the Senate through rejection or inaction. This last development is the usual senatorial method for withholding consent to controversial treaties without unnecessarily consuming legislative resources. Since treaties may remain before the Senate for an indefinite interval, a question may arise as to whether one is unperfected or pending. If its text or international conditions do not provide a clear answer, one would have to consult sources discussed in the last portion of this chapter.

The Senate may adopt a sense-of-the-Senate resolution or Congress may adopt a concurrent resolution concerning international policy. Though there are no limitations on the content of such measures, they have no binding effect and are in the nature of recommendations or opinions. Their political significance can influence executive action if aimed at a treaty that is under negotiation, pending in the Senate, or in effect.

PRESIDENTIAL ACTION

When the Senate makes its consent conditional upon certain understandings, reservations, or amendments, the President must accept the understandings, approve the reservations, or renegotiate the treaty based upon the amendments before he can ratify it. Such alterations may be made at the request of the President. He has the authority to judge what international effect is intended by the Senate's action and may decide that its statement is not a qualification, in which case the instrument of ratification will not mention it. If the President is persuaded that a reservation or understanding is intended, these conditions must be included in the instrument of ratification or it must otherwise be made known that United States approval is subject to the terms added by the Senate.

The President may find that the Senate has advised him to be reasonably certain, without linking the matter with the formalities of ratification, that the treaty be given a definite interpretation. This may entail additional correspondence or a supplementary agreement with the other party. Whether induced by senatorial language or the result of executive initiative, a "statement of understanding," "agreed minute," or "exchange of notes" between chiefs of state serves to construe the precise meaning of treaty provisions. Such clarifications are legally binding in the absence of any further or inconsistent Senate statements.

Should the President accept reservations or understandings adopted by the Senate, he communicates them to the other party. Ratification is normally deferred until the views of the other government on Senate action have been ascertained. Informally, such views are exchanged while Senate consideration is in progress. Presidential acceptance of Senate pronouncements is followed by the signing of the formal instrument of ratification, which is prepared by the Department of State and contains the full text of all Senate conditions or qualifications. The President is not obligated to accept any Senate action and if, in his judgment, it is undesirable, he may express disapproval by resubmitting the treaty at any time or terminating the process.

In response to Senate statements with which the President agrees, the other party has several options. It may accept or reject such conditions, request further negotiations, or attach conditions of its own which the United States may, in turn, accept or reject. The other signatory may choose to remain silent rather than issue a formal reply regarding reservations or understandings. If it exchanges instruments of ratification, its silence is interpreted as official consent to statements incorporated into the instrument. Another government's understandings may be rejected without affecting ratification. One party may proceed to exchange instruments while protesting or resisting an understanding. In this case, a treaty relationship is established with the parties in disagreement as to the application or intent of certain provisions.

A treaty may be withdrawn from the Senate any time after it is submitted and prior to approval of a resolution of ratification. Withdrawal may be the result of executive or legislative initiative or collaboration. This procedure begins with the receipt of a presidential message requesting that a treaty be returned to the executive. The message is referred to the Foreign Relations Committee, which reports an executive resolution directing the Secretary of the Senate to comply with the request. Upon Senate approval the resolution and all original treaty papers are delivered to the White House. Requests for withdrawal are invariably accorded favorable consideration.

Among the reasons for withdrawal are changed international conditions, a later international agreement, altered domestic political circumstances, or objections by members of the Senate. The President prefers to withdraw a treaty when it encounters serious opposition in the Foreign Relations Committee or on the floor rather than risk major amendments or formal rejection, which would jeopardize the possibility of concluding any agreement. Withdrawal, as an indirect method of disposing of unacceptable treaties, offers the President a diplomatic means to engage in further negotiations, which may result in the submission of a revised compact. A treaty withdrawn and resubmitted will be assigned a new designation. Even treaties disapproved by less than a two-thirds floor vote remain in the Senate until withdrawn.

RATIFICATION

An instrument of ratification includes the title of the treaty; its date of signature; the countries involved; the languages in which it is signed; its text; a statement regarding Senate action and the text of any amendments, reservations, or understandings; the text of any correspondence or other documents, such as lists, tables, charts and maps, that affect its content; and a declaration by the President that he has reviewed the compact and ratifies it.

Under the terms of a treaty, the ratifications are exchanged at a specified location and it becomes effective upon the date of such action. A "Protocol of Exchange of Ratifications," sometimes referred to as a *proces-verbal*, attesting the exchange is signed by an official of each party at this time. The effective date can almost always be derived from the text but may vary as to whether international or domestic law is involved. The treaty may contain provisions or the Senate may have added stipulations that make its effectiveness contingent upon certain conditions. Any Senate qualification to its approval of a treaty and included in the instrument of ratification takes effect as domestic law along with the treaty itself.

Although the exchange of ratifications is customarily the final step needed to bring a treaty into force, it is always proclaimed by the President. Receipt of a protocol of exchange by the Department of State is the prerequisite to the promulgation of a treaty through a presidential proclamation. This document, prepared by the Department of State, includes the title and date of the compact, names of all signatories, all particulars concerning its effectiveness, a list of all significant dates in its history, its text, and a statement that it is being made public so that its terms may be observed by all citizens. Since promulgation is a national act, its timing or absence does not affect the international obligation incurred.

At every stage in the treatymaking process, except for senatorial advice and consent to ratification — initiation, negotiation, signature, ratification, exchange or deposit of ratification and promulgation, the judgment of the President predominates. He may decide to terminate negotiations; if negotiated, he may prevent a treaty from being signed on behalf of the United States; if signed, he may decline to submit it to the Senate; if submitted, he may request it be withdrawn; if approved by the Senate, he may refuse to ratify it; if ratified, he may choose not to exchange ratifications. Though the President and the Senate may each exercise an unqualified veto in the making of treaties, the President has greater discretion and more opportunities to use it. While treaties cannot be concluded without presidential approval, they can be terminated despite the President's disapproval by the passage of legislation that is subject to his veto, but which may be overridden.

MULTILATERAL TREATIES

Some practices that apply to multilateral treaties differ from those employed for bilateral pacts. Most multilateral agreements are negotiated and publicly discussed at international conferences convened for the purpose. The text of a treaty is usually made available to the press at or before signature. The Final Act of such a conference summarizes its proceedings, lists the participants, describes its organization, and contains all resolutions adopted. The draft treaty prepared for consideration by interested governments is issued as a separate document.

The original copy of a multilateral treaty is deposited with an international organization or one of the signatories, and certified copies are furnished each party. Any conditions added by the Senate in the process of approving such a compact are communicated to the depository, which corresponds with other governments regardng the matter. An instrument of ratification is deposited with the original treaty; the depository notifies each party when one is received. Multilateral agreements become effective after a certain number or all parties, as stipulated in the treaty, have deposited their instruments. If it has gone into force for some signatories, it becomes effective for others upon the deposit of their ratifications. Thus, its effectiveness for a given government may be years later than its ratification.

The United States may adhere to a multilateral treaty rather than participate in its negotiation and ratification. Adherence refers to a nonsignatory that becomes a party to a treaty under terms that provide for such a contingency. United States adherence to a multilateral compact requires Senate approval in the form of a resolution of adherence, and it would go into force upon the deposit of an instrument of adherence.

ALTERING OBLIGATIONS

Treaties may be modified by legislation, formal amendment, or executive agreement. When a statute conflicts with an existing treaty provision or vice versa, the later action supersedes the earlier. In the former instance the treaty text is repealed as domestic law, but the international obligation remains valid and, if not otherwise honored, may produce political repercussions. Legislation may expressly modify or suspend a treaty or authorize the President to take such action through an executive agreement or upon the determination that certain conditions exist. To amend an existing treaty by revising or adding provisions would usually require senatorial consent. The President may modify a treaty without legislative action if domestic law or congressional prerogatives are not affected. An exchange of notes by the chief executives of each government may serve to clarify or interpret a disputed provision.

Treaties may be terminated by their expiration, abrogation, or repudiation. The terms of a compact may provide for its own expiration at a certain date or stipulate that upon the arrival of a designated date one party, after giving notice of its intention to do so, may sever the relationship. Governments may also negotiate treaties that supersede earlier ones or jointly decide to terminate a pact. Treaties about to expire would have to be extended through another if it was agreed that all provisions remained desirable. If only some of its terms were considered as worth renewing, then the President would decide whether to negotiate a treaty or other form of agreement.

Treaties may also be unilaterally terminated by the United States when the President gives notice of an intention to do so pursuant to passage of a joint or concurrent resolution to that effect or following enactment of a law whose provisions are inconsistent with existing treaty obligations. In these cases, a treaty relationship, despite its political or moral aspects, is abrogated by legislation or legislative-executive cooperation.

The President may initiate action and give notice in the absence of formal or informal congressional approval. Such repudiation is most likely to occur when he determines that certain treaty provisions have lapsed or were breached due to actions of the other party or to its change of status in the international community. The rationale for this prerogative is that the presidency is the only governmental organ legally empowered to communicate with foreign governments. Thus, no other body can proscribe such action, nor can the other party question its legitimacy. Some actions and conditions that relate to the modification, termination, or renewal of treaties clearly lack the validity or certainty of those that lead to ratification. (See figure 15 for an overview of the treaty process.)

Figure 15
Key Steps and Decision Points in the Life of a Treaty

Executive Action
1. Initiation and negotiation
2. Approval and signature
3. Preparation of treaty papers
4. Transmittal to the Senate

Senate Action
5. Foreign Relations Committee hearings
6. Foreign Relations Committee deliberations and revisions*
7. Foreign Relations Committee drafts and files Executive Report*
8. Chamber debate and adoption of qualifications*
9. Chamber approves resolution of ratification*
10. Resolution and papers delivered to the President

Figure 15 (cont'd)

Presidential Action
11. Withdrawal* (may occur any time during steps 5-8)
12. Renegotiation (if necessary)
13. Resubmission (equivalent to step 4)
14. Ratification
15. Exchange of ratifications
16. Promulgation

Subsequent Action
17. Modification: Legislation*, formal amendment*, executive agreement
18. Termination: Expiration, legislation*, presidential action

---

*Indicates steps that may or usually involve roll-call votes.

TREATY STATUS AND PUBLICATIONS

Treaties are ordinarily neither printed by the United States in any quantity nor are their texts generally available before they become effective. They usually appear as Department of State press releases and Senate treaty documents or in printed hearings of the Foreign Relations Committee, its Executive Report, and the *Congressional Record.* Approximately six months to a year after a treaty has gone into force, it is issued by the Department of State as an unbound pamphlet in the official *Treaties and Other International Acts Series* (TIAS). They are numbered consecutively, though the order in which they are printed corresponds to their effective date rather than their numerical sequence. The TIAS print includes the English and foreign-language versions of the text, all important dates concerning its development and approval, the President's proclamation, and any correspondence affecting its content. The Final Acts of international conferences also appear in this series.

The *United States Treaties and Other International Agreements* (UST) is the official treaty series published by the Department of State and issued annually in a multivolume set that cumulates and replaces TIAS. Each volume of UST has an index arranged by subject and country that covers that volume only. Each treaty is also printed in the *Statutes-at-Large* in conjunction with the presidential proclamation that promulgates it.

A commercial publication entitled *UST Cumulative Index,* edited by Igor I. Kavass and Adolf Sprudzs, provides comprehensive access to United States treaties. The initial four-volume set issued in 1973 covers the period 1950-1970, and a one-volume supplement appeared in 1977 for the years 1971-1975. This source contains a numerical list in TIAS order, along with chronological, country, and subject indexes. The first three aids include citations to TIAS and UST, while the last cites UST only. *Treaties and Other International Agreements of the United States of America 1776-1949,* compiled by Charles I. Bevans and published in 13 volumes by the Department of State, including a comprehensive subject index, contains the text of all pre-1950 compacts.

There is no definite duration for each stage of or for the entire treatymaking process. It is possible for a treaty to be in part executed, in part expired, and in part effective. A single source that provides all pertinent information about the status of any treaty—whether pending, unperfected, modified, suspended, terminated, or renegotiated—does not exist. The most comprehensive volume on this subject is the annual *Treaties in Force* (TIF) issued by the Department of State. It covers all international agreements irrespective of their nature or nomenclature to which the United States is a party and whose terms are still in effect. The first part of TIF lists bilateral compacts arranged by country and by subject thereunder, and the second part lists multilateral agreements arranged by subject and by country thereunder. To facilitate efforts to ascertain the status of treaties, those publications that can be consulted in regard to each stage of their consideration and approval, as well as subsequent action, are discussed below.

1)   Initiation: Public statements by the President or Secretary of State about the decision to negotiate a treaty appear in the *Weekly Compilation of Presidential Documents* (WCPD) or the Department of State *Bulletin*, respectively. The latter publication appears weekly and an index is issued semiannually. The *Bulletin* normally contains some facts that apply to all subsequent stages as well, but will only be mentioned when it is the only or best source available.

2)   Negotiation: Information about this stage relates to both positions and progress. If an existing international agreement or earlier legislation authorized negotiations, either might contain stipulations or guidelines to be followed. The course of proceedings may be monitored through the sources noted in (1) or Department of State press releases.

3)   Signature: The *Bulletin* or a Department of State press release confirms that this stage has been reached.

4)   Transmittal to the Senate: Receipt by the Senate is noted in the *Congressional Record*, Senate *Executive Journal*, and WCPD. All three sources include the President's message, and the last two cite the appropriate Senate executive or treaty document. Both documents are indexed in *CIS/Index*; the latter appears in the Serial Set as of the Ninety-Seventh Congress (1981).

5)   Foreign Relations Committee action: Printed hearings or a committee report can be located through the *Monthly Catalog* or *CIS/Index*. The bound volume of the *Daily Digest* section of the *Congressional Record* indicates whether hearings have been held. The *Daily Digest, Executive Journal*, and *CIS/Index* identify all executive reports, which also appear in the Serial Set as of the Ninety-Seventh Congress (1981).

6)   Senate action: All Senate amendments, reservations, and understandings, as well as the resolution of ratification, appear in the *Congressional Record* and *Executive Journal*. The latter publication also lists all treaties received from the President during prior sessions and still pending and contains a separate list of those submitted during the immediate session. The Foreign Relations Committee calendar provides a legislative history of all treaties either pending or on which action has been taken during the Congress for which it is issued. However, neither the *Executive Journal* nor the committee calendar are necessarily definitive sources on pending treaties because some are submitted only as an international gesture or for informational purposes rather than as a step toward ratification.

7)   Withdrawal: The *Congressional Record, Executive Journal, Daily Digest*, and WCPD furnish information regarding this procedure.

8) Renegotiation: This development may occur prior or subsequent to final Senate action. Information on this possibility appears in WCPD or a Department of State press release.

9) Ratification: The *Bulletin* and WCPD record the facts on this presidential action.

10) Exchange or Deposit of Ratification: The *Bulletin* should be consulted for this development.

11) Promulgation: The issuance of a presidential proclamation is noted in the *Bulletin*, while its text first appears in WCPD. Proclamations, which may include the text of Senate conditions and qualifications accepted by the President, are also printed in the *Statutes-at-Large*. The treaty text and some related documents are included and citation is given to UST, which contains a more complete compilation of material.

12) Modification, Termination, Renewal: Treaties whose status or terms have been altered are listed in *Shepard's United States Citations—Statutes Edition*. Amended or superseded compacts are identified by their TIAS/UST number and each entry cites the action that embodied the change. When the President gives notice to another government about United States action under the terms of a treaty, it is usually conveyed by a proclamation. The general lack of uniform standards for interpreting governmental actions at this stage contributes to the difficulty of ascertaining execution or effects.

Since the date of domestic implementation of a treaty may differ from the effective date of the international obligation, information in sources noted under (10) and (11) may be insufficient to determine its status. Executive orders issued by the President are used to implement treaty provisions that require action within the executive branch. The *Bulletin*, WCPD, or *Federal Register* should be consulted for this or other presidential action relating to implementation. The legislative activity report issued by the Senate Foreign Relations Committee following the final adjournment of each Congress contains a complete account of the most recent congressional action on all treaties submitted to the Senate, including information about implementing legislation. It appears in the Serial Set and also presents a legislative history of each treaty and lists all congressional publications on specific treaties and the subject of treaties.

Additional sources of information may be cited in a treaty, which may refer to earlier treaties between the same or other parties, to treaties that did not go into force, or to other official acts of the parties involved. Two documents of some importance that were not mentioned above as sources of information are the action memorandum, which covers stages (1) and (2), and the instrument of ratification. The reason for this omission is that neither is printed by the United States government. It is understandable that the memorandum would be kept confidential since its text or tenor may cover a discussion of negotiating positions and potential reactions, as well as other sensitive matters. Less compelling reasons exist for not publishing the instrument of ratification, which is the only document that includes the text of all presidential, congressional, and foreign pronouncements pertaining to a treaty.

The Department of State *Bulletin, Treaties in Force*, and *Shepard's United States Citations—Statutes Edition* are the main sources of information on current treaty developments. It is always possible for the print media to supplement or supplant these or other official sources in any given situation. The Treaty Office of the Department of State or the Senate executive clerk may be contacted when all efforts to ascertain the status of a treaty prove unavailing or further information is needed on this or some other aspect of United States treaties. The most comprehensive bibliographic coverage of recent treaty publications is provided by the *Monthly Catalog* or the combination of *CIS/Index* and WCPD, which is indexed quarterly.

BIBLIOGRAPHY

Byrd, Elbert M., Jr. *Treaties and Executive Agreements in the United States.* The Hague: Martinus Nijhoff, 1960.

U.S. Congress. Senate. *The Constitution of the United States of America: Analysis and Interpretation.* Senate Document No. 92-82, 92nd Congress, 2nd Session. Washington: U.S. Government Printing Office, 1973.

U.S. Congress. Senate. *Senate Legislative Procedural Flow.* 95th Congress, 2nd Session. Washington: U.S. Government Printing Office, 1978.

U.S. Congress. Senate. *Senate Procedure.* Senate Document No. 93-21, 93rd Congress, 1st Session. Washington: U.S. Government Printing Office, 1974.

U.S. Congress. Senate. Committee on Foreign Relations. *International Agreements: An Analysis of Executive Regulations and Practices.* Committee Print, 95th Congress, 1st Session. Washington: U.S. Government Printing Office, 1977.

U.S. Congress. Senate. Committee on Foreign Relations. *The Role of the Senate in Treaty Ratification.* Committee Print, 95th Congress, 1st Session. Washington: U.S. Government Printing Office, 1977.

U.S. Congress. Senate. Committee on Foreign Relations. *Treaty Termination Resolution.* Senate Report No. 96-119, 96th Congress, 1st Session. Washington: U.S. Government Printing Office, 1979.

U.S. Department of State. *List of Treaties Submitted to the Senate 1789-1934.* Washington: U.S. Government Printing Office, 1935.

U.S. Department of State. *List of Treaties Submitted to the Senate 1789-1931, Which Have Not Gone into Force.* Washington: U.S. Government Printing Office, 1932.

U.S. Department of State. *The Making of Treaties and International Agreements and the Work of the Treaty Division of the Department of State.* Washington: U.S. Government Printing Office, 1938.

U.S. Department of State. *Treaties and Other International Acts of the United States of America.* Volume 1 (Short Print). Washington: U.S. Government Printing Office, 1931.

U.S. Department of State. "Treaties and Other International Agreements." *Foreign Affairs Manual.* Volume 11, Chapter 700 (October 25, 1974).

U.S. Department of State. "Treaties and Other International Agreements: Procedure, Formalities, and the Information Facilities of the Department of State." *Bulletin*. Volume X, No. 255 (May 13, 1944). Washington: U.S. Government Printing Office, 1944.

Appendix

SURVEY OF THE STANDING COMMITTEES
OF CONGRESS, 1789-1981

Until the close of the nineteenth century, congressional committee documents are only available, with few exceptions, in the *American State Papers* or the Serial Set. Since the dates noting the life span of a committee suggest which sources or volumes to consult for locating its publications, this survey is intended to serve as a guide to such material. Another aim is to clarify some facts of committee history. The questions specifically addressed concern their origin as Senate, House, or joint panels, their status as standing or select committees, and their relationship to earlier and later units.

Since 1816, when the House created 6 and the Senate 12 standing committees, for respective totals of 20 and 16, these panels have exercised decisive influence in Congress regarding the enactment of public policy. The two attributes that define a standing committee are continued existence until some express action is taken to terminate it and authority to recommend legislation to the parent body, though this latter power is not usually granted to joint standing committees.

Most have been established by resolutions adopted in each chamber, while some have been authorized by law. Among the reasons for their formation are as a response to emerging or recurring issues, to provide a forum for certain legislators or societal interests, to monitor the operation of newly created or existing government agencies, or to cope with changing committee workloads or legislative priorities. A common denominator of these or other reasons is to maintain or enhance the political influence of the legislative branch.

The first major overhaul of standing committees was undertaken by the Senate in 1921, when it reduced their number from 74 to 34. The House followed with a more moderate reform in 1927 by eliminating 14 of 58 standing committees. Both houses reconstituted their committee structures via the Legislative Reorganization Act of 1946 (60 Stat. 812), which became effective at the start of the Eightieth Congress in January 1947. Standing committee totals were pruned from 33 to 15 in the Senate and from 48 to 19 in the House, while 4 joint committees remained in existence and 2 joint panels were created by statute. Unlike the earlier endeavors, which involved the dissolution of inactive committees, this action represented a consolidation of panels. As of December 1981 there existed 16 Senate, 22 House, and 4 joint standing committees.

The first column of this survey lists all committees in alphabetical order, with separate series for Senate, House, and joint panels. Existing committees are in capitals and an asterisk denotes that a panel existed as a select committee prior to its status as a standing committee. The numbers in the first column serve to identify immediate predecessor and successor panels in the second and fifth columns and enable one to trace the complete lineage of any committee by following the numerical references. When a committee was dissolved and its functions merged with an existing one, the former is not considered a predecessor, though the latter is a successor.

In the third and fourth columns, the Congress and session appear in parentheses following the dates, and an "S" indicates a special session. The final column notes the Superintendent of Documents classification number. A blank entry means the information was either not applicable or could not be ascertained. Facts in the first, third, and fourth columns were compiled primarily from an examination of the journals of each house, supplemented by recourse to the *Congressional Record* or one of its predecessors when necessary. Information in the second and fifth columns was obtained mainly from the sources listed in the bibliography.

A change of committee name does not necessarily mean its jurisdiction was significantly altered. The extent of each change determined whether a committee was assigned another number in this survey. Though it was not feasible to clearly distinguish between changes of name and function, some facts that concern this distinction appear in the fourth paragraph of this introduction, the second and fifth columns, and the notes.

Senate Committees

Senate Committees	P	Created	Dissolved	S	Y4
1. Additional Accommodations for the Library of Congress*		22 Mar 1909(61-1)	18 Apr 1921(67-1)	66	
2. Aeronautical and Space Sciences*		24 Jul 1958(85-2)	4 Feb 1977(95-1)	17	Ae8
3. AGRICULTURE, NUTRITION AND FORESTRY[1]		12 Dec 1825(19-1)			Ag8/2
4. APPROPRIATIONS	43	7 Mar 1867(40-1)			Ap6/2
5. ARMED SERVICES	68, 73	6 Jan 1947(80-1)			Ar5/3
6. Audit and Control the Contingent Expenses of the Senate		4 Nov 1807(10-1)	6 Jan 1947(80-1)	97	Se5
7. BANKING, HOUSING AND URBAN AFFAIRS[2]	43	15 Mar 1913(63-S)			B22/3
8. BUDGET[3]		12 Jul 1974(93-2)			B85/2
9. Canadian Relations*[4]		13 Jan 1892(52-1)	18 Apr 1921(67-1)	46	C16
10. Census		12 Dec 1887(50-1)	18 Apr 1921(67-1)	11	C33/2
11. Civil Service[5]		4 Dec 1873(43-1)	17 Apr 1947(80-1)	81	C49/2
12. Claims		10 Dec 1816(14-2)	6 Jan 1947(80-1)	63	C52/2
13. Coast and Insular Survey		15 Dec 1899(56-1)	18 Apr 1921(67-1)	59	C63
14. Coast Defenses		13 Mar 1885(48-2)	18 Apr 1921(67-1)		
15a. Commerce	16	12 Dec 1825(19-1)	6 Jan 1947(80-1)	58	C73/2
15b. Commerce	58	13 Apr 1961(87-1)	4 Feb 1977(95-1)	17	C73/2

(Senate Committees continue on page 170; notes begin on page 182.)

Senate Committees (cont'd)

Senate Committees	P	Created	Dissolved	S	Y4
16. Commerce and Manufactures		10 Dec 1816(14-2)	12 Dec 1825(19-1)	15a, 67	
17. COMMERCE, SCIENCE AND TRANSPORTATION	2, 15b	4 Feb 1977(95-1)			C73/7
18. Conservation of Natural Resources		22 Mar 1909(61-1)	18 Apr 1921(67-1)	59	
19. Corporations Organized in the District of Columbia*		19 Mar 1896(54-1)	18 Apr 1921(67-1)	22	
20. Cuban Relations[6]		15 Dec 1899(56-1)	18 Apr 1921(67-1)	46	C89
21. Disposition of Useless Papers in the Executive Departments[7]		22 Mar 1909(61-1)	18 Apr 1921(67-1)		
22. District of Columbia		11 Dec 1817(15-1)	4 Feb 1977(95-1)	50	D63/2
23. Education		8 Mar 1869(41-1)	14 Feb 1870(41-2)	24	Ed8/3
24. Education and Labor	23	14 Feb 1870(41-2)	6 Jan 1947(80-1)	65	Ed8/3
25. ENERGY AND NATURAL RESOURCES	56	4 Feb 1977(95-1)			En2
26. Engrossed Bills		26 Mar 1806(9-1)	18 Apr 1921(67-1)	J5	
27. ENVIRONMENT AND PUBLIC WORKS	56, 90	4 Feb 1977(95-1)			P96/10
28. Epidemic Diseases*		13 Mar 1885(48-2)	19 Mar 1896(54-1)	88	Ep4/2
29. Examine the Several Branches of the Civil Service*		13 Mar 1885(48-2)	18 Apr 1921(67-1)	11	
30. Expenditures in the Agriculture Department*		22 Mar 1909(61-1)	18 Apr 1921(67-1)	33	
31. Expenditures in the Commerce and Labor Department		5 Apr 1912(62-2)	25 Jun 1914(63-2)	32, 36	
32. Expenditures in the Commerce Department	31	25 Jun 1914(63-2)	18 Apr 1921(67-1)	33	

33. Expenditures in the Executive Departments	30, 32, 34-41	18 Apr 1921(67-1)	3 Mar 1952(82-2)	49	Ex7/14
34. Expenditures in the Interior Department*		22 Mar 1909(61-1)	18 Apr 1921(67-1)	33	
35. Expenditures in the Justice Department*		22 Mar 1909(61-1)	18 Apr 1921(67-1)	33	
36. Expenditures in the Labor Department	31	25 Jun 1914(63-2)	18 Apr 1921(67-1)	33	
37. Expenditures in the Navy Department*		22 Mar 1909(61-1)	18 Apr 1921(67-1)	33	
38. Expenditures in the Post Office Department		22 Mar 1909(61-1)	18 Apr 1921(67-1)	33	
39. Expenditures in the State Department		17 Dec 1907(60-1)	18 Apr 1921(67-1)	33	
40. Expenditures in the Treasury Department*		22 Mar 1909(61-1)	18 Apr 1921(67-1)	33	
41. Expenditures in the War Department*		22 Mar 1909(61-1)	18 Apr 1921(67-1)	33	
42. Expenditures of Public Moneys		5 Feb 1884(48-1)	12 Mar 1889(51-S)	74	
43. FINANCE		10 Dec 1816(14-2)			F49
44. Fisheries[8]		5 Feb 1884(48-1)	18 Apr 1921(67-1)	59	F53
45. Five Civilized Tribes of Indians*		22 Mar 1909(61-1)	18 Apr 1921(67-1)	53	
46. FOREIGN RELATIONS		10 Dec 1816(14-2)			F76/2
47. Forest Reservations and the Protection of Game*		19 Mar 1896(54-1)	18 Apr 1921(67-1)	89	F76/3
48. Geological Survey		15 Dec 1899(56-1)	18 Apr 1921(67-1)	89	
49. Government Operations	33	3 Mar 1952(82-2)	4 Feb 1977(95-1)	50	G74/6
50. GOVERNMENTAL AFFAIRS	22,49,81	4 Feb 1977(95-1)			G74/9

(Senate Committees continue on page 182.)
(Senate Committees continue on page 172; notes begin on page 182.)

Senate Committees (cont'd)

Senate Committees	P	Created	Dissolved	S	Y4
51. Human Resources	65	4 Feb 1977(95-1)	7 Mar 1979(96-1)	64	H88
52. Immigration		12 Dec 1889(51-1)	6 Jan 1947(80-1)	63	Im6/2
53. Indian Affairs		4 Jan 1820(16-1)	6 Jan 1947(80-1)	89	In2/2
54. Indian Depredations*		15 Mar 1893(53-S)	18 Apr 1921(67-1)	53	In2/4
55. Industrial Expositions*		22 Mar 1909(61-1)	18 Apr 1921(67-1)		In2/8
56. Interior and Insular Affairs	89	28 Jan 1948(80-2)	4 Feb 1977(95-1)	25, 27	In8/13
57. Interoceanic Canals*		15 Dec 1899(56-1)	6 Jan 1947(80-1)	58	In8/1
58. Interstate and Foreign Commerce	15a, 57, 67	6 Jan 1947(80-1)	13 Apr 1961(87-1)	15b	In8/3
59. Interstate Commerce*		12 Dec 1887(50-1)	6 Jan 1947(80-1)	58	In8/3
60. Investigate Trespasses Upon Indian Lands*		22 Mar 1909(61-1)	18 Apr 1921(67-1)	53	
61. Investigation and Retrenchment		14 Dec 1871(42-2)	4 Dec 1873(43-1)	11	
62. Irrigation and Reclamation*9		17 Dec 1891(52-1)	6 Jan 1947(80-1)	89	Ir7/1
63. JUDICIARY		10 Dec 1816(14-2)			J89/2
64. LABOR AND HUMAN RESOURCES	51	7 Mar 1979(96-1)			L11/4
65. Labor and Public Welfare	24	6 Jan 1947(80-1)	4 Feb 1977(95-1)	51	L11/2
66. Library		25 Feb 1806(9-1)	6 Jan 1947(80-1)	97	L61/3

67.	Manufactures[10]	16	12 Dec 1825(19-1)	6 Jan 1947(80-1)	58	M31/2
68.	Military Affairs[11]		10 Dec 1816(14-2)	6 Jan 1947(80-1)	5	M59/2
69.	Militia		10 Dec 1816(14-2)	16 Dec 1857(35-1)	68	
70.	Mines and Mining		8 Mar 1865(38-2)	6 Jan 1947(80-1)	89	M66/2
71.	Mississippi River and Its Tributaries*[12]		19 Mar 1879(46-1)	18 Apr 1921(67-1)	59	
72.	National Banks*		29 Apr 1912(62-2)	18 Apr 1921(67-1)	7	
73.	Naval Affairs		10 Dec 1816(14-2)	6 Jan 1947(80-1)	5	N22/2
74.	Organization, Conduct and Expenditures of the Executive Departments		12 Mar 1889(51-S)	17 Dec 1907(60-1)	39	
75.	Pacific Islands and Porto Rico		15 Dec 1899(56-1)	18 Apr 1921(67-1)	100	P11/1
76.	Pacific Railroad		22 Dec 1863(38-1)	12 Mar 1873(43-S)	91	
77.	Pacific Railroads*		30 Dec 1895(54-1)	18 Apr 1921(67-1)	59	P11/2
78.	Patents[13]		8 Sep 1837(25-1)	6 Jan 1947(80-1)	63	P27/2
79.	Pensions		10 Dec 1816(14-2)	6 Jan 1947(80-1)	43	P38/2
80.	Philippines		15 Dec 1899(56-1)	18 Apr 1921(67-1)	100	P53
81.	Post Office and Civil Service	11	17 Apr 1947(80-1)	4 Feb 1977(95-1)	50	P84/11
82.	Post Office and Post Roads		10 Dec 1816(14-2)	6 Jan 1947(80-1)	11	P84/2
83.	Printing		15 Dec 1841(27-2)	6 Jan 1947(80-1)	97	P93/3
84.			26 Dec 1826(19-2)	18 Apr 1921(67-1)		P93/7

(Senate Committees continue on page 174; notes begin on page 182.)

Senate Committees (cont'd)

Senate Committees	P	Created	Dissolved	S	Y4
85. Privileges and Élections		10 Mar 1871(42-1)	6 Jan 1947(80-1)	97	P93/6
86. Public Buildings and Grounds[14]		6 Dec 1838(25-3)	6 Jan 1947(80-1)	90	P96/7
87. Public Expenditures		22 Mar 1909(61-1)	27 Apr 1911(62-1)		
88. Public Health and National Quarantine	28	19 Mar 1896(54-1)	18 Apr 1921(67-1)	24	P96/9
89. Public Lands[15]		10 Dec 1816(14-2)	28 Jan 1948(80-2)	56	P96/1
90. Public Works	86	6 Jan 1947(80-1)	4 Feb 1977(95-1)	27	P96/10
91. Railroads	76	12 Mar 1873(42-3)	18 Apr 1921(67-1)	59	R13/2
92. Retrenchment		18 Feb 1842(27-2)	16 Dec 1857(35-1)		R31/1
93. Revision of the Laws of the U.S.[16]		10 Dec 1868(40-3)	10 Dec 1923(68-1)		
94. Revolutionary Claims		28 Dec 1832(22-2)	18 Apr 1921(67-1)		R32/2
95. Roads and Canals*[17]		18 Jan 1830(21-1)	16 Dec 1857(35-1)		R53
96. Rules*		9 Dec 1874(43-2)	6 Jan 1947(80-1)	97	R86/2
97. RULES AND ADMINISTRATION	6, 66, 83, 96	6 Jan 1947(80-1)			R86/2
98. SMALL BUSINESS*		25 Mar 1981(97-1)			Sm1/2
99. Standards, Weights and Measures*		22 Mar 1909(61-1)	18 Apr 1921(67-1)	59	St2
100. Territories and Insular Affairs[18]		25 Mar 1844(28-1)	6 Jan 1947(80-1)	89	T27/2

		Created	Dissolved	S	Y4
101. Transportation and Sale of Meat Products*		22 Mar 1909(61-1)	18 Apr 1921(67-1)	59	
102. Transportation Routes to the Seaboard*		19 Mar 1879(46-1)	18 Apr 1921(67-1)	59	T68
103. University of the U.S.*[19]		19 Mar 1896(54-1)	18 Apr 1921(67-1)		Un3/1
104. VETERANS' AFFAIRS[20]		26 Oct 1970(91-2)			V64/4
105. Woman Suffrage*		22 Mar 1909(61-1)	18 Apr 1921(67-1)		W84

House Committees

House Committees	P	Created	Dissolved	S	Y4
1. Accounts*		17 Dec 1805(9-1)	3 Jan 1947(80-1)	39	Ac2
2. AGRICULTURE		3 May 1820(16-1)			Ag8/1
3. Alcoholic Liquor Traffic*		18 Aug 1893(53-1)	5 Dec 1927(70-1)		Al1/2
4. APPROPRIATIONS	91	2 Mar 1865(38-2)			Ap6/1
5. ARMED SERVICES	57, 62	3 Jan 1947(80-1)			Ar5/2
6. BANKING, FINANCE AND URBAN AFFAIRS[21]	91	2 Mar 1865(38-2)			B22/1
7. BUDGET[22]		12 Jul 1974(93-2)			B85/3
8. Census*		5 Dec 1903(58-1)	3 Jan 1947(80-1)	67	C33/1
9. Civil Service*[23]		18 Aug 1893(53-1)	3 Jan 1947(80-1)	67	C49/1
10. Claims		13 Nov 1794(3-2)	3 Jan 1947(80-1)	50	C52/1
11. Coinage, Weights and Measures[24]		21 Jan 1864(38-1)	3 Jan 1947(80-1)	6, 47	C66

(House Committees continue on page 176; notes begin on page 182.)

House Committees (cont'd)

House Committees	P	Created	Dissolved	S	Y4
12. Commerce	13	8 Dec 1819(16-1)	19 Dec 1891(52-1)	47	C73/1
13. Commerce and Manufactures		14 Dec 1795(4-1)	8 Dec 1819(16-1)	12, 53	
14. Disposition of Executive Papers[25]		11 Apr 1911(62-1)	3 Jan 1947(80-1)	39	Ex3/2
15. DISTRICT OF COLUMBIA		27 Jan 1808(10-1)			D63/1
16. Education	17	19 Dec 1883(48-1)	3 Jan 1947(80-1)	17	Ed8/2
17. EDUCATION AND LABOR[26]	16, 51	21 Mar 1867(40-1)		16, 51	Ed8/1
18. Election of President, Vice-President and Representatives in Congress*		18 Aug 1893(53-1)	3 Jan 1947(80-1)	39	El1/1
19. Elections[27]		13 Apr 1789(1-1)	3 Jan 1947(80-1)	39	El2/2
20. ENERGY AND COMMERCE	47	25 Mar 1980(96-2), effective 3 Jan 1981(97-1)			En2/3
21. Engraving		16 Mar 1844(28-1)	16 Mar 1860(36-1)	J8	
22. Expenditures in the Agriculture Department		20 Dec 1889(51-1)	5 Dec 1927(70-1)	25	Ex7/1
23. Expenditures in the Commerce and Labor Department		11 Dec 1905(59-1)	27 May 1913(63-1)	24, 28	Ex7/2
24. Expenditures in the Commerce Department		27 May 1913(63-1)	5 Dec 1927(70-1)	25	Ex7/2
25. Expenditures in the Executive Departments	22, 24, 26-34	5 Dec 1927(70-1)	4 Jul 1952(82-2)	38	Ex7/13
26. Expenditures in the Interior Department		16 Mar 1860(36-1)	5 Dec 1927(70-1)	25	Ex7/3
27. Expenditures in the Justice Department		16 Jan 1874(43-1)	5 Dec 1927(70-1)	25	Ex7/4
28. Expenditures in the Labor Department		3 Jun 1913(63-1)	5 Dec 1927(70-1)	25	

Committee					
29. Expenditures in the Navy Department		30 Mar 1816(14-1)	5 Dec 1927(70-1)	25	Ex7/5
30. Expenditures in the Post Office Department		30 Mar 1816(14-1)	5 Dec 1927(70-1)	25	Ex7/6
31. Expenditures in the State Department		30 Mar 1816(14-1)	5 Dec 1927(70-1)	25	Ex7/8
32. Expenditures in the Treasury Department		30 Mar 1816(14-1)	5 Dec 1927(70-1)	25	Ex7/9
33. Expenditures in the War Department		30 Mar 1816(14-1)	5 Dec 1927(70-1)	25	Ex7/10
34. Expenditures on Public Buildings		30 Mar 1816(14-1)	5 Dec 1927(70-1)	25	Ex7/7
35. Flood Control		3 Feb 1916(64-1)	3 Jan 1947(80-1)	74	F65
36. FOREIGN AFFAIRS*[28]		13 Mar 1822(17-1)		46	F76/1
37. Freedmen's Affairs		4 Dec 1866(39-2)	20 Dec 1875(44-1)		
38. GOVERNMENT OPERATIONS	25	4 Jul 1952(82-2)			G74/7
39. HOUSE ADMINISTRATION	1, 14, 18, 19, 52,54,69	3 Jan 1947(80-1)			H81/3
40. Immigration and Naturalization*		18 Aug 1893(53-1)	3 Jan 1947(80-1)	50	Im6/1
41. Indian Affairs*		17 Dec 1821(17-1)	3 Jan 1947(80-1)	73	In2/1
42. Industrial Arts and Expositions*		11 Dec 1905(59-1)	5 Dec 1927(70-1)		In2/7
43. Insular Affairs		8 Dec 1899(56-1)	3 Jan 1947(80-1)	73	In7/1
44. INTERIOR AND INSULAR AFFAIRS	73	2 Feb 1951(82-1)			In8/14
45. Internal Security	87	18 Feb 1969(91-1)	14 Jan 1975(94-1)	50	In8/15
46. International Relations (see FOREIGN AFFAIRS and note 28)					In8/16

(House Committees continue on page 178; notes begin on page 182.)

House Committees (cont'd)

House Committees	P	Created	Dissolved	S	Y4
47. Interstate and Foreign Commerce[29]	11, 12, 53, 63, 75	19 Dec 1891(52-1)	3 Jan 1981(97-1)	20	In8/4
48. Invalid Pensions		10 Jan 1831(21-2)	3 Jan 1947(80-1)	89	In8/5
49. Irrigation and Reclamation*[30]		18 Aug 1893(53-1)	3 Jan 1947(80-1)	73	Ir7/2
50. JUDICIARY*		3 Jun 1813(13-1)			J89/1
51. Labor	17	19 Dec 1883(48-1)	3 Jan 1947(80-1)	17	L11
52. Library		27 Feb 1806(9-1)	3 Jan 1947(80-1)	39	L61/1
53. Manufactures	13	8 Dec 1819(16-1)	5 Apr 1911(62-1)	47	M31/1
54. Memorials		3 Jan 1929(70-2)	3 Jan 1947(80-1)	39	
55. MERCHANT MARINE AND FISHERIES[31]		21 Dec 1887(50-1)			M53
56. Mileage		15 Sep 1837(25-1)	5 Dec 1927(70-1)	1	M58
57. Military Affairs*		13 Mar 1822(17-1)	3 Jan 1947(80-1)	5	M59/1
58. Military Pensions	79	13 Dec 1825(19-1)	10 Jan 1831(21-2)	79	
59. Militia*		10 Dec 1835(24-1)	5 Apr 1911(62-1)	57	M59/3
60. Mines and Mining		19 Dec 1865(39-1)	3 Jan 1947(80-1)	73	M66/1
61. Mississippi Levees*[32]		10 Jan 1875(44-1)	5 Apr 1911(62-1)	80	M69/2
62. Naval Affairs*		13 Mar 1822(17-1)	3 Jan 1947(80-1)	5	N22/1

63. Pacific Railroads*[33]		2 Mar 1865(38-2)	5 Apr 1911(62-1)	47	P11/3
64. Patents*		15 Sep 1837(25-1)	3 Jan 1947(80-1)	50	P27/1
65. Pensions	79	2 Mar 1880(46-2)	3 Jan 1947(80-1)	89	P38/1
66. Pensions and Revolutionary Claims		22 Dec 1813(13-2)	13 Dec 1825(19-1)	78	
67. POST OFFICE AND CIVIL SERVICE	8, 9, 68	3 Jan 1947(80-1)			P84/10
68. Post Office and Post Roads		9 Nov 1808(10-2)	3 Jan 1947(80-1)	67	P84/1
69. Printing		22 Dec 1847(30-1)	3 Jan 1947(80-1)	39	P93/2
70. Private Land Claims		29 Apr 1816(14-1)	5 Apr 1911(62-1)		P93/5
71. Public Buildings and Grounds*[34]		15 Sep 1837(25-1)	3 Jan 1947(80-1)	74	P96/6
72. Public Expenditures[35]	91	26 Feb 1814(13-2)	2 Mar 1880(46-2)		P96/5
73. Public Lands		17 Dec 1805(9-1)	2 Feb 1951(82-1)	44	P96/2
74. PUBLIC WORKS AND TRANSPORTATION[36]	35, 71	3 Jan 1947(80-1)			P96/11
75. Railways and Canals*[37]		15 Dec 1831(22-1)	5 Dec 1927(70-1)	47, 80	R13/1
76. Revisal and Unfinished Business		14 Dec 1795(4-1)	25 Jul 1868(40-2)	77	
77. Revision of the Laws[38]		25 Jul 1868(40-2)	3 Jan 1947(80-1)	50	L44/2
78. Revolutionary Claims	66	13 Dec 1825(19-1)	2 Dec 1873(43-1)	90	R32/1
79. Revolutionary Pensions*[39]		9 Dec 1825(19-1)	2 Mar 1880(46-2)	58, 65	
80. Rivers and Harbors		20 Dec 1883(48-1)	3 Jan 1947(80-1)	74	R52
81. Roads		2 Jun 1913(63-1)	3 Jan 1947(80-1)	74	R53/2

(House Committees continue on page 180; notes begin on page 182.)

House Committees (cont'd)

House Committees	P	Created	Dissolved	S	Y4
82. RULES*40		2 Mar 1880(46-2)			R86/1
83. SCIENCE AND TECHNOLOGY*41		21 Jul 1958(85-2)			Sci2
84. SMALL BUSINESS*		3 Jan 1975(94-1)			Sm1
85. STANDARDS OF OFFICIAL CONDUCT		13 Apr 1967(90-1)			St2/3
86. Territories		13 Dec 1825(19-1)	3 Jan 1947(80-1)	73	T27/1
87. Un-American Activities*		3 Jan 1945(79-1)	18 Feb 1969(91-1)	45	Un1
88. Ventilation and Acoustics*		18 Aug 1893(53-1)	5 Apr 1911(62-1)	1	V56
89. VETERANS' AFFAIRS	48,65,93	3 Jan 1947(80-1)			V64/3
90. War Claims	78	2 Dec 1873(43-1)	3 Jan 1947(80-1)	50	W19
91. WAYS AND MEANS*		21 Dec 1795(4-1)			W36
92. Woman Suffrage		24 Sep 1917(65-1)	5 Dec 1927(70-1)		
93. World War Veterans' Legislation		14 Jan 1924(68-1)	3 Jan 1947(80-1)	89	W89

Joint Committees

Joint Committees	P	Created	Dissolved	S	Y4
1. Atomic Energy[42]		1 Aug 1946(79-2)	20 Sep 1977(95-1)	S5, S25, S27, H5, H36, H44, H47, H83	At7/2
2. Congressional Operations[43]		26 Oct 1970(91-2)	1 Oct 1977(95-1)	S97, H39, H82	C76/7
3. Defense Production[44]		8 Sep 1950(81-2)	1 Oct 1977(95-1)		D36
4. ECONOMIC[45]		20 Feb 1946(79-2)			Ec7
5. Enrolled Bills		(H) 27 Jul 1789(1-1) (S) 6 Aug 1789(1-1)	3 Jan 1947(80-1) 6 Jan 1947(80-1)	H39 S97	
6. Internal Revenue Taxation[46]		26 Feb 1926(69-1)	4 Oct 1976(94-2)	10	In8/11
7. LIBRARY[47]		21 Feb 1806(9-1)			L61/2
8. PRINTING[48]		3 Aug 1846(29-1)			P93/1
9. Reduction of Federal Expenditures[49]		20 Sep 1941(77-1)	12 Jul 1974(93-2)		R24/4
10. TAXATION[50]	6	1 Feb 1977(95-1)			T19/4

(Notes begin on page 182.)

Notes

1. Originally named Agriculture; dissolved 16 Dec 1857(35-1); reestablished 14 Dec 1863(38-1); redesignated Agriculture and Forestry 5 Feb 1884(48-1); assigned present name 4 Feb 1977(95-1).

2. Originally named Banking and Currency; redesignated 26 Oct 1970(91-2) by law (84 Stat. 1163).

3. Authorized by law (88 Stat. 300).

4. Originally named Relations with Canada; redesignated 23 Nov 1903(58-1).

5. Originally named Civil Service and Retrenchment; redesignated 18 Apr 1921(67-1).

6. Originally named Relations with Cuba; redesignated 23 Nov 1903(58-1); dissolved 15 Mar 1913(63-S); reestablished 5 Jun 1914(63-2).

7. Occasionally functioned as a joint committee in collaboration with its House counterpart.

8. Originally named Fish and Fisheries; redesignated 13 Mar 1885(48-2).

9. Originally named Irrigation and Reclamation of Arid Lands; redesignated 18 Apr 1921(67-1).

10. Dissolved 16 Dec 1857(35-1); reestablished 10 Feb 1864(38-1).

11. Redesignated Military Affairs and Militia 16 Dec 1857(35-1); original name restored 10 Dec 1868(40-3).

12. Originally named Improvement of the Mississippi River and Its Tributaries; redesignated 18 Dec 1905(59-1).

13. Originally named Patents and the Patent Office; redesignated 8 Mar 1869(41-1).

14. Existed as a standing committee for the 16th Congress, 16 Dec 1819—4 Mar 1821, and originally named Public Buildings; redesignated 16 Dec 1857(35-1); occasionally functioned as a joint committee in collaboration with its House counterpart.

15. Redesignated Public Lands and Surveys 18 Apr 1921(67-1); original name restored 6 Jan 1947(80-1).

16. Occasionally functioned as a joint committee in collaboration with its House counterpart.

17. Existed as a standing committee for the 16th Congress, 8 Feb 1820-20 Dec 1822.

(Notes continue on page 184.)

18. Originally named Territories; redesignated Territories and Insular Possessions 18 Apr 1921(67-1); redesignated 17 Jun 1929(71-1).

19. Originally named Establish the University of the United States; redesignated 23 Nov 1903(58-1).

20. Authorized by law (84 Stat. 1164).

21. Originally named Banking and Currency; redesignated Banking, Currency and Housing 3 Jan 1975(94-1); assigned present name 4 Jan 1977(95-1).

22. Authorized by law (88 Stat. 299).

23. Originally named Reform in the Civil Service; redesignated 14 Jan 1924(68-1).

24. Originally named Uniform System of Coinage, Weights and Measures; redesignated 2 Mar 1867(39-2).

25. Originally named Disposition of Useless Executive Papers; redesignated 9 Apr 1935(74-1); occasionally functioned as a joint committee in collaboration with its Senate counterpart.

26. Divided into 2 committees 19 Dec 1883(48-1); reunited 3 Jan 1947(80-1).

27. Divided into 3 Committees on Elections 17 Dec 1895(54-1).

28. Redesignated International Relations 19 Mar 1975(94-1); original name restored 5 Feb 1979(96-1).

29. Redesignated Commerce and Health 3 Jan 1975(94-1); original name restored 14 Jan 1975.

30. Originally named Irrigation of Arid Lands; redesignated 14 Jan 1924(68-1).

31. Redesignated Merchant Marine, Radio and Fisheries 4 Jan 1932(72-1); original name restored 26 Feb 1935(74-1).

32. Redesignated Levees and Improvements of the Mississippi River 7 Nov 1877(45-1).

33. Originally named Pacific Railroad; redesignated 2 Mar 1880(46-2).

34. Occasionally functioned as a joint committee in collaboration with its Senate counterpart.

35. Reestablished 21 Dec 1881(47-1) and dissolved 3 Mar 1883(47-2).

Notes (cont'd)

36. Originally named Public Works; redesignated 3 Jan 1975(94-1).

37. Originally named Roads and Canals; redesignated 9 Apr 1869(41-1).

38. Occasionally functioned as a joint committee in collaboration with its Senate counterpart.

39. Redesignated Military Pensions 13 Dec 1825(19-1); original name restored 10 Jan 1831(21-2).

40. Existed as a standing committee for the 31st Congress, 27 Dec 1849-3 Mar 1851.

41. Originally named Science and Astronautics; redesignated 3 Jan 1975(94-1).

42. Authorized by law (60 Stat. 772); abolished by law (91 Stat. 884).

43. Authorized by law (84 Stat. 1187).

44. Authorized by law (64 Stat. 820).

45. Authorized by law (60 Stat. 25); originally named Economic Report and redesignated 18 Jun 1956(84-2) by law (70 Stat. 290).

46. Authorized by law (44 Stat. 127); abolished by law (90 Stat. 1835).

47. Authorized by law (2 Stat. 350).

48. Authorized by law (9 Stat. 114).

49. Authorized by law (55 Stat. 726) and originally named Reduction of Nonessential Federal Expenditures; redesignated 23 Jul 1968(90-2) by law (92 Stat. 404); abolished by law (88 Stat. 304).

50. Authorized by law (90 Stat. 1835).

BIBLIOGRAPHY

Galloway, George B. *The Legislative Process in Congress.* New York: Thomas Y. Crowell, 1953.

U.S. Congress. House. *Hinds' and Cannon's Precedents of the House of Representatives.* Washington: U.S. Government Printing Office, 1936.

U.S. Congress. House. Select Committee on Committees. *Committee Reform Amendments of 1974.* House Report No. 93-916, Part II, 93rd Congress, 2nd Session. Washington: U.S. Government Printing Office, 1974.

U.S. Congress. Senate. Temporary Select Committee to Study the Senate Committee System. *First Report, with Recommendations.* Senate Report No. 94-1395, 94th Congress, 2nd Session. Washington: U.S. Government Printing Office, 1976.

U.S. Congress. Senate. Temporary Select Committee to Study the Senate Committee System. *The Senate Committee System.* Committee Print, 94th Congress, 2nd Session. Washington: U.S. Government Printing Office, 1976.

U.S. National Archives and Records Service. *Records of the House of Representatives 1789-1946.* Preliminary Inventory No. 113. Washington: National Archives, 1959.

Document Index

Subject Index